Paula. Cronjo.

THE ECUMENICAL FUTURE

THE ECUMENICAL FUTURE

Background Papers for
In One Body through the Cross:
The Princeton Proposal for Christian Unity

Edited by

Carl E. Braaten and Robert W. Jenson

WILLIAM B. EERDMANS PUBLISHING COMPANY
GRAND RAPIDS, MICHIGAN / CAMBRIDGE, U.K.

Wm. B. Eerdmans Publishing Co.
255 Jefferson Ave. S.E., Grand Rapids, Michigan 49503 /
P.O. Box 163, Cambridge CB3 9PU U.K.

Printed in the United States of America

09 08 07 06 05 04   7 6 5 4 3 2 1

ISBN 0-8028-2671-7

www.eerdmans.com

Contents

Preface

After the Second Vatican Council expectations ran high that the many ecumenical dialogues that followed would succeed in placing the major blocs of world Christianity on converging paths. The concept of the church as a communion *(koinonia)* of churches seemed to offer hope for the ecumenical movement to reach its goal of church unity. Pope John Paul II placed the highest priority on reconciliation between the Eastern and Western branches of Christianity. The dialogues succeeded not only in changing attitudes of Christians toward one another, but also in producing interchurch agreements with far-reaching implications. The Leuenberg Agreement had brought Lutheran and Reformed Churches into closer fellowship in Europe and around the world. The *Joint Declaration on the Doctrine of Justification* was signed by the Vatican and the Lutheran World Federation, stating that the mutual condemnations of the Reformation period are no longer church-dividing. The *Called to Common Mission,* accepted by the Evangelical Lutheran Church in America and the Episcopal Church USA, is an agreement resulting in full communion and shared ministries. These, along with many similar ones, are the fruits of the many interdenominational dialogues that changed the ecclesial landscape also in North America.

Yet, in spite of these significant gains the perception is widespread that the ecumenical train is stalling or has even run off the tracks. Churches have cut back on their financial support to ecumenical organizations. The official ecumenical councils of churches are struggling to become more inclusive of Evangelical and Pentecostal communities that have traditionally been left out. These are among the fastest growing; yet they often look upon ecumenism as a waste of time and energy, a distraction from the Great Commission of our Lord to evangelize and make disciples of all nations. To complicate things further the ecumenical leadership at the world (WCC) and national (NCC) levels invariably takes the liberal side on highly divisive theological, ethical, and cultural issues, provoking conservatives in every denomination to regard ecumenism as the enemy of the gospel. It is not an exaggeration to say that the kind of ecumenism the churches have practiced in the years since Vatican II is in a state of crisis.

The Center for Catholic and Evangelical Theology is an ecumenical organization that was founded twelve years ago in the firm conviction that ecumenism is not a passing fad with which Christians and churches may or may not choose to become involved. Ecumenism is a function of authentic Christian faith; the ecumenical quest for church unity is based on Jesus' high-priestly prayer in Chapter 17 of St. John's Gospel that all who believe in him "may be one so that the world may believe." Here ecumenism and evangelism are two sides of the same coin. As long as Christians and churches are separated and relate to each other as rivals, they dis-grace the gift of unity given in the gospel they profess to believe. In order that world evangelization may not be impeded, every cause of division and obstacle to the visible unity of the members of Christ's body must be overcome. That calls for serious theological work of the kind the contributors to this volume on the renewal of ecumenism have done.

Four years ago the directors of the Center for Catholic and Evangelical Theology invited sixteen theologians and ecumenists representing various traditions to undertake an intensive study of the ecumenical future of the divided churches. The result of that study is the publication of an ecumenical statement, *In One Body through the Cross: The Princeton Proposal for Christian Unity.* In part this document is a protest against much of present-day ecumenism that subordinates matters of faith and doctrine to social and political agendas. But it is more importantly also a venture of hope that churches might be ready for a renewal of ecumenism that would not only reconnect with its promising missionary origins and but also seize upon unprecedented opportunities to invite new players onto the ecumenical field. This volume contains the background papers written by members of the Study Group in preparation for the drafting of the Princeton Proposal.

CARL E. BRAATEN & ROBERT W. JENSON

viii

A Survey of Ecumenical Reflection about Unity

WILLIAM G. RUSCH

The purpose of this essay is to survey briefly the ecumenical reflection about the theme of unity, especially within the framework of *koinonia/communio*. The material is assembled as a resource for the ecumenical text, *In One Body through the Cross: The Princeton Proposal for Christian Unity*. Its intended usefulness is that it is a brief summary of a rather extended process. The thesis of this presentation is simple, and I trust, clear: attention to the concept of unity has had a long history in the ecumenical movement.

Not all of this activity has been conducted within the context of the World Council of Churches. "Faith and Order" both within and without conciliar structures has usually been one of the major focal points for such thinking, although by no means the only one. Nevertheless for present purposes it is helpful to organize the presentation by and large around assemblies for the World Council.

At the outset it should be noted that within the general discussion of unity there is a recent tendency to conclude that ecumenical attention to *koinonia/communio* is a recent development. While it is certainly true that there has been a new stress on this concept, as a quick review of ecumenical literature would disclose, preoccupation with *koinonia/communio* is neither a novel idea, nor has it been restricted to the dialogues. This will be made clearer in what follows.

A convenient time span to examine this history is the years between the Third Assembly of the World Council of Churches, New Delhi in

I

1961 and the Eighth, and last, Assembly of the Council in Harare in 1998. Still, a few comments should be made about the earlier periods.

In virtually every century of church history since the breaks between the Eastern and Western churches, and the sixteenth-century Reformation, there have been attempts to restore the unity of the church. These efforts were often the enterprise of committed individuals with varying degrees of indifference or hostility from their churches. These attempts were usually characterized by the lack of consideration of the nature of unity being sought or naïve assumptions that recovered unity meant return to some previous location in the history of those separated.

A new seriousness came to the concern with the unity of divided churches in the nineteenth century. This attentiveness was motivated by the scandal of Christian division on the missionary fields of Africa and Asia. As different missionary societies and churches entered into world mission, their separation, and even antagonism, became painfully obvious detriments to their desired goals. One of the wellsprings of the twentieth-century ecumenical movement was the world missionary movement of the previous century.

As is well known, the origin of the modern ecumenical movement is normally identified as the World Missionary Conference of 1910, held in Edinburgh. Two factors were not accidental. First, this gathering across many denominational lines was occasioned by a century of world missionary movements. Second, many individual leaders at Edinburgh became the custodians of the first generation of the ecumenical movement. The step from concerned world missionary to committed ecumenist was easy for many in this group.

Yet their vision was hampered by some limitations. They indeed saw the intimate connection between unity and mission, but too often unity was viewed as only something expedient for mission and not a desired goal in its own right under the mandate of Scripture and confessional documents of certain churches. They also suffered from a lack of vision of an ecumenical comprehension of unity. Too often they understood unity as merely defined within their own separated traditions.

Nevertheless, even with these constrictions, the years after Edinburgh recorded the further development of what along with world mission would become the two major components of the ecumenical movement: Faith and Order, concerned with the theological issues that kept the churches divided, and Life and Work, occupied with the issues of society and justice, confronting and often dividing the churches. Frequently these two elements were portrayed as competitive. In reality their emphases were different but their alliance to a common, but multidimensional, movement, was obvious.

The period between 1910 and 1948 discloses several characteristics of the emerging modern ecumenical movement.[1] First, as indicated above, this movement has never been a homogeneous phenomenon. The differing views of ecumenism are seen in the variety of reasons for participation in the movement and in its very perception. Second, the ecumenical movement is profoundly shaped by the differing understandings of the church and its unity carried to the ecumenical enterprise by the various churches. Third, like all of human life this movement is lodged in the changing context of human history. The historical setting has conditioned, and does condition, the ecumenical movement.

Yet, even in the midst of all this fluidity, there has been a large degree of consensus that the goal of the movement is the unity of Christians, or the unity of the church, or the unity of the churches. Whatever else the ecumenical movement may concern itself with, the ecumenical movement at its heart must always be about the unity of the church of Jesus Christ, or it is not the ecumenical movement. Since the year 1910 this insight has not always been obvious, and its lack of clarity has been to the detriment of the entire movement.

This fundamental conviction of the ecumenical movement has claimed rootage in three basic presuppositions, viz., the ecumenical conviction, the ecumenical indicative, and the ecumenical imperative. The first briefly put is that unity belongs to the nature of the church. The second is that the essential unity of the church is presupposed in every effort for unity. The third is that the essential unity of the church must be lived and be made visible.

This last element, stated expressly in the constitutions of the World Council of Churches and of the Commission on Faith and Order, did not always appear as such in ecumenical documents. "Visible unity" endeavors to keep the distinction between God's action as gift and the human response and to underscore that the unity being sought is not separate from

1. As examples, see the reports of the first two world conferences on Faith and Order: H. N. Bates, ed., *Report on the World Conference on Faith and Order, Lausanne, Switzerland, August 3 to 21, 1927* (London: SCM, 1927) and Leonard Hodgson, ed., *The Second World Conference on Faith and Order, Held at Edinburgh, August 3-18, 1937* (Edinburgh: Lothian, 1938).

the visible, empirical reality of Christian life and action. It also implies that even in their separation the churches already share a certain level of fellowship. Still there have been reservations about the expression in ecumenical work that have continued, although not to the point of preventing churches with disagreements about it from taking part in the one ecumenical movement.[2]

In 1948, after years of delay caused by the Second World War, the World Council of Churches came into being. This organization brought together the two movements of Faith and Order and Life and Work. Initially there had been some hesitation on the part of Faith and Order to join in such an organization, but by 1937 in Edinburgh these fears were overcome.

The early history of the Council discloses that the churches taking part in the ecumenical movement had no common view of church unity. This is demonstrated most vividly by "The Toronto Declaration" of 1950. This text, produced by the Council's Central Committee, showed that the formation of the World Council and the holding of its first assembly did not answer a number of fundamental questions about the nature of unity, the nature of the Council, and the relationship of the Council to its member churches.

"The Toronto Declaration" described a number of assumptions underlying the Council, but it contained a number of negative statements. It declared that the World Council is not and must never become a superchurch. It cannot and should not be based on any one particular conception of the church. Thus it does not prejudge the ecclesiological problem. Membership in the Council does not imply that a church treats its own conception of the church as merely relative. Finally, membership in the Council does not imply acceptance of a specific doctrine about the nature of church unity.[3] Thus the Declaration has often been pictured as a statement of "ecclesiological neutrality."

Clearly the World Council of Churches, and the ecumenical movement itself, could not labor long under such uncertainties about its goal. The Commission on Faith and Order, while respecting the views of the

2. For a full discussion of this material, see Harding Meyer, *That All May Be One* (Grand Rapids: Eerdmans, 1999), pp. 1-15.

3. See "The Toronto Declaration" in Michael Kinnamon and Brian E. Cope, eds., *The Ecumenical Movement: An Anthology of Key Texts and Voices* (Grand Rapids: Eerdmans, 1997), pp. 463-68.

Central Committee of 1950, began to develop a formula for unity that gave the characteristics and requirements for the visible unity of the church. This statement was accepted by the Third Assembly of the Council meeting in New Delhi in 1961. The importance of the New Delhi Declaration and its commentary for the ecumenical movement cannot be stressed too much. The Assembly stated:

> We believe that the unity which is both God's will and his gift to his Church is being made visible as all in each place who are baptized into Jesus Christ and confess him as Lord and Saviour are brought by the Holy Spirit into one fully committed fellowship, holding the one apostolic faith, preaching the one Gospel, breaking the one bread, joining in common prayer, and having a corporate life reaching out in witness and service to all and who at the same time are united with the whole Christian fellowship in all places and ages in such wise that ministry and members are accepted by all, and that all can act and speak together as occasion requires for the tasks to which God calls his people. It is for such a unity that we believe we must pray and work.[4]

The New Delhi Declaration built on the three basic convictions of the ecumenical movement. It saw church unity as a "fully committed fellowship" that must include several elements: a mutual recognition of baptism; a common confession of the apostolic faith and common proclamation of the gospel; a common celebration of the Lord's Supper; a common devotional worship with petition, intercession, and thanksgiving; a common life in witness and service to the world; a mutual recognition of ministries and members; and an ability to act and speak together in view of concrete tasks and challenges.[5]

In raising up "fellowship" the New Delhi statement was not referring to a general sociological concept, but to the biblical and patristic notion of *koinonia/communio*. Especially since 1961 "fellowship" has been a key idea in virtually all ecumenical texts on unity. If recently *koinonia/communio* has replaced "fellowship," this should not result in ignoring the long history of the basic idea.[6]

---

4. *The New Delhi Report: The Third Assembly of the World Council of Churches, 1961* (London: SCM, 1962), pp. 117-19.

5. See *The New Delhi Report,* pp. 118-29.

6. See *The New Delhi Report,* p. 119, and Harding Meyer, *That All May Be One,* pp. 44-45, and material presented later in this essay.

Since 1961 the basic ideas of the New Delhi Declaration have been repeated in ecumenical texts of the World Council of Churches, the Commission on Faith and Order, Christian world communions, and bilateral dialogues. As Harding Meyer has pointed out, since New Delhi the issue has not been to define the ecumenical goal again, but to develop further and explain with greater clarity the contents of New Delhi.[7]

This was done in Uppsala at the Fourth Assembly of the World Council of Churches in 1968, where the stress was on the catholicity of the church. According to this assembly, the unity of the church also means the "fullness, the integrity, and the totality of life in Christ." This catholicity is developed in the quest for diversity, for continuity, for the unity of the whole church, and for the unity of humankind.[8] All four of these aspects played an important role in ecumenical thinking in the following years, and were taken up at subsequent assemblies of the World Council, in work of Christian world communions and the dialogues.

It was the Uppsala Assembly that also gave clear expression to the subject of church and mission. This assembly saw the church not only in itself, but as a church for others. Mission was viewed as participation by the church in the mission of God for the renewal of creation. This mission involved the struggle in the world's search for reconciliation, renewal, and humanity's unity.[9] These themes of both unity and mission continued to have a leading place in ecumenical discussion and action.

For example, the next assembly of the World Council of Churches in Nairobi in 1975 spoke of the one universal church to be envisioned in a conciliar fellowship of local churches. It promoted discussion of diversity by underlining that the unity of the church is not monolithic. The assembly recognized the gifts of member churches and local churches. It spoke of the diversity of the church as grounded in the Trinity. Thus diversity in the church was something to be not only acknowledged but actively sought.[10]

7. See Harding Meyer, *That All May Be One*, p. 48.

8. See *The Uppsala Report 1968: Official Report of the Fourth Assembly of the World Council of Churches* (Geneva: WCC, 1968), pp. 13-18.

9. See *The Uppsala Report*, pp. 12, 27-36, and also Kinnamon and Cope, eds., *The Ecumenical Movement*, pp. 325-92.

10. See David M. Patton, ed., *Breaking Barriers, Nairobi 1975: The Official Report of the Fifth Assembly of the World Council of Churches, Nairobi, 23 November–10 December, 1975* (London: SPCK, 1976), pp. 59-61.

This positive assessment was continued at the next assembly in 1983. The Sixth Assembly committed itself to develop further and to stand in continuity with the earlier declarations of New Delhi and Nairobi. It stated that the Eucharistic vision of unity coming to the fore gives new appreciation for the richness of the diversity of the church.[11]

It was the Seventh Assembly in Canberra in 1991 that added even greater clarity to the continuing discussion about unity with its statement, "The Unity of the Church as Koinonia: Gift and Calling." In describing the unity of the church as *koinonia,* the assembly was putting forth an understanding of the unity of the church as a whole.[12] By specifically using the Greek *koinonia* and the Latin *communio,* the assembly was indicating an obvious connection with the thinking of the New Testament and patristic churches.

In this step the Canberra Assembly was reaching back into a long ecumenical history, at least in terms of the content, if not always the actual words. Early Faith and Order Conferences in Lausanne and Edinburgh pictured the church as a *communio.*[13] The assembly at Evanston in 1954 spoke of the communion *(koinonia)* of the church as not merely a human fellowship.[14] As mentioned earlier, it was at New Delhi that this idea became prominent, although its full implications were yet to be recognized.

The heritage of New Delhi began to become obvious during the decade of the 1980s in the work of the bilateral dialogues, especially as they addressed the topic of the church. These dialogues were influenced not only by the eucharistic ecclesiology of Orthodox churches and by Roman Catholic communion ecclesiology particularly during and after the Second Vatican Council, but also by the New Delhi Declaration.[15]

11. See David Gill, ed., *Gathered for Life: Official Report of the Sixth Assembly of the World Council of Churches* (Geneva: WCC, 1983), pp. 44-45.

12. See Michael Kinnamon, ed., *Signs of the Spirit: Official Report of the Seventh Assembly of the World Council of Churches* (Geneva: WCC, 1991), pp. 173-74.

13. See *Conference on Faith and Order, Lausanne,* p. 463; *Conference on Faith and Order, Edinburgh,* pp. 237-38.

14. See W. A. Visser 't Hooft, ed., *The Evanston Report, the Second Assembly of the World Council of Churches, 1954* (London: SCM, 1955), p. 85.

15. See Harding Meyer and Lukas Vischer, eds., *Growth in Agreement: Reports and Agreed Statements of Ecumenical Conversations at the World Level* (New York: Paulist, 1984); Harding Meyer, Jeffrey Gros, and William G. Rusch, eds., *Growth in Agreement II: Reports and Agreed Statements of Ecumenical Conversations on a World Level, 1982-1988* (Grand

The concept of *koinonia/communio* employed by the dialogues in the 1980s did not add anything to the understanding of unity as pictured in the New Delhi Declaration, but it did indeed deepen the idea of unity, not least because of its New Testament and patristic connections. It also made more concrete than some terminology both the vertical and horizontal dimensions of the life of the church.

Harding Meyer has offered several points that reveal the integrative force of *koinonia/communio* for ecumenical theology. In summary form they are: *koinonia/communio* keeps the connection between church and its unity; it roots the church and its unity in the area of visibility; it anchors communion in faith, worship, and the sacraments, not in sociological superficiality; it keeps faith and ethical action together; it has as a constitutive element the positive recognition of diversity; it insists that there are structural and institutional aspects of the church and its unity; and finally, *koinonia/communio* places the church and its unity in the context of God's act of salvation.[16]

Thus *koinonia/communio* offers real ecumenical potential for advance. It expresses a continuity with an understanding of unity and the ecumenical goal. It does not offer a formulation to solve all ecumenical problems, as it has sometimes been portrayed. The Canberra Assembly in its acceptance of "The Unity of the Church as Koinonia: Gift and Calling" presented a viable resource for ecumenical work. Its influence can be seen in the Fifth World Conference on Faith and Order and in the ongoing work of Faith and Order's ecclesiology study both on the world level and in the United States.[17]

It is regrettable, although telling, that the eighth assembly of the World Council in Harare in 1998 made no advance beyond what the Council had said in 1991 on the church and its unity.

What has been observed in this concise summary has been the development and sharpening of an ecumenical understanding of the church

---

Rapids: Eerdmans, 2001), the various dialogue reports and indices. See also Harding Meyer, *That All May Be One,* pp. 63-65.

16. See Harding Meyer, *That All May Be One,* pp. 67-70.

17. See Thomas F. Best and Günther Gassman, eds., *On the Way to Fuller Koinonia: Official Report of the Fifth World Conference on Faith and Order* (Geneva: WCC, 1993) and "Nature and Purpose of the Church," Faith and Order Paper 181 (Geneva: WCC, 1998). The Commission on Faith and Order in the United States has conducted its own studies on ecclesiology and may soon publish a volume that will be an American commentary on the Canberra statement.

and its unity. From unarticulated assumptions from the world missionary movement to the creation of the modern ecumenical movement the need has been more and more acknowledged for an expression of the goal of the ecumenical movement, the nature of the unity being sought.

Even at the time of the establishment of the World Council of Churches it was not possible in any significant way to express this goal. In 1950 it was necessary to declare an ecclesiological neutrality in order for churches to participate in the ecumenical movement. Only eleven years later in New Delhi was a breakthrough to occur. The New Delhi Declaration with its stated aim of "one fully committed fellowship" set in motion a trajectory that led to Canberra, to Santiago de Compostela, and to numerous dialogues. This trajectory deepened and developed the insights of the Third Assembly to the point that today in some circles there is an unrealistic notion that *koinonia/communio* is the solution to all that divides the churches.

Still, it is recognized today that *koinonia/communio* has potential yet unrealized to move the churches from their separation to greater expressions of visible unity. In this process it will challenge the churches to affirm and correct their individual understandings of *koinonia/communio*.[18]

It is in the light of this maturation of thought about *koinonia/communio* that the notion of full communion has entered into ecumenical deliberation. The patent advantage of the term is that it can grant that a level of communion exists among divided churches as they strive to receive the gift of full communion. It also clearly articulates a goal without restriction to any one model of unity. In fact full communion has the potential to be lived out in a variety of models.

While there is a general recognition that the concept of full communion requires further definition as the divided churches enter into this relationship and begin to live it out, e.g., a current study topic of the Commission on Faith and Order in the United States is precisely the "continuing definition of full communion," there is also a common acknowledgment that full communion has certain characteristics.

18. A useful summary of individual church views of *koinonia/communio* as well as the biblical background and ecumenical discussion is found in "Communio/Koinonia: A New Testament–Early Christian Concept and Its Contemporary Appropriation and Significance" of the Institute for Ecumenical Research at Strasbourg (1990) published in William G. Rusch, ed., *A Commentary on "Ecumenism: The Vision of the ELCA"* (Minneapolis: Augsburg, 1990), pp. 119-41.

They include: (1) a common confessing of the Christian faith; (2) a mutual recognition of baptism and a sharing of the Lord's Supper, allowing for the exchangeability of members; (3) a mutual recognition and availability of ordained ministers to the service of all members of churches in full communion, subject only but always to the disciplinary regulations of the other churches; (4) a common commitment to evangelism, witness, and service; (5) a means of common decision-making on critical common issues of faith and life; and (6) a means for mutual lifting of any condemnations that exist between the churches.[19]

Thus recent dialogues have employed the expression "full communion" to indicate not only the ultimate goal of their work, but as a resource to describe where the presently divided churches are in their relation to each other. A useful survey of this material was drawn up by Michael Root in 1990.[20] His overview and conclusions can be updated by consulting the recent volume *Growth in Agreement II.*[21]

The material referred to here discloses that indeed the ecumenical movement in its various forms is a movement. As part of that dynamic process, reflection about the nature of unity, which is the goal of the ecumenical movement, has advanced. Understanding of the goal of unity has become clearer, even if not yet complete. While impressive progress has occurred, in many ways the goal seems as elusive as, and perhaps more challenging than, it did to the first generation of ecumenical leaders after Edinburgh.

19. This formulation comes from *Ecumenism: The Vision of the Evangelical Lutheran Church in America* (Chicago: Evangelical Lutheran Church in America, 1991), but similar expressions can be found in numerous ecumenical texts.

20. See "The Phrase 'Full Communion' as a Statement of the Ecumenical Goal as Described in the Proposed Ecumenical Policy Statement of the ELCA," in William G. Rusch, ed., *A Commentary on "Ecumenism: The Vision of the ELCA,"* pp. 142-53.

21. See Meyer, Gros, and Rusch, eds., *Growth in Agreement II,* esp. the indices.

The Global Structures of Ecumenism

GEOFFREY WAINWRIGHT

The *Oikoumene*

The word *oikoumene,* by its Greek etymology, refers to the "inhabited" world. In antiquity the term carried the cultural connotation of "civilized" world, as opposed to barbary; and the political connotation of "imperial" world, as distinct from those regions where the emperor's writ did not (yet) run. In Christian usage, the term's potential thrust towards universality has made it suitable for speaking in connection with a mission to "go into all the world and preach the gospel to the whole creation" (Mark 16:15), to bear witness to Jesus Christ "among all nations" (Luke 24:47) and "to the end of the earth" (Acts 1:8). This geographical extension assumes an eschatological horizon in Christianity, for "this gospel of the kingdom will be preached throughout the whole world, as a testimony to all nations, and then the end will come" (Matthew 24:14). The definitive kingdom of God will amount to a new creation, "a new heaven and a new earth" (Revelation 21:1); it can be called "the *oikoumene* to come" (Hebrews 2:5). Culturally, the city of God will include "the treasures of all nations" (Haggai 2:7; cf. Revelation 21:26).

From the time of the imperial recognition and establishment of Christianity under Constantine and Theodosius in the fourth century, the adjective "ecumenical" came into regular churchly usage to signify councils or decisions that concerned the entire church. Clearly there was considerable overlap between the imperial and the ecclesiastical references, although of course "Christendom" could at various times and for various reasons be either less or more extensive than "Empire." A problem arises at schisms: both the Byzantine and the Roman churches, divided since the eleventh century, stake "ecumenical" claims for themselves — respectively and therefore conflictingly (the same applies even if the Latin word used is *universalis* or *generalis*). In such cases, the very word "ecumenical" carries an implicit imperative towards reconciliation and re-union.

The modern usage of the word "ecumenical," as in the phrase "the ecumenical movement," derives from the Protestant revivals in the eighteenth and nineteenth centuries that stimulated both a recovered obligation to universal mission and a sense of Christian fellowship embracing disciples from among the multiple nations — clear implicates of Matthew 28:18-20; but it also signals the problem of confessional and institutional divisions that historically exist among the several communities claiming to be "church." Both tension and opportunity come to expression in the need to relate the two concerns epitomized in two formulas dating from the turn into the twentieth century: "the evangelization of the world in this generation" (the project of the Student Volunteer Movement) and "that they all may be one" (the motto of the World's Student Christian Federation). In the one direction, unity among Christ's witnesses appears as an aid, even a requirement, for evangelistic mission, according to the syntax of Jesus' prayer for his disciples in John 17:21: "that they all may be one, that the world may believe." In the other direction, the very spread of the faith throughout the world — by God's grace in spite of a disunited witness — constitutes an invitation, indeed a summons, to universal Christian unity.

Catholicity

By the second and third centuries, the word "catholic" was used to designate the "universal" church — the church that is found "everywhere." The *Martyrdom of Polycarp* refers to "the whole catholic Church throughout the inhabited world" (8.1). Already Ignatius of Antioch supplies a christological basis for this universal extension: "Wherever Christ Jesus is, there is the catholic Church" (*Letter to the Smyrneans* 8.2). This may seem to beg a question when, in the case of controversy among communities variously claiming to be Christian, the saving presence of Christ is in dispute. Nevertheless, universality was regularly a factor advanced in the "catholic" case against local schismatics and heretics.

In the mid-fourth century, Cyril of Jerusalem fuses "quantitative" and "qualitative" elements when he expounds to the catechumens the meaning of "catholic" in the Creed: "The Church is called catholic because it is spread throughout the world, from end to end of the earth; also because it teaches universally and completely all the doctrines which man should know concerning things visible and invisible, heavenly and earthly; and also because it subjects to right worship all mankind, rulers and ruled, lettered and unlettered; further because it treats and heals universally every sort of sin committed by soul and body, and possesses in itself every conceivable virtue, whether in deeds, words, or in spiritual gifts of every kind" *(Catechetical Lecture XVIII)*.

Cyril's definition sounds like a good checklist for all claimants to ecclesiality. It certainly suggests that ecumenism, in its aspects of both mission and unity, will be concerned with faith and order, with spiritual and sacramental communion, with corporate life and conduct, as they embody and transmit the full range of divine grace and truth that are found in Christ.

From Para-Ecclesiastical to Ecclesiastical Structures

The earliest structures of the modern ecumenical movement were in some sense para-ecclesiastical. I am thinking, for instance, of the (World's) Evangelical Alliance (1846), where membership belonged to individuals on the basis of core beliefs in the inspiration and authority of Scripture, the unity and triunity of God, the fallenness of humankind, the incarnation and atonement of Jesus Christ, justification by faith alone, and resurrection and final judgment; the character and functions of the Evangelical Alliance seem to have been taken up by the World Evangelical Fellowship, founded in 1951. Or again there were the Young Men's Christian Associations and the Young Women's Christian Associations. The 1855 "Paris basis" of the former was also adopted *mutatis mutandis* by the latter in 1898: "The YMCAs seek to unite those young men who, regarding Jesus Christ as their God and Saviour according to the Holy Scriptures, desire to be his disciples in their faith and in their life, and to associate their efforts for the extension of his Kingdom among young men." Or yet again, the World's Student Christian Federation, founded in 1895, linked what were usually known at the national levels as Student Christian Movements. For all their pioneering work, the limitations — and comic potential — of such structures are illustrated by Garrison Keillor's fictitious ascription of sponsorship of his Prairie Home Companion to the "Association of Federated Organizations" or the "Federation of Associated Organizations" or the "Organization of Federated Associations" (he hardly cares about the word order).

To be fair, these early ecumenical moves were what made possible the World Missionary Conference of Edinburgh 1910, from which *the* ecumenical movement is conventionally dated.[1] From Edinburgh 1910 sprang, in the 1920s, both the International Missionary Council and, with missionary bishop Charles Henry Brent as catalyst, Faith and Order. It was Faith and Order that took the ecumenical movement beyond the level of good will among individual Christians, cooperation among mission boards, and satisfaction with peaceful coexistence among doctrinally and institutionally unreconciled denominations.

On his return from Edinburgh, Bishop Brent persuaded the General Convention of the Protestant Episcopal Church in the USA to call for a world conference on Faith and Order. With Peter Ainslie of the Disciples of Christ, Brent thenceforth became a leader in the movement to overcome the ecclesiastical divisions that Ainslie castigated as "the scandal of Christianity." Already in 1886, the bishops of the Episcopal Church, in face of "the sad divisions which affect the Christian Church in our own land," and with a view to "the restoration of the organic unity of the Church," had proposed the "Chicago Quadrilateral" of the canonical Scriptures, the Nicene Creed, the dominical sacraments of baptism and the Lord's supper, and the historic episcopate "locally adapted in the methods of its administration." With a mention of the Apostles' Creed alongside the Nicene, these four items were endorsed by the worldwide Lambeth Conference of Anglican bishops in 1888 and figured in the "Appeal to All Christian People" issued by the Lambeth Conference of 1920.

---

1. It might, of course, be said that, rather than being "para-ecclesiastical," nineteenth-century ecumenism operated with a *different* ecclesiology, more "invisibilist" and less "sacramental" than that of historic Christianity or what came to prevail in the ecumenical movement. It is an ecclesiology still characteristic of many "evangelicals" and a point of differentiation between themselves and those they term "ecumenicals."

They came to provide, if not the lineaments of a full portrait of ecclesial unity, then at least the main items on the agenda of the Faith and Order movement throughout the twentieth century, beginning from its first world conference at Lausanne, Switzerland in 1927.

Beside "Faith and Order" and "Mission and Evangelism," a third strand in the international ecumenical movement was constituted by "Life and Work" or *praktisches Christentum.* In 1920 the Orthodox Patriarchate of Constantinople issued an encyclical letter "to the churches of Christ everywhere" proposing, by analogy with the nascent League of Nations, a "fellowship of churches," part of whose purpose would consist in a common social witness in face of the lingering consequences of the First World War. At the same time, the Swedish Lutheran archbishop Nathan Söderblom began preparing for the Universal Christian Conference on Life and Work that would take place in Stockholm in 1925 and carry forward the movement for "practical Christianity" in the interests of liberty, justice, and peace. The activist slogan of "doctrine divides, service unites" made for tense relations with Faith and Order, while the relation between direct evangelism and humanitarian service remained a debated question in the International Missionary Council.

Nevertheless, following their respective world conferences at Edinburgh and Oxford in 1937, the Faith and Order and the Life and Work movements began a process that, after the Second World War, would result in the foundation of the World Council of Churches. For its part, the meeting of the International Missionary Council at Tambaram, India in 1938 had come to a stronger recognition of the mutual implication of church and mission, thus preparing the way for an eventual integration with the World Council of Churches in 1961.

The World Council of Churches

After the Second World War, the inaugural assembly of the World Council of Churches took place at Amsterdam in 1948 under the theme of "Man's Disorder and God's Design." The constitution of the WCC formulated its basis of membership thus: "The World Council of Churches is a fellowship of churches which accept our Lord Jesus Christ as God and Saviour." The WCC was not understood by its member churches to be "above" them as the "church universal" or an incipient "world church"; it was rather their instrument — what the first general secretary W. A. Visser 't Hooft called "an emergency solution, a stage on the road, . . . a fellowship which seeks to express that unity in Christ already given to us and to prepare the way for a much fuller and much deeper expression of that unity."[2]

"The Toronto Declaration" of 1950 sought to clarify the ecclesiological implications of membership in the WCC.[3] The WCC "is not and must never become a super-church." It does not negotiate union between churches. It "cannot and should not be based on any one particular conception of the church." Membership does not "imply that a church treats its own conception of the Church as merely relative" or accepts a "specific doctrine concerning the nature of the Church." Nevertheless, the common witness of the members "must be based on the common recognition that Christ is the divine head of the body." Membership in the church of Christ "is more inclusive" than membership in one's own Christian community, but this "does not imply that each church must regard the other member churches as churches in the true and full sense of the word." In practice, however, member churches "should recognize their solidarity with each other, render assistance to each other in case of need, and refrain from such actions as are incompatible with brotherly relationships."

In *The Household of God* (1953), Lesslie Newbigin — then a bishop in the newly united Church of South India — opined that while the WCC was "a meeting-place," "forum for discussion" and a tool for joint action in "witness" and "service," it should not be viewed as a "model" for unity; for it would favor a unity that was "federal" rather than "organic" — and a unity that was "bureaucratic," to boot.

In 1961, at the New Delhi Assembly, the WCC made its membership basis doctrinally more precise by adding a mention of Holy Scripture and of the Triune God: "The World Council of Churches is a fellowship of churches which confess the Lord Jesus Christ as God and Saviour according to the Scriptures, and therefore seek to fulfill together their com-

---

2. W. A. Visser 't Hooft, *The Genesis and Formation of the World Council of Churches* (Geneva: WCC, 1982), pp. 66-67. The cohesion of the WCC in the first decades of its existence owed much to this brilliant and theologically astute Dutch pastor who, having devoted himself to ecumenical work since his youth, served as the Council's general secretary from 1948 to 1966.

3. See M. Kinnamon and B. E. Cope, eds., *The Ecumenical Movement: An Anthology of Key Texts and Voices* (Geneva: WCC and Grand Rapids: Eerdmans, 1997), pp. 463-68.

mon calling to the glory of the one God, Father, Son, and Holy Spirit."[4] Here, too, the WCC adopted a description of "the unity we seek" that was heavily indebted to a paragraph drafted by Bishop Newbigin:

> We believe that the unity we seek which is both God's will and his gift to his Church is being made visible as all in each place who are baptized into Jesus Christ and confess him as Lord and Saviour are brought by the Holy Spirit into one fully committed fellowship, holding the one apostolic faith, preaching the one Gospel, breaking the one bread, joining in common prayer, and having a corporate life reaching out in witness and service to all and who at the same time are united with the whole Christian fellowship in all places and all ages in such wise that ministry and members are accepted by all, and that all can act and speak together as occasion requires for the tasks to which God calls his people.[5]

The assembly recognized that "the achievement of unity will involve nothing less than a death and rebirth of many forms of church life as we have known them. We believe that nothing less costly can finally suffice."

In the years immediately after New Delhi, the attention was focused on "all in each place," but the Uppsala Assembly of 1968 expanded the horizons again to the universal. The Nairobi Assembly of 1975 consequently endorsed a Faith and Order description of "conciliar fellowship":

> The one Church is to be envisioned as a conciliar fellowship of local churches which are themselves truly united. In this conciliar fellowship of local churches, each local church possesses, in communion with the others, the fulness of catholicity, witnesses to the same apostolic faith, and therefore recognizes the others as belonging to the same Church of Christ and guided by the same Spirit. . . . [E]ach church aims at maintaining sustained and sustaining relationships with her sister churches, expressed in conciliar gatherings whenever required for the fulfilment of their common calling.[6]

The Nairobi text explicitly stated that the term "conciliar fellowship" does "*not* look towards a conception of unity different from that full organic

4. Kinnamon and Cope, eds., *The Ecumenical Movement*, p. 469.
5. Kinnamon and Cope, eds., *The Ecumenical Movement*, pp. 88-92.
6. Kinnamon and Cope, eds., *The Ecumenical Movement*, pp. 110-11.

unity sketched in the New Delhi statement, but is rather a further elaboration of it." Nevertheless, it became used — as Newbigin feared it would be — to justify the maintenance of *confessionally* distinct congregations, and indeed the maintenance of global networks among them (see below: The Christian World Communions). (Incidentally, Newbigin himself came to allow that even "a local church truly united" might as a temporary measure have to allow for different *cultural* groupings within it, though he had discountenanced the — unofficial — continuance of "caste" in the Indian churches.)[7]

The 1991 Canberra Assembly of the WCC provided a more elaborate description of "The Unity of the Church as Koinonia: Gift and Calling."[8] Notable additions included integration of the "pain" and "scandal" of divisions among "the churches," the experience of "common suffering" as a unitive factor, a hint at the common "decision-making" that had come to be seen as necessary over the previous couple of decades, and express mention of "justice, peace, and the care of God's creation" among the areas of and for cooperation. For our question of structures, the most important paragraph was this (notice that there is no definition of what "the churches" — plural — might comprise):

> The unity of the church to which we are called is a koinonia given and expressed in the common confession of the apostolic faith; a common sacramental life entered by the one baptism and celebrated together in one eucharistic fellowship; a common life in which members and ministries are mutually recognized and reconciled; and a common mission witnessing to the gospel of God's grace to all people and serving the whole of creation. The goal of the search for full communion is realized when all the churches are able to recognize in one another the one, holy, catholic and apostolic church in its fulness. This full communion will be expressed on the local and universal levels through conciliar forms of life and action. In such communion churches are bound in all aspects of their life together at all levels in confessing the one faith and engaging in worship and witness, deliberation and action.

Meanwhile the ecumenical movement, as seen from the Geneva headquarters of the World Council of Churches, was undergoing a "para-

7. Kinnamon and Cope, eds., *The Ecumenical Movement*, pp. 114-21.
8. Kinnamon and Cope, eds., *The Ecumenical Movement*, pp. 124-25.

digm shift" — the image used by the soon-to-be-successful candidate for general secretary of the WCC, Konrad Raiser, in a book first published in German in 1989.[9] A major change had indeed been introduced by the official entrance of the Roman Catholic Church onto the ecumenical scene with Vatican II (see below: The Roman Catholic Church). But that was not what Raiser meant. For him, the key shift took place at the WCC Uppsala Assembly in 1968, and he wanted to bring it to completion: it entailed a move from "christocentric universalism" to "full trinitarianism" (though it is hard to see how one can have either without the other; and his own references to the Trinity are rather vacuous); from "salvation history" to "care for the planet"; from concentration on Christian unity to common life in the one human household. Between the lines of Raiser's book it is easy to detect a scorn for "high-church" ecumenism and an anti-Roman sentiment. Further: while the sixties had been "secular," the swing took place in the seventies to "religion" and "spirituality"; and from that point on, the WCC bureaucracy has been more interested in interreligious dialogue than in mission and evangelism.

My implied criticisms of the World Council of Churches are close to those voiced at the end of the 1991 Canberra Assembly in statements by the Orthodox delegates and by Evangelical participants. Having observed in recent years a general shift away from the doctrines epitomized in the constitutional basis of the WCC, the Orthodox now roundly declared: "We miss from many WCC documents the affirmation that Jesus Christ is the world's Saviour. We perceive a growing departure from biblically-based understandings of (a) the Trinitarian God; (b) salvation; (c) the 'good news' of the gospel itself; (d) human beings as created in the image and likeness of God; (e) the Church." Through the 1990s the WCC struggled to find a "Common Understanding and Vision"; but the Harare Assembly of 1998 was widely recognized as a flop. Attempts continue to allow the Orthodox churches more of a say in WCC matters and to create some kind of a "forum" for ecumenical endeavors across the broadest possible range (including the WCC, the RCC, the Christian World Communions, and some "para-ecclesiastical" organizations), but clearly the WCC is no longer the leading player in the ecumenical movement.

9. Konrad Raiser, *Ökumene im Übergang: Paradigmenwechsel in der ökumenischen Bewegung?* (München: Kaiser, 1989); expanded English translation as *Ecumenism in Transition: A Paradigm Shift in the Ecumenical Movement?* (Geneva: WCC, 1991).

The Christian World Communions

"Christian world communions" is now the favored term for what were for quite a while called "world confessional families." They are a roughly recognizable genus, though the species vary considerably in their self-understanding and organization. Their officers meet together annually. Among the largest are:

The (Eastern) Orthodox Churches

These are autocephalous or autonomous churches whose original range was largely geographical or territorial; but modern geopolitical and demographic factors both make them less "national" churches than they long were and also face them with the problem of overlapping jurisdictions that run counter to their traditional ecclesiology ("one bishop in one place"). They view the see of Constantinople as first among equals. A Pan-Orthodox Synod has been in preparation for the past half-century. These — the Byzantine/Chalcedonian churches — and the "Oriental Orthodox" or "pre-Chalcedonian" churches have recently reached "theological" agreement on Christology, but no institutional steps have yet been taken to restore ecclesial communion.

The Anglican Communion

Since 1867 the "Lambeth Conference" of Anglican bishops worldwide has met roughly every ten years. The 1930 Lambeth Conference described the Anglican Communion as "a fellowship, within the one holy catholic and apostolic Church, of those duly constituted dioceses, provinces or regional churches in communion with the see of Canterbury." The 1968 Lambeth Conference set up the Anglican Consultative Council, which is made up of bishops, presbyters, and laypeople from each geographical unity and meets every two years; it has central offices in London. A more recent development has been the regular meeting of the primates of each church. Other major factors in holding global Anglicanism together were the English language and several closely related "Books of Common Prayer." Strains have appeared in the communion during the past few decades over such controversial issues as the ordination of women and sexual ethics; and there is said to be an "impairment" of communion as among certain provinces or within them. The 1998 Lambeth Conference witnessed varying and perhaps conflicting tendencies towards independent provincial action, transprovincial admonition, and a strong primatial role for Canterbury. The Chicago-Lambeth Quadrilateral of 1866-88 (Scriptures; ancient Creeds; baptism and Lord's Supper; "the historic episcopate, locally adapted") dominated the Faith and Order agenda for most of the twentieth century. Anglicans long favored an "organic" model of unity (though the bishops of the Church of South India were not admitted as full members of Lambeth until 1998 because the terms of that organic union of 1947 appeared unsatisfactory to many Anglicans elsewhere); but in more recent years they have tended to a "communion of communions" model.

The World Alliance of Reformed Churches

Founded in 1875, the Alliance of Reformed Churches specified that its members held to the Presbyterian church order. Since 1970 it has been joined with the International Congregational Council to form the World Alliance of Reformed Churches. The member churches cherish their autonomy. The WARC has central offices in Geneva. It is renowned for its social and political interests. The theological dialogues held with other global bodies have usually treated "church-and-world" themes. There is a strong emphasis on the *semper reformanda* character of the church, and some churches renew their book of confessions quite frequently.

The Lutheran World Federation

Established in 1947, the Lutheran World Federation saw itself as a "free association of Lutheran churches" joined together for the sake of united witness, theological study and research, ecumenical engagement with others, and common response to human need and questions of social justice. The LWF has central offices in Geneva. In the 1980s and 90s efforts were undertaken to promote the character of Lutheranism as a "communion." The model most favored by the LWF in the search for wider Christian unity has been that of "reconciled diversity." A major achievement of the LWF has been the production and, in 1999, the signing of the *Joint Declaration on the Doctrine of Justification* with the Pontifical Council for Promoting Christian Unity on behalf of the Roman Catholic Church — though the process as well as the content of the JDDJ has provoked much unease among German Lutheran theologians in the matter of the authority of the LWF so to act and speak.

The World Methodist Council

From 1881 "Oecumenical Methodist Conferences" were held roughly every ten years, until the World Methodist Council was constituted in 1951, which now meets quinquennially. Administered by a minimal bureaucracy, it has no legislative powers over its member churches but serves for fellowship, mutual information and advice, and the management of cooperative programs in evangelization, social action, and the international exchange of pastors. It has acquired a certain "theological" status as the agency through which Methodist churches are engaged in international bilateral dialogues; and in 1996 it approved a short statement of "Wesleyan Essentials of Christian Faith." In Methodist denominations, supreme oversight characteristically resides with (their own) "Conference" composed of ministers and laypeople. "Methodist Conferences have always accepted the Scriptures as the supreme rule of faith and practice, and have been guided in their reading of them by Wesley's *Sermons* and *Explanatory Notes upon the New Testament*. In understanding these authorities, the Conference is the final interpreter."[10]

By far the largest of the eighty or so member churches of the World Methodist Council is the United Methodist Church. While having its origin and basis in the United States, the UMC considers itself a "global" church by virtue of its overseas annual conferences. Delegates from these bodies make for cultural diversity in the quadrennial meetings of the UMC's general conference, and the positions of the overseas delegates in theology and morals generally favor those of historic Christianity. Meth-

---

10. So the 2001 Brighton Report of the bilateral dialogue between the World Methodist Council and the Roman Catholic Church, *Speaking the Truth in Love: Teaching Authority among Catholics and Methodists*, para. 96.

odist churches in the British tradition have sought — sometimes successfully (as, for instance, in South and North India and in Australia) — to enter into organic unions with other Christians at the national level.

The Roman Catholic Church

The Roman Catholic Church is represented at the annual meetings of the officers of the Christian world communions. Its official entrance on the ecumenical scene occurred with Vatican II and the decree *Unitatis redintegratio.* It did not join the World Council of Churches (there would have been no constitutional objection on the WCC side to Roman Catholic membership, even if the massive size of the Roman Catholic Church would have posed technical and representational problems); but a Joint Working Group between the WCC and the Vatican has met annually since 1966 for consultation. So far, the biggest single effect of Roman Catholic ecumenism on our question of global structures has occurred through the new emphasis on bilateral relations that finds a focus in the international dialogues. No doubt those dialogues are the most significant that have the Roman Catholic Church as one of the two partners; but bilateral dialogues occur also between other pairs of Christian world communions. In the long run, the most dramatic potential in global ecumenism is contained in the claim and offer of a "Petrine ministry" made by the see of Rome.

A Petrine Ministry

The World Council of Churches has been hesitant to take up the scarcely separable themes of the papacy and a Petrine ministry; and that remains the case with Faith and Order's latest interim statement on *The Nature and Purpose of the Church* (1998).[11]

Some of the world Christian communions have been quicker off the

11. I have placed this matter in a broader context in my contribution to *Church Unity and the Papal Office,* ed. C. E. Braaten and R. W. Jenson (Grand Rapids: Eerdmans, 2001): "*Ut Unum Sint* in light of 'Faith and Order' — or 'Faith and Order' in light of *Ut Unum Sint?*" pp. 76-97.

mark in the matter of a Petrine office understood as universal ministry of unity, especially in their bilateral dialogues with the Roman Catholic Church. The Anglican–Roman Catholic International Commission (ARCIC) has characteristically discussed the matter in terms of "primacy."[12] Even the Methodist-Catholic 1986 Nairobi report, "Towards a Statement on the Church," could venture that "it would not be inconceivable that at some future date in a restored unity, Roman Catholic and Methodist bishops might be linked in one episcopal college and that the whole body would recognize some kind of effective leadership and primacy in the bishop of Rome. In that case Methodists might justify such an acceptance on different grounds from those that now prevail in the Roman Catholic Church" (paragraph 62).

It is, however, the words of Pope John Paul II in his 1995 encyclical *Ut Unum Sint* that have brought the matter into greatest prominence. Noting that "many of those involved in ecumenism today feel a need for such a ministry," the Bishop of Rome invites the leaders of the churches and their representatives to "a patient and fraternal dialogue" with himself in order to "find a way of exercising the primacy which, while in no way renouncing what is essential to its mission, is none the less open to a new situation." This is how John Paul II, in paragraph 94, describes the responsibilities of the Bishop of Rome as Successor of Peter:

> With the power and the authority without which such an office would be illusory, the Bishop of Rome must ensure the communion of all the churches. For this reason, he is the first servant of unity. This primacy is exercised on various levels, including vigilance over the handing down of the Word, the celebration of the Liturgy and the Sacraments, the Church's mission, discipline and the Christian life. It is the responsibility of the Successor of Peter to recall the requirements of the common good of the Church, should anyone be tempted to overlook it in the pursuit of personal interests. He has the duty to admonish, to caution, and to declare at times that this or that opinion being circulated is irreconcilable with the unity of faith. When circumstances require it, he speaks in the name of all the Pastors in communion with him. He can

---

12. See the 1976 Venice Statement on "Authority in the Church," paragraphs 12 and 19-25, and the 1986 Windsor Statement "Authority in the Church, II," in H. Meyer and L. Vischer, eds., *Growth in Agreement* (Geneva: WCC and Ramsey, N.J.: Paulist, 1984), pp. 93-94, 96-98, 104-5, and 106-15; and the 1998 report, "The Gift of Authority."

also — under very specific conditions clearly laid down by the first Vatican Council — declare *ex cathedra* that a certain doctrine belongs to the deposit of faith. By thus bearing witness to the truth, he serves unity.

In technical terms, the Petrine ministry claimed by the Bishop of Rome involves the various issues subsumed under such words as primacy, collegiality, synodality, subsidiarity, the community of the faithful, infallibility, universal immediate jurisdiction — where the nuances are debated even within Roman Catholic theology and practice. Moreover, this cluster of issues is historically and controversially freighted in both theory and experience. Journalistically, it might be remarked that Pope John Paul II has been very widely appreciated among other Christians for his witness to the gospel even while being criticized on many scores by Catholics "of Roman obedience." Even that notorious inopportunist John Henry Newman, in the approach to the First Vatican Council, saw that "An honorary head, call him primate or premier duke, does not affect the real force, or enter into the essence of a political body, and is not worth contending about. We do not want a man of straw, but a bond of unity."[13]

Furthermore, though only to state the obvious: the papacy is embedded in the entire ecclesiological self-understanding of the Roman Catholic Church. Communion with the Bishop of Rome as Successor of Peter is an essential feature of that one Church of Jesus Christ such as it is said to "subsist in" the (Roman) Catholic Church.

Units of Communion

It is obvious that there is a mutual conditioning between global structures and the units that are (to be) held together in universal communion. The ecumenical vision of the Evangelical Church in Germany, as expressed in a statement of 2001, rises no higher than a "geordnetes Miteinander konfessionsverschiedener Kirchen," which might roughly be translated as "peaceful coexistence in conditions of cold war." This "unreconciled denominationalism" represents the danger inherent in a model of unity as "reconciled diversity." More promising are the ecclesiological implications

---

13. Letter of March 23, 1867, to E. B. Pusey, in *Letters and Diaries,* vol. 23, ed. C. S. Dessain and T. Gornall (Oxford: Clarendon, 1973), p. 106.

of what has been described, in connection with the Lutheran-Catholic *Joint Declaration on the Doctrine of Justification,* as "differentiated consensus"; but even this need entail no more than a "communion of communions," understood as a federation among continuing "world Christian communions." Ecclesial unity would seem to require greater topographical visibility.

An older pattern of universal communion is, in fact, that constituted by the network of local churches, usually understood since Constantinian times as dioceses presided over by a single bishop. But the purely geographical understanding of the units of communion has been complicated by linguistic, ethnic, and cultural diversity on the same territory, the mobility of populations, and the development of various spiritual traditions even within a single confession.

What then, in a universal communion still to be realized, would be the appropriate structures to carry forward the positive inheritance of various traditions coming together after a history of separation? I am thinking in the line of Cardinal Willebrands's "ecclesial *typoi.*"[14] Given agreement in the faith, each such *typos* might maintain its "characteristic theological method and approach," its "characteristic liturgical expression," its "characteristic canonical discipline." Might they be seen as "spiritual families" analogous to "religious orders" within a global church? If so, they would surely need also to be bound with others in their local situations for the sake of visibility of unity on the ground as well as being linked with others at the universal level for the sake of ultimate harmony in doctrine and practice. At the local level, one might think of a collegial oversight exercised by *episcopoi* in and from the several cultural and spiritual traditions.[15] On the global plane, one might think of a conciliar pattern of authority that would both draw from and operate towards the local units and the broader "spiritual families." In the intermediate ranges, one might think of "conferences" with a geographical or a familial scope that would serve theological consultation though not dogmatic definition, that would regulate liturgical practices though not vary sacramental or euchological doctrine, that would plan and monitor evangelistic out-

14. See Johannes Willebrands, "Moving towards a Typology of Churches" (1970), in the Kinnamon and Cope anthology, pp. 99-101.

15. See Geoffrey Wainwright, "In favour of a perichoretic and peripatetic episcopate — perhaps . . ." in H. Meyer, ed., *Gemeinsamer Glaube und Strukturen der Gemeinschaft* (Frankfurt am Main: Otto Lembeck, 1991), pp. 198-207.

reach though not modify the gospel. In its own terms, of course, the Roman Catholic Church already has such structures in place; and the basic ecumenical question may be that of their expansion and reform so as to integrate other Christians and their communities in ways that are not understood and experienced on any side as a simple "return" of wanderers to the fold. John Paul II's *Ut Unum Sint* seems to imply an invitation to explore that possibility.

Future Prospects

In the world but not of it, the Church and the churches live in a secular context that they will hope to influence but cannot and should not control. The twentieth-century ecumenical movement thus developed its structures, in part at least, *in response* to such geopolitical factors as colonialism and decolonization, two world wars, between-the-wars fascisms, and the rise of communism and the fall of the Soviet empire. Prediction is hazardous, but it seems likely that ecumenism in the twenty-first century will have to take into account an increased international interdependence in economics and politics, a worldwide web of information and communication, a series of technological advances affecting the beginning, shaping, and ending of life, and a clash of civilizations on a quasi-religious basis. Internally, progress towards Christian unity will correspondingly face the challenges and opportunities of finding theological and practical agreement in the areas of justice and peace, truth-telling, bioethics, and relation to other religions.

Demographically, and perhaps providentially, Christianity's global center of gravity appears to be shifting southward; and a cause, symptom, or result of that shift is a spiritual style that may roughly be designated pentecostal.[16] In the long term, the most significant ecumenical relationship may be that foreshadowed, in a very preliminary way, by the current dialogue between the Roman Catholic Church and some representatives of Pentecostalism.[17] What the Pentecostal factor may turn out to entail in

16. See Philip Jenkins, *The Next Christendom: The Rise of Global Christianity* (New York: Oxford University Press, 2002).

17. See Geoffrey Wainwright, "The One Hope of Your Calling? The Ecumenical and Pentecostal Movements after a Century," in *Pneuma: Journal of the Society for Pentecostal Studies* 25 (2003): 7-28.

the way of more precise ecclesial structures beggars the present imagination. Meanwhile the modest duty of those churches and spiritual families that have carried the ecumenical movement until now remains that of continuance in prayer, thought, and action for the realization of the New Delhi vision among them.

The Ecclesial Context of Ecumenical Reception:
A Case Study

DAVID S. YEAGO

In this paper, I want to discuss very briefly a few aspects of the large question of what ecumenists call the "reception" of ecumenical agreements, particularly in light of the recent history of my own Lutheran denomination. During the first ten years of its life, the Evangelical Lutheran Church in America took on an unusually ambitious ecumenical agenda, approving a denominational statement of ecumenical policy, three full communion agreements with church bodies of other traditions, and one major doctrinal accord.[1] While I do not suggest that what has happened in the ELCA is universally relevant, it may nonetheless be instructive to look at its "ecumenical decade" as a sort of laboratory of ecumenical reception.

---

1. A proposed ecumenical policy document was the subject of debate at the first ELCA Churchwide Assembly (1989); it was adopted in 1991 after further study. Cf. *Ecumenism: The Vision of the Evangelical Lutheran Church in America* (Chicago: ELCA, 1991). At the Churchwide Assembly of 1997, the ELCA entered into full communion agreements with the North American Province of the Moravian Church, and with the United Church of Christ, the Presbyterian Church in the United State of America, and the Reformed Church of America. The 1997 Assembly also approved the *Joint Declaration on the Doctrine of Justification,* worked out between the Vatican and the Lutheran World Federation and presented by the Federation to its member churches for approval. A full communion agreement with the Episcopal Church failed by a few votes to achieve the necessary two-thirds majority at the 1997 Assembly; a revised version was approved in 1999. Ecumenical controversy continued to be central to the political life of the ELCA until the 2001 Assembly, at which compromise was achieved (at least for the time being) on internal disputes arising from the agreement with the Episcopal Church.

"Reception" in an ecumenical context has been defined to include

all phases and aspects of an ongoing process by which a church under the guidance of God's Spirit makes the results of a bilateral or multilateral conversation a part of its faith and life because the results are seen to be in conformity with the teachings of Christ and of the apostolic community, that is, the gospel as witnessed to in Scripture.[2]

Reception here is defined as a process in which "a church" acts as subject; there are therefore *ecclesial presuppositions* of the process of reception. My concerns arise from the uncomfortable observation that in many recent instances these ecclesial presuppositions of reception seem to be absent or else insufficiently in place to allow an authentic reception-process to occur. This raises ecclesiological questions precisely about the *subject* of the ecumenical process: when it is said that "a church" receives the results of ecumenical dialogue, just what is the concrete referent of that term? Within the constraints of this paper, only a few aspects of this issue can be touched upon.

1. Through the process of reception, according to the definition cited above, ecumenical results become "part of the faith and life" of "a church." There is an assumption here that "a church" is a community with a sufficient *density* of distinctive "faith and life" for this to be a meaningful proposition. Reception assumes that the issues of the dialogues figure in the accounts the communities involved in dialogue give of their faith, and that these issues are intertwined with their distinctive practices, in such a way that the results of ecumenical discussion bear on their communal *identities,* their "faith and life" in that communally constitutive sense.

It is difficult, I fear, to avoid doubt about the validity of this assumption, especially in the well-established churches of the Northern Hemisphere — North American "mainline" denominations[3] and Northern European *Volkskirchen* — which took the lead in the twentieth-

2. William G. Rusch, *Reception: An Ecumenical Opportunity* (Philadelphia: Fortress, 1988), p. 31. These words are italicized in the original.

3. I will refer to these denominations as "mainline" because this term continues to describe their self-understanding better than any other. Sociologically, of course, these churches are no longer in fact the "main line" of North American Christianity.

century ecumenical movement. The second half of the twentieth century saw a rapid and consequential thinning-out of the communal density of these churches. Serious catechesis has become a rarity; traditional languages of proclamation and spiritual counsel have yielded to a universal therapeutic *patois;* worship has become less formalized and liminal, in the process losing much of its character as a formative *discipline;* ancient practices of devotion have fallen into oblivion. In all these areas the older practice of the churches undoubtedly needed reform; the point is that no such reform has occurred. Christian formation has not taken substantial new forms; it has to a considerable extent simply ceased to occur.

This thinning of density sometimes (not always) makes ecumenical agreement easier, but may also make it less significant.[4] For example, I am deeply supportive of the *Joint Declaration on the Doctrine of Justification,*[5] but I cannot help admitting that its approval by my own denomination was made easier by the fact that, beyond a few slogans, very few Lutherans any longer employ the language of justification and grace to talk about anything central to their lives.[6] Indeed, a crucial element in the context of modern ecumenical agreement on justification has been the alienation of Western churches generally from the Augustinian tradition of discourse in which the Reformation disputes were born. This theological alienation has both conditioned and been conditioned by the wholesale (and in large measure deliberate) abandonment in nearly all of Western Christianity of Augustinian penitential piety and its associated

---

4. In the dialogue-report urging full communion between the Evangelical Lutheran Church in America and three denominations from the Reformed tradition (cf. note 1 above), the alienation of both Lutheran and Reformed churches from their own normative traditions is actually adduced as part of the rationale for ecumenical rapprochement. Cf. Keith F. Nickle and Timothy Lull, *A Common Calling: The Witness of Our Reformation Churches in North America Today* (Minneapolis: Augsburg, 1993), pp. 30-31.

5. The Lutheran World Federation and the Roman Catholic Church, *Joint Declaration on the Doctrine of Justification* (Grand Rapids: Eerdmans, 2000).

6. After the ELCA accepted the *Joint Declaration on the Doctrine of Justification,* professors at ELCA seminaries were among the signers of a letter sent by dissident Lutheran theologians to Cardinal Cassidy, then President of the Pontifical Council for Promoting Christian Unity, declaring their rejection of the *JDDJ* and their intention of teaching in opposition to it. That this dramatic demonstration of our internal discord on the doctrine "by which the church stands or falls" had *no consequences whatsoever* — not even a formal call by denominational leadership for internal dialogue — is indicative, I fear, of the *real* status of the doctrine, beyond the level of slogans, in our denominational life.

practices. *Can* the doctrine of justification, in anything like *either* its Reformation *or* its Counter-Reformation forms, be pastorally and spiritually important to churches that have renounced or forgotten the whole Augustinian paradigm of perpetual penitence, the web of vision and practice that gave form to the never-ending Christian struggle with the world, the flesh, and the devil, lived out in sorrow for sin and lowliness before God?

2. Where this loss of density in faith and life has occurred, the languages of inherited confessional commitments lose their reference points in the common life of the churches. In terms coined by the nineteenth-century Lutheran theologian A. F. C. Vilmar, the idiom of a theological tradition loses its constitutive grounding in the *Tatsachen* of ecclesial life, and becomes a mere *Rhetorik,* a reservoir of powerful and evocative language ready to be deployed in arbitrary ways in the service of all manner of interests and projects.[7]

This intersects with another phenomenon of considerable importance in the contemporary experience of reception: the often unexamined and unacknowledged role of *cultural modernity* in sustaining Christian division and at the same time transforming its character. This is a large theme that can only be touched on here. Ecumenical dialogues often proceed under the assumption that the "faith and life" commitments of the participating churches are adequately defined by confessional writings of the Reformation era or even earlier. Yet in the process of reception what often becomes clear is that the functioning sense of identity in our churches is just as much, if not more, determined by various ways in which they participate in or else resist modern culture and its ideologies.

Thus dialogues which assume that "being Lutheran" is essentially a particular way of being a western Augustinian may run afoul of the fact that "being Lutheran" has for many Lutherans become far more centrally a way of being *modern.* This is not to say that being modern is always and in every case a bad thing. But the more our churches have undergone the "thinning of density" just mentioned, the more likely they are to be "modern" in uncritical and problematic ways. Moreover, the commitments to modernity that are cherished in our churches have often not

---

7. Cf. August Ferdinand Christian Vilmar, *Die Theologie der Tatsachen wider die Theologie der Rhetorik: Bekenntnis und Abwehr* (Marburg, 1857).

been acknowledged cleanly and straightforwardly. Instead they have taken possession of the symbols and concepts of older theological controversies and transformed them covertly from within.

In my own setting, the most striking example of this phenomenon is the role played by the concept of "Christian freedom" among those who have fought the reception of the historic episcopate by the ELCA in the context of *Called to Common Mission* (CCM), a full communion agreement with the Episcopal Church.[8] The content of the concept in these circles seems to be almost wholly modernist: "Christian freedom" means the gospel's liberation of the believing individual from external constraints, a "freedom" to which *any* public order of meaning embodied in the outward world can only be threatening and oppressive.[9] Thus opponents of CCM have generally insisted that disagreement with ecclesiastical decisions is a basis for individual entitlement; ordinands who reject CCM "as a matter of conscience" have a *right*, it has been claimed, to special treatment by the denomination. Here the "Lutheran identity" supposedly threatened by ecumenical agreement has devolved into little more than a modernist demand that the community defer to the autonomy of the individual self. Such a "Lutheranism" arguably owes more to John Stuart Mill than to Martin Luther.[10]

A further aspect of this problem needs mention: the commitments to cultural modernity which in many cases have taken possession of older theological and confessional languages are by no means simply a matter of theological abstractions. They express the outlook and protect the interests of groups and institutions within our churches. To continue with the example just given, the power of a modernist account of "freedom" among American Lutherans cannot be fully grasped if one does not un-

---

8. The official text of *Called to Common Mission* can be most conveniently found online at http://www.elca.org/ea/Relationships/episcopalian/ccmresources/contents.html.

9. On the theological background, cf. my essay, "Gnosticism, Antinomianism, and Reformation Theology: Reflections on the Costs of a Construal," *Pro Ecclesia* 2 (Winter 1993): 37-49.

10. Other traditions could doubtless tell similar stories about the co-option of traditional theological categories: perhaps the fate of "experience" in Methodism would be an example. There is also the possibility that ways of *resisting* modernity could play a similar role in transforming the meaning of confessional idioms. One can perhaps see this in some of the difficulties ecumenical reception has encountered in the Roman Catholic Church.

derstand how bitterly angry many Lutheran clergy become at the very suggestion of institutionalized accountability.

As North American Lutheran church life has developed, the pastor of a local congregation is an almost entirely autonomous agent. He or she must of course maintain a mutually tolerable relationship with the congregation, but there are no functioning structures of oversight. This institutional reality is then the social base on which there has been constructed a manifold superstructure of pastoral self-images that share a common individualism. Examples include the pastor as martyr-prophet, the pastor as sensitive therapeutic presence, the pastor as church programming specialist, and most recently, the pastor as freewheeling church-marketing entrepreneur. The perceived threat to "freedom" posed by the symbolism of the historic episcopate is perhaps more than anything else a threat to these professional self-images and their social-institutional base.

3. The definition of reception with which we began also contains two further assumptions that might well be treated together. It assumes, first, that "a church" is a community in which there are communally recognized norms in terms of which ecumenical results will be evaluated — "the teachings of Christ and of the apostolic community, that is, the gospel as witnessed to in Scripture." But looking at the contemporary experience of reception, one does not find that scriptural argument typically plays any significant role in the process. Strategic and tactical concerns about the effect of ecumenical proposals on institutional life and especially on "church growth" play a much larger role, along with a sort of ecclesiastical identity-politics: "What will adoption of this proposal do to our sense of who we are? Does the proposal assert the value of our 'identity' with sufficient force? Or will we lose our self-respect by 'giving up' too much, by truckling to our ecumenical partner?"

At the same time, the definition of reception also assumes that the reception-process is capable of *resolution* — that our churches are capable, as corporate subjects, of giving authoritative accounts of their faith and life into which the results of ecumenical dialogue might be received. The challenge implied here was stated clearly by the formulator of the definition:

> Ecumenical reception will remain incompletely realized until the churches themselves face more directly in the new ecumenical setting

their need for a clear conception of authoritative teaching which includes theologians, other church leaders, and the faithful.[11]

In other words, the very idea of ecumenical reception brings forward the question of *doctrinal magisterium*. This does not imply that ecumenical results enter into the faith and life of a church only or even mainly by a formal exercise of teaching authority. Such entry may be accomplished chiefly by informal processes extending over many years in which ecumenical perspectives gradually permeate the common mind of a church. But ecumenical reception will indeed "remain incompletely realized" where there is no authority competent to declare publicly the reception of ecumenical agreement into that which is not just widely accepted but *normative* in the community's faith and life.[12]

I have suggested elsewhere that the incomprehensibility of the very idea of teaching authority in North American mainline churches is deeply rooted in powerful though not always fully articulate accounts of the *mission* of the church.[13] Mainline churches in Europe and North America typically and most deeply conceive of themselves, I would argue, not as intentional communities of witness to a specific message — "the gospel as witnessed to in Scripture" — but as providers of the consolations of religion to extensive populations. As a service-provider, the first obligation of the church is not to speak a particular truth with clarity but to remain *available* to the populations it is called to serve. Doctrinal contention and authoritative teaching on any model, Reformation or Roman, seem to hamper that availability, and so to deprive the denominational constituency of services to which it has a rightful expectation.

To look once again at my own setting, it has been painful to see the leadership of the ELCA struggle to defend the Churchwide Assembly ac-

---

11. Rusch, *Reception*, p. 63.

12. For example, the non-reaction of the ELCA to public dissent from the *Joint Declaration on the Doctrine of Justification* (cf. note 6, above) surely raises questions about the meaning of the action of the 1997 Churchwide Assembly which approved the *JDDJ*. Since the Churchwide Assembly is the final locus of authority in the ELCA structure, it would seem that if the Assembly cannot make a binding doctrinal decision, then such decisions simply *cannot be made* in the ELCA.

13. Cf. David S. Yeago, "The Papal Office and the Burdens of History: A Lutheran View," in Carl E. Braaten and Robert W. Jenson, eds., *Church Unity and the Papal Office: An Ecumenical Dialogue on John Paul II's Encyclical* Ut Unum Sint *(That All May Be One)* (Grand Rapids: Eerdmans, 2001), pp. 98-123; here especially pp. 112-20.

tion of August 1999 approving *Call to Common Mission* while remaining true to the principle that "all must win and all must have prizes." What is clearly impossible — ruled out by the implicit rules of the game we play as a North American mainline church — is for anyone in authority to suggest that some forms of support for or opposition to CCM might be the expression of *false doctrine,* perhaps even legitimately church-dividing false doctrine. We are simply not the sort of corporate body in which it is a possible role of leadership to make such suggestions or to initiate that sort of discussion.

4. What has been coming into view in these considerations is the problem of what might be called *implicit ecclesiologies* — deeply embedded forms of communal self-understanding that are seldom fully articulate and stand in a complex relationship to formal academic theologies and inherited confessional teaching. Another locus of such "implicit ecclesiology" is of course the *institutional structures* of denominations. Here again, I will use my own church as an example.

In the official ecclesiology of the Evangelical Lutheran Church in America, the church is said to exist in congregational, synodical,[14] and churchwide "expressions." In organizational fact, these three "expressions" are organized *pyramidally* — local congregations relate to one other through "synod," and the synods relate to one other through a "churchwide" denominational center. In other words, communion between the churches is embodied in the subordination of all to a higher instance — a formally perfect reproduction of the ecclesiology of Pope Gregory VII, except that at the top of the pyramid is not the symbolically plausible figure of the successor of Peter, but an office suite in Chicago.

If proposed as an institutional realization of communion between, say, Lutherans and Presbyterians, this structure would simply be laughed out of court. The implication thus seems to be that *Lutheran* unity is something more or other than *Christian* unity. Within this peculiar Lutheran unity, which we would not want to experience with any other Christians, each congregation or synod lives in a horizontal vacuum, with

---

14. A "synod" in the ELCA corresponds to what other churches might call a diocese or a district. The term is used differently in the Lutheran Church — Missouri Synod (LCMS), another Lutheran denomination that grew from a "synod" of immigrant Lutheran congregations located primarily in Missouri.

few significant *lateral* relationships, bound to the larger ecclesial context chiefly by virtue of its *vertical* connection with the "expression of the church" located above it.

The self-enclosure and top-heaviness of this mode of organization reflect the long aspiration of American Lutherans to unite in a cohesive denominational structure that would allow them appropriate influence and prestige on the American religious scene. Having substantially achieved this goal, however, mainline American Lutheranism has found itself paralyzed rather than empowered. Local initiatives in mission are discouraged by a central-planning mentality and a central bottleneck of resources. Denominational mission planning is tacitly but tightly controlled by the exigencies of feeding the institutional elephant we have installed in our backyard. The political life of the denomination is dominated on all sides by the fear that some hostile "other" on the Right or on the Left will gain or has gained control of the institutional power-center.

Ecumenically, this structure makes it impossible for any congregation or synod to move very far towards communion with other churches except insofar as the whole institutional pyramid moves along with it. Only "churchwide" can make binding ecumenical commitments. This hinders the sort of untidily open-ended growth toward unity from the ground up that is envisioned, for example, in the *Facing Unity* document of the Lutheran–Roman Catholic Joint Commission on Unity,[15] and at the same time implicates every ecumenical proposal in the dynamic of power-struggle for control of the "churchwide" high ground.

5. It would be a great mistake, however, to assume that the ELCA's pyramidal structure implies a common life rigidly controlled from above. The outcome (so far) of the strife over the historic episcopate in the ELCA may illustrate the complexity of the situation. The 2001 Churchwide As-

---

15. Roman Catholic–Lutheran Joint Commission, *Facing Unity: Models, Forms, and Phases of Catholic–Lutheran Church Fellowship* (Geneva: Lutheran World Federation, 1985). This report described a process by which visible unity could grow "from below" through multiple officially sanctioned agreements at the diocesan/synodical level, rather than through a single agreement binding each communion universally "from above." While specifically addressed to the Lutheran–Roman Catholic relationship, the model could be adapted to other situations. Perhaps not surprisingly, *Facing Unity* was very poorly "received" by the sponsoring churches.

sembly voted that candidates for ordination would be allowed to request an "exception" to the rule that the synodical bishop is the ordinary minister of ordination. Such requests may be granted or denied by the synodical bishop, whose decision is final and without appeal. Should the exception be granted, the ordinand will be ordained by a pastor not installed in the episcopal office, thus avoiding any "hierarchical" defilement of his or her conscience.

This action was remarkable in several respects. The 1999 Assembly had adopted *Called to Common Mission* on the *explicit* understanding that its terms would not permit "planned exceptions" to the rule of ordination by a bishop, and it was on this understanding that the Episcopal Church adopted the proposal at its General Convention in 2000. The 2001 ELCA action therefore constituted the *unilateral* amendment of an agreement to live in "full communion" — which suggests, to say no more, a rather peculiar notion of what "communion" means. Furthermore, with rich but unconscious irony, the Assembly made provision for the consciences of those who reject "hierarchy" by giving ELCA bishops arbitrary power over an important aspect of the denomination's ordination practice.

Both in the Assembly action itself, and in the power conferred thereby on synodical bishops, a peculiar pattern emerges: the pyramidal structure functions not to impose a corporate rule of life from the top down, but *to ensure that there shall be no such rule*. The move in twentieth-century American Lutheranism from primarily lateral to primarily vertical bonds of communion correlates directly with our gradual loss of the capacity to sustain a common rule of life together. This incapacity is masked by self-approving talk of "diversity," and the celebration of "pastoral" rather than "legalistic" ways of dealing with issues. Inevitably, however, a "pastoral" approach — whether to divorce or clergy misconduct or our ecumenical commitments — involves the renunciation of a doctrinally coherent and communally recognized rule of life; instead, the pastor or bishop is given arbitrary power to deal with each case as it arises, with no significant accountability to any corporate norm.[16]

16. Along with these developments, there has appeared recently in the ELCA a peculiar rhetoric of "trusting the church," i.e., the ELCA structure and its processes, which often goes to the point of demanding that the outcome of institutional processes be regarded *a priori* as the work of the Holy Spirit. The irony of such a glorification of formal institutional procedure in a *Lutheran* setting is obvious and exquisite.

Behind these developments is undoubtedly the service-provider ecclesiology mentioned above. The institutional structure of the denomination is shaped by this self-understanding; therefore when the denomination attempts to act according to a different ecclesiology, when it occasionally acts as though it were an intentional community of gospel witness, its institutional life is threatened. The ELCA simply did not realize what it was getting into when it accepted *Called to Common Mission,* which obliged it to observe certain practices as an embodied witness to our unity in the apostolic faith with the Episcopal Church, and more broadly with the church through the ages. When it became clear that such witness might have institutional costs, that congregations and pastors might withdraw from the ELCA, creating painful and messy legal and pastoral tangles, the denomination and its leaders acted consistently with the service-provider ecclesiology embedded in the denominational structure: we must make room for everyone, we must accommodate those who sincerely disagree, we must deal with this situation "pastorally," and so on. Above all, we must never, never suggest that our inability to agree on the practices mandated in CCM might be the tip of an iceberg of deeper internal divisions in faith.

A church body that cannot adopt a common rule of faith and life and stick with it cannot *in principle* carry out the full reception of ecumenical agreements. Christian unity is not achieved by paper declarations of theological agreement and formal expressions of mutual recognition;[17] it is achieved only when those "in each place" who have been separated begin to *live together* as one people of God "in one fully committed fellowship."[18] In the words of the Lutheran theologian Peter Brunner, such unity can only be realized "through an abundance of actually lived, concrete, historical, and of course, constitutionally formulated relationships and forms of expression. . . ."[19] Unity in the gospel calls for unity in

---

17. It is clear that the ELCA's full communion agreements with the Moravians and the Reformed have caused less controversy precisely because they commit us to less at the level of concrete practice.

18. Phrases in quotation marks are from the classic account of visible unity articulated at the New Delhi Assembly of the World Council of Churches in 1961. Cf. *The New Delhi Report: The Third Assembly of the World Council of Churches, 1961,* ed. W. A. Visser 't Hooft (London: SCM, 1962), p. 116.

19. Peter Brunner, "The Realization of Church Fellowship," in *The Unity of the Church: A Symposium,* Papers presented to the Commission on Liturgy and Theology of

ecclesial life and mission; such unity requires that separated bodies *commit themselves* to shared forms and practices and arrangements that give expression to their unity in the gospel and bind them together concretely as a single people. Church bodies that are not organized to embody communion in a specific faith and mission, but are formed on some other ecclesiological principle, will therefore find ecumenical reception exceedingly painful, and in all likelihood prohibitively costly.[20]

The full dimensions of the situation only become clear, moreover, when we realize the "implicit ecclesiologies" that frustrate ecumenical reception are themselves by and large the product of Christian division. The "service-provider" ecclesiology, for example, is rooted deeply in the need of separated churches to protect their own *separate* existence, to carve out a piece of demographic turf on which independent institutional life can be securely grounded. There is a relatively straight line from state-establishment in post-Reformation Europe to church-marketing and other ways of catering to class-defined constituencies in contemporary mainline churches. The common element is the search for a mechanism by which to bind a particular population firmly to a particular institutional structure, in order to ensure the vigor and indeed the survival of the latter. In the unfolding logic of division, the separate institutions initially formed to sustain sharply defined confessional commitments end by blurring and suppressing those commitments, as separate institutional existence becomes an end in itself.

6. Every "mainline" denomination is organized differently, and each lives out of a distinctive theological and institutional history. The details of the ELCA's situation and experience will not, therefore, be reproduced in other settings. Nevertheless, it is safe to say that every mainline North American denomination today faces similar issues in its own distinctive

---

the Lutheran World Federation (Rock Island, Ill.: Augustana Press, 1957), pp. 17-18. English translation altered following Michael Root, "What Are We Doing? The Unity of the Church and the Unity of the Churches," in Gabriel Fackre and Michael Root, *Affirmations and Admonitions: Lutheran Decisions and Dialogue with Reformed, Episcopal, and Roman Catholic Churches* (Grand Rapids: Eerdmans, 1998), p. 76.

20. It is true that *Called to Common Mission* has been received far more easily by the Episcopal Church than by the ELCA. However, by the logic of this particular relationship, the Episcopalians were chiefly asked to *relax* certain rules temporarily in order to achieve full communion with the ELCA, not to adopt new and controversial practices.

way: the "thinning out" of ecclesial density and Christian formation; the confusing interaction of theological tradition and cultural modernity in the formation of denominational identity; the conflict of doctrinal and ecumenical aspiration with the "implicit ecclesiologies" that inform church structures and frustrate such aspiration; and above all, the looming doubt that mainline denominations any longer have the capacity to sustain commitment to any common rule of faith and life whatsoever. I would suggest, therefore, that the general dynamics of the ELCA's disappointing experience of ecumenical reception, if not its specific forms, are likely to reappear in other mainline settings.

All these observations raise in one way or another the question of the *ecclesial subject* of ecumenical reception. What exactly is the referent of the term "church" when it is said that in reception "a church" makes ecumenical results part of its faith and life? More pointedly: Where can we identify corporate ecclesial subjects that are *competent* to carry out ecumenical reception? The twentieth-century ecumenical movement typically assumed that the denominations would ordinarily be sufficient acting subjects of the ecumenical process. In recent years, however, Michael Root and Ephraim Radner have both questioned this assumption, from different but in the end convergent perspectives.

Michael Root has asked how we ought to assess "the ecclesial character of the denomination"[21] if unity is an *essential* mark of the church:

> Perhaps neither the denominations nor the world communions can be churches in the full sense of the word, because they are social forms which inherently lack the mark of unity in that both are social forms created by (and that can only exist within) a situation of church division.[22]

Root's point is not to deny altogether the ecclesial significance of denominations; like the Christian world communions, they may be "the home and expression of social process that would give them a certain 'ecclesial density,' i.e., that would make them church to a degree."[23] As the concrete forms of visible church unity that actually exist, denomina-

---

21. Michael Root, "The Unity of the Church and the Reality of the Denominations," *Modern Theology* 9 (1993): 385-401; here 397.
22. Root, "The Unity of the Church," p. 396.
23. Root, "The Unity of the Church," p. 396.

tions deserve a certain critical respect from ecumenists, however distant they are from the unity to which we are called. But as a form of unity that presupposes and perpetuates disunity, the denominational embodiment of ecclesial communion is inherently flawed, indeed, self-contradictory.

In light of this insight, Root goes on to challenge the assumption that denominations, in contrast to the world communions, have a *unique* ecclesial integrity that renders them privileged subjects in the ecumenical process.

> For most Protestant (including Anglican) groups, only the denomination or national church can make binding decisions. The decisions of the world body do not themselves commit the member churches. Often, this decision has been justified precisely by the claim that the denomination or national church is a church in the full sense and the world body is not. Can this distinction, however, withstand careful scrutiny? If the denomination or national church must itself be understood as a strictly provisional institution, should it be the sole body capable of making binding decisions, e.g., to enter into a relation of full communion with another church?[24]

The line of thought that Root here follows "upward" from the denominations to the Christian world communions might surely also be followed "downward" from the denomination to the smaller ecclesial communities contained within the denominational structure. If it is not obvious that the denomination is a more sufficient or competent ecclesial agent than a synod or diocese, or even a congregation, is it so obvious that binding ecumenical decisions cannot be made at these levels also? This question gains pertinence, I would suggest, at a time when, by default or set purpose, mainline denominational bodies are increasingly leaving central questions of faith and life to be decided at the diocesan/synodical or congregational level.[25]

In a different theological key, Ephraim Radner has suggested, in ef-

24. Root, "The Unity of the Church," p. 398.
25. For example, the implication of the ELCA's "exceptions" clause is that when a congregation decides whether or not to call an "exceptionally" ordained pastor, it will also be deciding whether or not to live in full communion with the Episcopal Church. The most glaring case of devolution towards "local option," is of course that of moral teaching on sexuality, which in most mainline churches is now determined on a congregation-by-congregation basis.

fect, that our existing denominational unities relate to the visible unity to which God's people are called much as the *palaios anthrōpos*, the "Old Adam" (Rom. 6:6; Eph. 4:22), relates to the *kainos anthrōpos*, the new human being "created according to the likeness of God in true righteousness and holiness" (Eph. 4:24).[26] The old and the new cannot be connected by any developmental process, but only by a christologically shaped *dying and rising*. Just as the *palaios anthrōpos* cannot move itself into newness of life, but can only suffer the baptismal act of God by which it is co-crucified with Christ (cf. Rom. 6:1-11), so our present denominational bodies cannot be seen as competent ecclesial subjects of ecumenical movement: "A prophetic understanding of denominationalism answers with a curt No the question as to whether divided churches can, by definition, possess integrity at all."[27]

Despite this austere judgment, the future Radner prophesies for the divided churches is not mere dissolution, but rather death and resurrection, a corporate conformation to the crucified Christ that can be embraced in the sobriety of hope. This *conformitas Christi* contains three moments that Radner describes as the "disappearance of denomination," the "formation of a remnant," and the acceptance of the limits of a "constricted penitence."[28] That is, the identities and unities formed through division are dispersed under the providential pressures of history; new forms of ecclesial communion, to which the old divisions are essentially irrelevant, begin to take form in the wake of this dispersal; and these new

---

26. This is not Radner's way of putting the matter, but a restatement of what I take to be his central claim in the idiom of baptismal theology. Cf. Ephraim Radner, *The End of the Church: A Pneumatology of Christian Division in the West* (Grand Rapids: Eerdmans, 1998), as well as his somewhat more accessible essay, "The Cost of Communion: A Meditation on Israel and the Divided Church," in *Inhabiting Unity: Theological Perspectives on the Proposed Lutheran-Episcopalian Concordat*, ed. Ephraim Radner, R. R. Reno, and Wolfhart Pannenberg (Grand Rapids: Eerdmans, 1995), pp. 134-52. For a lucid analysis of Radner's work, cf. Bruce D. Marshall, "The Divided Church and Its Theology," *Modern Theology* 16 (2000): 377-96.

27. Radner, "The Cost of Communion," p. 135. Radner describes the situation of the divided churches theologically by way of a typological reading of the division and re-unification of Israel. Just as the unity of Israel was not restored except by the exile-death of the Northern and Southern Kingdoms and the resurrection of return, so too the unity of the church entails the dying of the unities created by division. "Prophetic" here therefore essentially means "scriptural."

28. Cf. Radner, "The Cost of Communion," pp. 143-51.

configurations of communion find themselves "constricted," driven back to the apostolic origin, to the rock that remains when the wood, hay, and stubble of our pretensions and illusions are consumed by divine judgment (cf. 1 Cor. 3:10-15).

Radner's work does not, it should be noted, call *us* to dismantle our denominational homes. His work is a *prophecy* of the "disappearance of denomination" at *God's* hands, not a program for the demolition of denomination on our initiative. His counsel for those living amidst the decomposition of the denominations is not anger and rebellion, but rather, in a wonderful phrase, "a profound kind of staying put even while the place in which we stand is beaten down and reconfigured from its bottom up into a new household."[29] Nor does Radner counsel despair about denominational ecumenism (though he might, to be sure, treat it with more understanding[30]), even as he calls into question the capacity of our denominations to act as competent ecumenical subjects. The *conformitas Christi* which is our future can "include the ecumenical actions of divided churches in its grasp,"[31] so that in and through the process of ecumenical reception there can occur one dimension of our submission to the humiliation of denominational self-sufficiency and the reconfiguration of the ecclesial remnant.

In this diagnosis, Radner is only confirming and expounding with unprecedented depth what the twentieth-century ecumenical movement at its spiritual core always knew. Ecumenical reception must be understood not as an action by which competent ecclesial subjects move themselves from division into communion, but as the *suffering* of God's acts of judgment and mercy by which the ecclesial subject is being re-formed amid the exposure of our present incompetence as a divided people. As

---

29. Radner, *The End of the Church,* p. 352.

30. Radner undoubtedly does not give professional ecumenists, whose public statements are often made under the constraints of official position and ecclesiastical appointment, enough credit for insight into the implications of Christian disunity. Cf. what Rusch says, to be sure in a far milder tone, about the implications of reception as a spiritual process, in *Reception,* pp. 55ff. What it could mean when Rusch says that reception "goes to the core of a church's being" (p. 55) if *not* the sort of corporate dying and rising with Christ of which Radner speaks? It would, however, be an even greater mistake for ecumenists to fail in turn to see that Radner is attempting to supply a theological metanarrative adequate to the deepest insights of the ecumenical movement itself.

31. Radner, "The Cost of Communion," p. 151.

the *New Delhi Report* expressed it, in words that follow closely upon its classic description of visible unity:

> The achievement of unity will involve nothing less than a death and rebirth of many forms of church life as we have known them. We believe that nothing less costly can finally suffice.[32]

---

32. *The New Delhi Report,* p. 117.

The Debilitation of the Churches

R. R. RENO

To a great extent, the current ecumenical impasse stems from difficulties faced by the churches themselves. Doctrinal aphasia seems widespread. The churches are shaped by a cultural captivity that overrides distinctively Christian commitments, and this has produced a crisis of mission and catechesis. Intra-ecclesial conflict paralyzes and increasingly diverse teaching and practices undermine the cogency of church traditions. In short, the ecumenical movement has stalled because the participant churches are too weakened to effectively motivate, participate in, and receive forward momentum.

This debilitation of the churches is, without doubt, a broad phenomenon. It is very much the preoccupation of modern theologians. Whether revisionary or restorative, what makes modern Christianity modern seems to be an acute sense that the public dimension of faith (the scriptural text, the creedal tradition, liturgy, and church discipline) suffers from a diminished cognitive, affective, and social potency. To present and assess this condition (whether imagined or real) would entail a history of modern Christianity. I cannot here pursue such ambitions. Instead, I wish to focus on the ecumenical debilitation of the churches, the fact that they appear unable to play the roles assigned to them by modern ecumenism. My goal is to explain how the churches, far from serving as agents of unity, are weakened and diminished by the Christian imperative of unity. In so doing, I hope to provide a diagnosis of the stalled ecumenical movement.

My plan is to advance a seemingly paradoxical thesis: the more seriously the churches take the imperative of unity, the less capable they become as ecumenical agents. This thesis depends upon the key logical and historical claim that division has a debilitating effect upon churches. In other words, the churches cannot see how they are both ecclesial subjects (churches in the proper sense) and ecumenical agents (Christian communities that recognize the present need to restore the unity of the church).[1]

The ecumenical process is stalled because the churches cannot square the circle. They cannot articulate their identities as churches, while at the same time admitting that they suffer an ecumenical need for unity with others.[2] This should not be surprising. The theological discipline devoted to defining the identity of the church, what we now call "ecclesiology," emerged out of the need to identify the true church amidst diverse and rival Christian bodies after the Reformation. The modern ecumenical movement focuses on the imperative of unity among divided churches, and this clashes with the tradition of Western ecclesiology and its fundamental project of justifying separation. As a result, great pressures develop that make the claims of post-Reformation ecclesiologies either implausible or incoherent. First and most obviously, the polemical thrust of traditional ecclesiologies is in fundamental tension with a growing sense of the already implicit reality of unity, as well as the desire for

---

1. Throughout I will presume to speak about Western Christianity. I am insufficiently informed about Orthodoxy to advance any claims. Nonetheless, Alexander Schmemann's essay, "A Meaningful Storm," in *Church, World, Mission* (Crestwood, N.Y.: St. Vladimir's, 1979), pp. 85-116, suggests certain parallels between Western Christian denominationalism and Orthodox ecclesial nationalism. "The national principle which, in a different ecclesiological context and in continuity with the genuine canonical tradition, had been indeed a principle of unity and thus a valid form of the Church's self-fulfillment ('one Church in one place'), became in America exactly the opposite: a principle of division, the very expression of the Church's subordination to the divisions of 'this world'" (pp. 102-3). Thus, in the American context, national churches now expatriated have calcified into *de facto* denominations, and "there appeared finally a hierarchy, a theology, even a spirituality defending all this as something perfectly normal, positive and desirable" (p. 105). Given such developments, unity becomes a threat to ecclesial identity.

2. In this analysis, I will give most of my attention to the intellectual dimension of church life, the plausibility structures, if you will. A more satisfactory account would trace the bureaucratic, liturgical, and pastoral debilitations that parallel and reinforce the theological aspects. I have attempted to do this elsewhere, although only in an ad hoc way, in an essay, "Toward a Postliberal Ecclesial Spirituality," in *In the Ruins of the Church: Sustaining Faith in an Age of Diminished Christianity* (Grand Rapids: Brazos, 2002), pp. 129-47.

more explicit forms of unity. More importantly, however, in the context of enduring separation, attempts to reformulate an account of the church that is not invested in division fail to identify an actual, existent church.[3] For both reasons, the most obvious sources of disciplined reflection about the nature and identity of the church — i.e., traditions of ecclesiological reflection in the West — turn out to offer only a debilitated voice to those who wish to articulate the conditions for and shape of Christian unity.[4] Not surprisingly, then, the churches are unable to play their roles in the ecumenical movement. But I am speaking too enigmatically. Let me turn to some historically detailed expositions of the problem.

Roman Catholic Debilitation

Surveying Roman Catholic ecclesiology since the Reformation, Gustave Thils suggests that systematic investigations into the features that identify the church as "one, holy, apostolic, and catholic" were not elements of pre-Reformation treatises. With rare exceptions, he reports, "the imposing literature provoked by the Eastern schism, the *Contra Iudaeos,* the *Adversus Saracenos,* the *Adversus Waldenses,* the *Contra Catharos,* had confined itself to the direct defense of the points of catholic doctrine raised by the dissidents or heretics. . . ."[5] In contrast, the sixteenth-century schism gave birth to a whole tradition of treatises *De vera Ecclesia.*[6] To be

---

3. Looking back on his attempt to construct a "third way" between Protestantism and Roman Catholicism, Newman identifies the vaporous and otherworldly unreality of his own proposal in comparison to the Protestant and Roman realities "that actually gripped men's minds and shaped nations." They are "real religions," while the position Newman advances was but an idea and, an idea that, however wonderful in itself, had no power to shape souls and govern institutions ("Preface to the Third Edition," *The Via Media of the Anglican Church* [Oxford: Clarendon, 1990], pp. 14-16). In the end, for Newman, real actualities triumphed over notional possibilities, because the latter lacked the ability to cure souls.

4. Ecumenical documents recognize this difficulty. See the Methodist–Roman Catholic Report of Nairobi 1986: "As we reflect on a re-united church, we cannot expect to find an ecclesiology shaped in a time of division to be entirely satisfactory" (para. 22).

5. Gustave Thils, *Les notes de l'église dans l'apologétique catholique depuis la réforme* (Paris: Desclée, 1937), p. xiii.

6. For a view that emphasizes continuity, see Scott H. Hendrix, "In Quest of the *Vera Ecclesia:* The Crises of Late Medieval Ecclesiology," *Viator: Medieval and Renaissance*

sure, traditional polemics relying on material charges of heresy continued. Shelves groan under the weight of the volumes. However, precisely as those polemics reinforced rather than diminished divisions, serious effort turned toward the formal question of what constitutes the "true" church over and against the "false." The upshot was an elaboration of the "notes" of the Church, famously developed by Bellarmine. These "notes" were to serve as positive criteria by which to judge between rivals.

Thils charts the development of Roman Catholic efforts to specify these criteria, and the note of unity tells an interesting tale. In the sixteenth and seventeenth centuries, Thils reports, Roman Catholic apologists were content to contrast the unity of Catholicism with the anarchy of Protestantism. The spirit of Protestant division seemed so evident that no precise account of Catholic unity was necessary. Protestants demonstrated their falsity by anathematizing each other. How could such a form of life honor the plain sense meaning of Christian unity? However, by the nineteenth century, Pan-Protestant cooperation, Anglicanism's newly articulate affirmations of certain features of catholic polity, and Eastern Orthodoxy's reappearance in the overall cultural consciousness of the West, blocked easy contrast. By the twentieth century, "Catholics . . . recognized a certain unity in dissident churches. They could no longer speak of non-Romans as a multitude of disparate and confused sects that swarm in the synagogue of Satan."[7] The facts on the ground, so to speak, began to put pressure on Roman Catholic ecclesiology. Given the increased unity among Protestants (to say nothing of Eastern Orthodoxy), what makes the Roman Catholic Church the proper subject of the apostolic predicate "one"?

Just this question forced greater precision. The difference between Roman Catholic and rival claimants to the title "one, holy, catholic, and apostolic church" had to be reestablished. Here, more than partisanship was at work. The fact of Christian division exerted logical pressure. Con-

---

Studies 7 (1976): 347-78. Hendrix surveys the tumultuous late medieval debates about papal authority and its relation to the presumptive spiritual authority of the life of poverty. It is not clear that Hendrix's account contradicts Thils's. The pre-Reformation debate was certainly fractious, but unlike post-Reformation debates, the issue was not that of identifying the church over and against rivals. Instead, the debate concerned identifying the pneumatic core of the church, its spiritual heart and proper source of authority over and against corrupted and deceptive forms of authority *within* a single ecclesial body.

7. Thils, *Les notes,* p. 211.

sider this line of reasoning. If more than one ecclesial body exhibits the notes of the church, then they all may rightly be called "church." Unity, however, is a note of the church. Therefore, if more than one church can be called "church," then either unity is not a note of the church, or the plain sense meaning of unity must be rejected.

To a great extent, the Reformed tradition has advanced the notion of "invisible unity," which adopts the second option in order to focus on unity in doctrine rather than institutional unity. Modern theological attempts to manage Christian conflict with pseudo-trinitarian theologies of diversity and difference are unfortunate stepchildren of this tradition. But this turn away from the plain sense meaning of unity was closed to Roman Catholic theologians. As a result, in the development of Roman Catholic ecclesiology, redoubled effort was put into identifying the visible features of the church that would warrant her claim to unity, as well as the other notes.

Thils charts this redoubled effort. Driven to find the distinctive feature of the Roman Catholic Church that differentiates it from rivals, ecclesiology — indeed, a great deal of Roman Catholic systematic theology — balanced on the narrow point of the juridical authority of the Bishop of Rome. The late-nineteenth-century textbook, *A Handbook of Fundamental Theology*, by John Brunsmann, illustrates. Turning to the notes of the Church, Brunsmann explains his purpose. "Here . . . our object is to demonstrate which of the different Christian denominations is the true Church."[8] Brunsmann is not motivated by mean-spirited fear of "the other." He is driven to this task by rather commonplace assumptions about the Christian life. As he observes, "A man can become a member of the true Church [and he has already demonstrated that this is a positive duty for all Christians] only if that Church is knowable as such, and can be with certainty distinguished from every other rival claimant. Since God in His wisdom and justice cannot make demands which it would be impossible for a man to comply with, the true Church must of necessity be visible, so that she may be recognized with certainty and distinguished from all false claimants" (p. 388). These assumptions, then, force Brunsmann to put an accent on that which distinguishes. "The notes of the Church cannot occur simultaneously in several denominations, because

---

8. Volume 3, p. 402. I am using the English edition, adapted and edited by Arthur Preuss (St. Louis: Herder, 1931). Page citations follow in parentheses.

in that case they would not enable us to distinguish the true Church from rival claimants" (p. 404), and we would not be able to discharge our duty as Christians.

In view of the breadth and depth of shared language and practice — wide varieties of Christian communities use Scripture, ordain ministers, baptize infants, and celebrate communion — Brunsmann narrows the focus to that one feature of Roman Catholicism that clearly divides its ecclesial life from others: the juridical primacy of the Bishop of Rome. The visible clarity of *that* feature of the church secures and defines all other features. As Brunsmann puts the matter, "Unity of doctrine and faith manifests itself . . . in the decisions of the infallible teaching office" (p. 411). The same holds for the other notes of the church. Catholicity is only evident in the visible structure of the church "subject to one common head, the pope" (p. 412). Apostolicity is secured by the juridically authorized succession of bishops. Brunsmann does not reduce the note of holiness to the juridical authority of the church, but as Ephraim Radner so effectively shows, in post-Reformation Catholic thought, holiness is only probative if its authenticity is secured by the magisterium.[9] In each instance, the notes of the church reduce to a nearly vacuous circularity. We can know that the Roman Catholic Church is the one true church because only the Roman Catholic Church has produced a machinery of juridical self-identification. And this is exactly what Brunsmann says. By his analysis, the "knowability" of the church "is based primarily upon the existence and exercise of the power of jurisdiction, culminating in the primacy of Peter and his successors, the Roman pontiffs" (p. 387).

The approach to ecclesiology adopted by Brunsmann debilitates the capacity of the Roman Catholic Church to function in the ecumenical movement. This occurs in two ways. First, in this ecclesiological tradition, the one thing that Roman Catholics *do not share* with other Christians (magisterial office culminating in the papacy) supersedes the many things they *do share* (Scripture, ancient creeds, sacraments) as the touchstone of identity and assurance. This is not a function of insularity,

---

9. See *The End of the Church: A Pneumatology of Christian Division in the West* (Grand Rapids: Eerdmans, 1998), pp. 57-134. This feature is clearly evident in the Jansenist controversy. See Radner's dissertation, "A Pneumatological Investigation of the Miracles of Saint-Medard and Their Rejection" (New Haven: Yale University, 1994), revised and published as *Spirit and Nature: The Saint-Medard Miracles in 18th Century Jansenism* (New York: Crossroad, 2002).

ecclesial nativism, or conservatism. It follows, as Brunsmann so painstak-
ingly shows, from the logic of affirming the necessary unity of the church
amidst divided Christianity. The second ecumenical dysfunction is sub-
tler. Brunsmann's analysis shifts the focus of Roman Catholic theology
and ecclesial life away from the primary apostolic tradition (because that
which is shared amidst division is unable to identify the church), and in
so doing, greases the skids toward cultural captivity. The power of jurisdiction is easily assimilated to the logic of modern bureaucracies: com-
mercial, military, and governmental. Thus, at the very moment that the
Roman Catholic Church is clearly distinguished from all other churches,
it blurs into the landscape of modern life. Thus, in ecumenical discussions, inevitable cultural differences become closely associated with
ecclesial identities.

The ecumenical dysfunction was not unknown to leading Roman
Catholic theologians, though they certainly did not label it as such. In Roman Catholicism, before the Second Vatican Council, an interest in ecumenism was often denounced as a species of "indifferentism" or "latitudinarianism," that is, a disregard for fundamental truths of the faith.[10] This
worry reflected both consequences of the logic that dominated post-
Reformation Roman Catholic ecclesiology. The standard ecclesiology sets
about to demonstrate the identity of the Roman Catholic Church as the
one, holy, catholic, and apostolic church, and this seems to require explicitly rejecting the need for the ecumenical movement. The one true Church
already exists; schismatics ought to abandon their deformed communities
and return. The charge of "indifferentism," however, reflected a worry
about ecumenism rather than a confident rejection. That worry was
straightforward. Should Roman Catholics act as if the difference between
Rome and, for example, Geneva was not fundamental and decisive, then,
by the analysis Brunsmann utilizes, the apostolic trustworthiness and visible clarity of the church would be in doubt. After all, that trustworthiness
and clarity depend upon the "power of jurisdiction" exercised by Roman
pontiffs — precisely the unbridgeable difference between Rome and
Geneva. To be indifferent about the latter throws into doubt the former.

10. On the condemnation of indifferentism and latitudinarianism, see the Syllabus
of Errors, sec. III. For a discussion representative of nineteenth-century Roman Catholic
sensibilities, see the entry, "latitudinaires," in the *Dictionnaire de théologie dogmatique*
(1851).

An episode on the eve of the Second Vatican Council illustrates the logic of the worry about "indifferentism." During the preparation of the schema *De Ecclesia,* Cardinal Bea floated a number of ecumenical ideas in public speeches, including the idea that non-Catholics were, in some sense, members of the Church. The conservative theologian Sebastian Tromp led the opposition to such ideas. As a historian of the Council observes, "Tromp took direct issue with Bea's position and explained that to admit that heretics and schismatics, forty-five percent of all Christians, are really members of the Church would make it difficult to defend the ecumenical character of Trent and Vatican I, would require that heretical and schismatical bishops be invited to Vatican II, would deny the unity of the Church, and would ruin its claims to infallibility."[11]

The logic of Tromp's concerns was unassailable then, and remains so today. His resistance to Cardinal Bea's ecumenical initiatives was not the consequence of "pride" in any ordinary sense; it was the result of clear thinking. The situation faced by Roman Catholic theologians was and remains unambiguous. If the Roman Catholic Church is *not* the only just claimant to the title "Church," then an unhappy disjunction seems to follow. Either no properly one, holy, catholic, and apostolic Church exists (since there cannot be many such churches), or the Protestant polemicists are right and all Catholics ought to flee to whichever Protestant (or Orthodox) church rightfully merits the title. Neither outcome was (or currently is) cognitively or spiritually tolerable. The genius of *Lumen gentium,* the final form of the Second Vatican Council's treatment of the church, was to finesse the problem and avoid the dilemma by stating that the one, holy, catholic, and apostolic church "subsists in" the visible church presently structured by the juridical authority of the Bishop of Rome.

To finesse a problem mitigates rather than avoids the consequences. The ecumenical imperative of unity debilitates the church as an ecumenical agent. Either the wedge of division must be re-driven after each and every recognition of some degree of unity among divided churches, or the reality of unity becomes obscure ("Where is unity if not in a particular church?"), and the notes of the church become increasingly invisible. If we press the first side of the dilemma, then we must insist that the "oneness" of the church "subsists" *uniquely* in the Roman Catholic Church.

11. *History of Vatican II,* ed. G. Alberigo and J. A. Komonchak (Maryknoll, N.Y.: Orbis, 1995), p. 292.

This rejuvenates Roman Catholic identity, but it is hardly a stance that encourages ecumenical progress. On the other hand, if we give up the claim to uniqueness, then, in a crucial sense, unity is invisible, "subsisting" in such a way that it might be present elsewhere, unrecognized until ecumenical discussions about doctrine bring it to light. But this possibility vindicates the theological assumptions of Reformed theology, and what seems to be ecumenical progress becomes capitulation. Thus, in both ways, a commitment to the unity of the church, itself a crucial necessity for the ecumenical movement, weakens the ability of Roman Catholicism to play its ecumenical role. Tromp's horrified reaction to Cardinal Bea's ecumenical initiatives seems altogether warranted.

The Fries/Rahner proposal, *Unity of the Churches,* offers further evidence in favor of Tromp's conclusion that post-Reformation ecclesiology cannot readily adapt itself to the ecumenical imperative.[12] Fries and Rahner's defense of this proposal is a perfect illustration of the way in which the imperative of unity evacuates the classical, denominational theologies of the West of their cognitive significance. For them, the unity of the churches cannot rest upon theological synthesis. The disparate vocabularies, historical development, and social situations of the churches make substantive consensus elusive. For Fries and Rahner, this need not impede, for they are not altogether convinced that it is possible for any particular church to provide universal, authoritative teaching. Therefore, the particular doctrinal forms that now seem to divide churches need not be taken as decisive. A more primitive and practical unity can obtain, based upon common baptism, a shared trinitarian confession, and a common acknowledgment of the unitive function of the Petrine office.

The analysis is complex. Fries and Rahner are aware of the postmodern intellectual situation: endlessly complex fields of knowledge without overarching syntheses. ("The universal scholar is extinct," p. 28.) They evoke the historicist thesis that religious consciousness is given life in the determinate social and historical matrices of particular traditions. ("Individual churches each have their own cultural and historical environment in which they actualize their Christianity in part determined by their environment," p. 34.) Nonetheless, the scholastic background of the argument does the real work. The epistemological minimalism is posi-

---

12. English translation published by Fortress and Paulist Presses in 1985. Citations follow in parentheses.

tively required by the imperative of unity. "If one rejects the notion that a unification of the churches is simply impossible in today's intellectual-political circumstances — a notion simply prohibited by the fundamental convictions of Christianity and the Church — then one will have to admit that in today's intellectual climate no unity in faith is possible other than the one just proposed. Therefore, it must be legitimate" (p. 38). The logic of the reasoning is clear, and it has nothing to do with modernity. "One must say this: either one declares the unity of faith to be an actually unachievable ideal to which one merely pays lip service, or one strives for a realistically conceivable unity of faith which one must then recognize as legitimate and attempt to make theologically comprehensible" (pp. 38-39). In other words, the only realistic possibility of unity requires epistemological minimalism; therefore, such minimalism must be legitimate. Otherwise, God compels us to do something — be one — which we cannot. The kind of thinking that animated Brunsmann recurs, though now the fundamental premise is that the Roman Catholic Church does not, in fact, uniquely and exclusively possess the note of unity.

In the Fries/Rahner proposal, two themes stand out. First, the proposal requires some form of papal primacy, and it does so in order to preserve the identity of the Roman Catholic Church as an ecumenical agent. Mere baptism and Trinitarian confession are insufficient to pick out the Roman Catholic Church from a wide array of other ecclesial bodies, and if Rome is to participate in unity, she must be identifiable in that unity. Yet, the epistemological minimalism that Fries and Rahner advance gives them *nothing to say* about why the Petrine office has apostolic significance. Indeed, were the papacy explained and justified, a range of contested theological judgments would reemerge. How can one formulate reasons why such an ecclesial practice is fundamental to the unity of the churches without reopening church-dividing issues about the mediation of salvation? Thus, the Fries/Rahner proposal represents a *reductio ad absurdum* of the post-Reformation ecclesiological tradition that it is designed to overcome. The manualists had articulate (though increasingly implausible) reasons for insisting upon the Petrine office. The Fries/Rahner proposal is programmatically inarticulate about this and any other contested matter between divided churches. The only way in which the divided churches can unite *as* divided churches is by preserving their distinguishing marks — but they can only unite if these distinguishing marks are both affirmed as necessary for unity (otherwise it would not be those particular churches uniting) and at the same time evacuated of all theological content (otherwise the unity would be contrary to the truth of the gospel).

The second theme involves this evacuation of content, which is, after all, exactly what nineteenth-century Roman Catholicism denounced as "latitudinarianism" and "indifferentism." Joseph Cardinal Ratzinger has expressed dismay at the proposal's insouciance regarding authoritative doctrine (especially, one imagines, because Fries and Rahner slyly conscript Ratzinger's earlier publications to their cause, see p. 40). Ratzinger's concern is about what I would call the "ecumenical trump." As Ratzinger puts the matter, "the only thing that is clearly visible . . . is Christ's command of unity." How, he wonders, is the command of unity exempt from the overarching epistemological uncertainty that the proposal evokes? Yet, even if Fries and Rahner were able to defend the ecumenical imperative, absent substantive convergences and a thick magisterial context, Ratzinger questions, "What kind of unity is it really? A formal unity without any clear content is fundamentally no unity at all, and a mere linking together of institutions is no value in itself. Unity conceived of in this way is based on common skepticism, not on common knowledge."[13] The unity proposed would seem no more "real" and "living" than the restrictive manualism of Brunsmann's juridically defined notes of the church.[14]

By my analysis, both Fries/Rahner and Ratzinger are right. As a matter of fact, for many complex reasons, modern Christians find it increasingly difficult to inhabit the doctrinal and disciplinary traditions that emerged after the Reformation. Something like epistemological

13. Both quotes from *Church, Ecumenism and Politics: New Essays in Ecclesiology* (New York: Crossroad, 1988), p. 131. I owe these citations, and the insights they provide into the logic of Christian division, to Ephraim Radner, *The End of the Church*, pp. 1-19. He cites Ratzinger on p. 18.

14. As a regular reader of Rahner, I offer the following observation. The way in which his approach to Christian unity circles back to the debilitations of the manualist tradition (now redoubled by the doubts he raises about that very tradition) is typical. Even though Rahner's project is motivated by a deep conviction that the traditional language and practice of the church lack immediate plausibility for "modern man," and that they require theological redescription, guided by a transcendental anthropology, to secure existential potency, he often completes his most important syllogisms by recourse to authoritative church doctrine. The effect is to draw attention in two directions, both away from the very language and practice he seeks to commend. Either the weight of argument is carried by the transcendental anthropology, or it is carried by Denzinger. The weight is not carried by the primary language or logic of Scripture and worship.

minimalism is the functional attitude of great numbers of faithful church members, not the least because the plausibility of classical post-Reformation theologies depends upon an *intra-ecclesial unity* created by insisting upon *extra-ecclesial division*. The explicit principle of epistemological minimalism does little more than baptize this implausibility. Yet, Ratzinger is surely right to note that such a condition leads to a debilitating vacuum, not only in ecumenical matters, but also across a range of ecclesial practices. Because we cannot inhabit the highly developed post-Reformation traditions with confidence, we either downplay the need for unity (after all, the very idea of unity is defined in conflicting fashions by these questionable ecclesiologies), or we downplay the adequacy of our traditions. Both contribute to the Gnostic sensibilities of the modern churches. Apostolic requirements that we actually do something in the world become shadowy, eschatological, and spectral. Particular ecclesial forms of life become partial, temporary, even inhibiting barriers to the fullness of faith. The actual cement that holds together the Christian life comes to be seen as something other than the determinate shape of ecclesial life: the inner spiritual life, the mystery beyond language, political liberation, bourgeois self-affirmation.

Protestant Debilitation

Roman Catholic ecclesiology is not uniquely invested in the logic of division. One of the clearest minds of the nineteenth century saw how Christian division colored all reflection upon the reality of the church. In his *Lectures on the Prophetical Office of the Church,* written while an Anglican, Newman observes that insofar as we wish to assert and affirm propositions about the church, "we necessarily come across the existing teachings of Rome, and are led to attack it, as the most convenient, or rather only, way of showing what our own views are. It has pre-occupied the ground, and we cannot erect our own structure without partly breaking it down, partly using what we find upon it. And thus . . . the following Lectures, as far as their very form goes, are written against Romanism, though their main object is not controversy, but edification."[15] Here, Newman is typi-

15. Republished in 1887 as *The Via Media of the Anglican Church.* This quote is found on p. 62 of the recent edition published by Clarendon Press (1990).

cal. In order to create space for the existence of non-Roman churches, the claims of Rome must be refuted. In this way, though different in emphases and argumentative techniques, the wide array of Protestant ecclesiologies, like their Roman Catholic alternatives, are driven by the logic of division. The upshot is a debilitating emphasis on doctrine that parallels a focus on the juridical.

One of the most irenic figures of the factious seventeenth century, the Puritan pastor Richard Baxter, demonstrates the difficulties. Baxter advances a straightforward argument. "The church of Christ being his body, is but one, and hath many parts, but should have no parties, but unity and concord without division."[16] In view of the fundamental imperative of unity, "no Christian must be of a party or sect, as such, that is, as dividing itself from the rest, causing schism or contention in the body . . ." (p. 396). It follows, then, that "nothing will warrant us to separate from a church as no church, but want of something essential to a church" (p. 397). In other words, one is only justified in separating from a body that has renounced the gospel, and in so doing, proves itself no church at all.

Now it is a plain fact that, by the time Baxter was writing, schism had occurred. Some have separated themselves from others. According to Baxter's logic, this is only justified if the assembly of people from which one has separated is not a church. In short, the consequences of the Reformation are only tolerable if Romanists have repudiated something essential, something that, once renounced, renders their form of life something other than a church. Baxter draws back from consigning Roman Catholicism to the nether regions of the "synagogue of Satan." Nonetheless, his horror of division leads him to conceive of the Reformation schism as an act of the Roman church. Indeed, for Baxter, the Reformation manifests the overall *Roman* pattern of separation. "Mistaking the just terms of union and communion," which, for Baxter, are properly understood as constituent elements of the profession of true faith, "and setting up a false center as that which all men must unite in," that is to say, insisting upon the authority of the church itself, "the Roman party divided themselves from the Greeks and protestants, and made the greatest schism in the church that ever was made in it" (p. 400). The Roman

---

16. Richard Baxter, *Practical Works*, vol. 16 (London: James Duncan), p. 395. Further citations follow in parentheses.

party, then, must bear the odium of division. Moreover, even if Baxter is mild (for his age), one cannot but conclude that a party that sets up "a false center" is a party that has, *de facto,* renounced the "true center," and is therefore opposed to true Christianity — the role, indeed, of the Anti-Christ.

Baxter does more than illustrate the divisive logic of post-Reformation ecclesiologies. He also gives evidence of the Protestant debil-itation of caring about unity in the context of division. Baxter's own pro-posal for unity tells the tale. He rejects the possibility of a general council as impractical (vast distances and a confusion of tongues). Moreover, the very notion of structured, institutional unity is "ill-grounded" and "un-holy," and various efforts to achieve such unity are themselves "a great cause of the division and distraction of the churches" (p. 407). After all, exactly these institutional matters constitute the "false center" of the Ro-man party. Against the vain quest for institutional unity, Baxter advances the standard Protestant claim that the true unity of the church is invisible. Yet, Baxter is aware that such a claim, taken alone, renders the imperative of unity vacuous. Some form of "Christian concord" must characterize the visible life of the church. Again, Baxter's solution is standard. The vis-ible unity of the church is based upon "a profession of true Christian faith, subscribed, with a renunciation of all that is contrary thereto . . ." (p. 407).

Baxter's understanding of "true Christian faith" is admirably ecu-menical. He writes, "when parties and sects do trouble the church, we must still hold to our mere Christianity. . . ."[17] He defines this "mere Christianity" in terms of an apostolic core not significantly different from most of the Fries/Rahner proposal: Scripture, the baptismal covenant, and the Creeds. Yet, Baxter cannot adopt epistemological minimalism. "Mere Christianity" is not a mere idea; for Baxter, it is necessarily a visible form of life. In the context of division, finding the proper body of Chris-tians with whom to affiliate is a pressing need. Thus, Baxter is forced to articulate three "notes" of the "true faith" that identifies the church: (1) in-ward assurance, (2) holiness of life, (3) profession of true doctrine.

What is crucial is that each "note" marks a path *away from* those ap-ostolic texts and practices that Christians share. Inward assurance all too easily drifts toward a pietism in which inward conviction supersedes visi-

---

17. Baxter, *Practical Works,* vol. 21, p. 396.

ble forms. Holiness migrates toward moralism. Profession of true doctrine signals a "doctrinal supersessionism" that parallels Roman Catholic "juridical supersessionism." In each case, the deracination that debilitates Roman Catholic ecclesiologies occurs here as well. What makes any particular ecclesial body the "true Church" involves something that stands at one remove from apostolic language and practice. Common use of Scripture and sacraments is insufficient. *Proper* use of the apostolic inheritance is necessary — proper subjectivity, proper moral enactment, proper doctrinal formulation. Thus, in stipulating a precise meaning of "proper" — and this must be done if Protestant theologians are to avoid the simple gnosticism of relying on an "invisible church" ecclesiology — the ways in which one identifies the true church supersede the primary elements of ecclesial life.[18]

The ways in which assurance descends into pious subjectivism are many, and the jump from Protestant ideals of holiness to the moralism of modern "Life and Work" ecumenism would require a careful genealogy. I can pursue neither. However, I wish to elaborate on what might be called a "doctrinal supersessionism" that debilitates a great deal of modern Protestantism. Here, I turn to Schleiermacher. His intellectual rigor brings out the problem that seems to emerge almost inevitably out of the need for post-Reformation theology to identify the proper form of "true faith" that marks the true church.

In *The Christian Faith,* Schleiermacher observes that Roman Catholicism exhibits "a spirit alien" to Evangelical Christianity (24.1), which he famously articulates in terms of the role of the church in relation to Christ. This alien juxtaposition, however, does not signal a polemic against Roman Catholicism. "We may leave it standing alongside our own religion; as being of a different formation but equally Christian" (24.1). Behind this irenicism is Schleiermacher's theory of the way in

---

18. Ever the harbinger, Baxter tries to avoid these debilitations in two ways. First, he anticipates the modern use of eschatology to preserve the cogency of Christianity against the contradictions of its present form: "Remember this advice: expect not a heavenly perfection of unity and concord till you come to heaven" (vol. 21, p. 331). Second, he appeals to the unitary function of national churches. Yet, Baxter cannot follow through with either strategy. The complacency of a too thorough use of eschatological delay is repugnant to him: "A peaceable spirit must be a public spirit, highly esteeming the welfare of the whole body . . ." (p. 333). Against political solutions, he writes, "If any would unite the church in Kings, in councils, in any human devices, they will but divide it" (p. 335).

which Jesus' universal saving potency is individuated and concretized in different historical and cultural contexts.[19] This removes any scandal from division: it simply follows from Schleiermacher's metaphysical assumptions about the universal and particular that different, *einheimisch* forms of communal faith will emerge from a single, spiritual potency. Nonetheless, the antagonism between the two forms of Christianity is real; and Schleiermacher rejects any attempt to mediate between the two. To try to reestablish a pre-Reformation form of unity would yield nothing but antiquarian dreams. More importantly, "the Apostolic Age cannot be brought back," writes Schleiermacher, "because we cannot sacrifice the precision of our ideas" (24.1). In other words, the antagonism of Protestant and Catholic has been theologically helpful. Both traditions have, by juxtaposition, advanced, clarified, and deepened their respective theological systems of thought. Given such fruitful division, "this naturally creates for the Evangelical theologian the task of bringing to clear consciousness the distinctive character of Protestantism in antithesis to Catholicism . . ." (24.2). If we are to function as sophisticated and conceptually precise church theologians, suggests Schleiermacher, then we must *intensify and formalize* the lines of division.

We can dismiss Schleiermacher's conception of the theological task as somehow unique to his modern methodology, but I think that dismissal is misguided. Schleiermacher wished to be a theologian of the church, not of an idea or a feeling, and I read his approach to the division between Protestant and Roman Catholic as central to his desire to avoid the Gnostic tendencies in his own theory of religion. Although his formulations are distinctively modern, his goal as a theologian was to undertake disciplined reflection in the service of an identifiable community of believers. Separation from Rome is necessary to maintain the identity of Protestant churches as the ecclesial subjects. For this reason, he insists upon the antithesis.

By contrast, consider Schleiermacher's approach to the historic differences between Reformed and Lutheran doctrine. Written after the Prussian Union of 1817, *The Christian Faith* is self-consciously committed to an ecumenical theology for an actually united body of Christians. Of

19. For a helpful summary, see Klaus Penzel, "A Chapter in the History of the Ecumenical Quest: Schelling and Schleiermacher," *Church History* 33, no. 3 (Sept. 1964): 322-37.

course, in keeping with his theory of religious language and practice, Schleiermacher insists that the two groups never manifested a "difference in the religious affections themselves" (24–postscript). However, his functional assumptions are more important: "Since in the confessional documents, at least in the second stage, Reformed modes of presentation are directed against Lutheran, and vice versa, it must be admitted at the outset that only that part of the confessional documents in which they all agree can be really essential to Protestantism" (27.2). The *actual unity* of the two groups (at least in Prussia) makes any doctrinal difference secondary and inessential. The "facts on the ground," if you will, provide positive indication of that which is central and that which is peripheral.

There are limits, however, to how much unity can disclose. The visible reality of the churches in the West is, in fact, marked by a fundamental divide between Roman Catholics and Protestants. If the actual and visible forms of division are inconsequential for our lives of faith, then we are easily tempted to think that any number of actual and visible forms of communal life and practice are inessential, and such a conclusion is exactly what Schleiermacher wishes to avoid. For this reason (as Thils charts on the Roman Catholic side), intra-Protestant comity intensifies the need to redrive the wedge of difference between Protestant and Catholic. An emergent and real unity must be juxtaposed to a real and enduring disunity. Here, Schleiermacher is insistent. A bright line must divide, "otherwise [the theologian] will no more be able to perform his work with some degree of security and completeness . . ." (24.2). Protestant thought and practice make no sense unless division is reinforced. Current arrangements must be justifiable.[20]

20. See also Schleiermacher's analysis of the conditions for spiritual unity and visible fellowship. Unity is very much a note of the church: "We enter into a fellowship of very particular acts and forms of self-expression, so as uniformly to occupy a common area with those who have closest affinity with ourselves . . ." (149.1). Unity, however, is bound to division, as every visible fellowship "seeks to repel what is alien . . ." (149.1). In this way, Schleiermacher builds division into the very essence of the visible church. "By the laws of physics," Schleiermacher insists, "the visible is always involved in separation and division" (149.2). To a great extent, the history of *Kulturprotestantismus* is shaped by these "laws of physics." The anti-Catholic polemic shifts from doctrine to culture. The free religious conscience is juxtaposed to slavish obedience. Progress is set against antiquarianism. However, as this strategy of separation gains ground, the distinction between the Protestant church and modern German culture blurs. Thus, modern German theology is involved in a zero-sum game. To distinguish Protestantism from Catholicism requires embedding the

Schleiermacher is a devilishly compressed author, and his arguments require slow unpacking. I have tried to suggest why he thinks that the antithesis between Roman Catholic and Protestant must be as clear as possible, but I can only report his conclusion regarding theological procedure. Because this difference is so central to "the precision of our ideas," "the confessional documents of the Evangelical Church, collectively, are, as it were, given a prior place to the New Testament Scriptures themselves" (27.1). The doctrinal supersessionism implied is mitigated by the "as it were." Schleiermacher certainly does not wish to undermine the central role of Scripture. Nonetheless, one could not hope for a clearer statement of the way in which "precise" ecclesial identity, as well as an articulate and sophisticated theology that serves actual ecclesial communities in a state of division, tends to supplant Scripture with doctrine. Just as in the case of the Roman Catholic tradition, this tendency is not some sort of isolated "sin" — a narrow scholastic mentality or a false intellectualism. Doctrinal supersessionism follows from the logic of division. That which divided churches share cannot be the basis for the identity of a divided church; otherwise, either division would be unjustified (and one begins to wonder whether the inherited traditions that put so much emphasis on justifying division are healthy and faithful), or division would not really be relevant (and one begins to wonder whether those same inherited traditions, so invested in division, are really worth the effort). Thus, to maintain loyalty to inherited forms of theological reflection and ecclesial identity, division must be reinforced. But even as division is justified, debilitation occurs, for only the second-order language of doctrine can give precise and cogent form to division, and this doctrinal supersessionism pushes theology (and ecclesial governance and pastoral practice) away from the first-order apostolic tradition that all share.[21]

---

church in that which makes German culture modern (e.g., Harnack's treatment of Catholicism). To distinguish the Protestant church from other modern bureaucratic institutions requires finding a way to lever the church away from the very cultural sources of anti-Catholic polemic. This push-and-pull is a major feature of *Kulturprotestantismus,* governing its method and content as much as the putative demands of modernity.

21. David Wells's polemic against doctrinal atrophy in the Evangelical Movement, *No Place for Truth, or Whatever Happened to Evangelical Theology?* (Grand Rapids: Eerdmans, 1993), misses this logic entirely. Wells assumes that modernity constitutes the primary explanation for the eclipse of theology in Evangelical churches, and he longs for a recovery of the glories of Reformed theology. If my analysis of Schleiermacher is correct,

The consequences for ecumenism follow the same logic as the Fries/ Rahner proposal. In order to participate in ecumenical discussion as Lutherans or Methodists, churches must identify themselves in terms of that which they do not share. They must apply Schleiermacher's principle of identity by antithesis. Yet, in order to contribute to ecumenical progress, something like Rahner's epistemological minimalism must obtain. Nothing theologically decisive can be said about the ecclesial identities of divided churches, or division will be re-justified rather than overcome. In this way, the ecumenical imperative of unity tends to evacuate the churches of theological resources for ecclesial self-description. The closer they get to unity, the more spectral and atavistic their identities — and the less functional they are as ecumenical agents.

Two Examples of Intra-Denominational Debilitation

In his essay, "Maintaining a Spirit of Unity in Face of Current Diversities," Waldemar Janzen identifies an "incline toward unity" in the biblical witness.[22] When unity is broken by sin, division becomes necessary. "Throughout both Testaments we hear a repeated call to the people of God to separate themselves from idolatry" (p. 217). Nonetheless, this separation always takes place on the "incline toward unity," and thus, "where separation for the sake of faithfulness to God seems necessary in any given context, it must always be seen as an emergency measure for a time" (p. 217).

Given these strictures, the burden of proof falls on those who would separate, and Janzen is naturally concerned to justify the separative practice of Free Churches. In so doing, he recapitulates, in contemporary id-

---

then a more plausible explanation of Evangelical doctrinal aphasia rests in the ecumenical spirit of the Evangelical Movement. How, for example, could one recover the vigor of Protestant theology without re-igniting the church-dividing issues of infant baptism, creedal authority, and ministerial office that have, historically, separated Nazarenes from Presbyterians, Baptists from Congregationalists, and all of them from Pentecostals? Just as Schleiermacher asserts that the past differences between Reformed and Lutheran, given emergent comity, are demonstrably inessential, so also do Wells's students, captive no doubt to modernisms of many sorts, recognize how little of classical Protestant theology, much of which is devoted to intra-Protestant polemic, is essential.

22. *Conrad Grebel Review* 7 (Fall 1989): 211-16. Citations follow in parentheses.

iom, a "low Protestant" polemic against the "artificial unity" imposed by more highly developed ecclesiologies. Recognizing the debilitation caused by doctrinal supersessionism, Janzen worries that "authority has been shifted, as least de facto, from scripture to creed" (p. 218). Against this implicit drift away from the primitive apostolic tradition, Janzen articulates an ecclesiology that emphasizes classical Free Church themes of voluntary association and non-creedal biblical faithfulness: "The church is defined as the people subjecting themselves to the supreme authority of the one God who is revealed in the biblical story" (p. 220). Free from the authoritarian demands of a hierarchy, untainted by the divisive logic of doctrinal dispute, "the biblical canon . . . allows for considerable diversity within an area surrounded by definite boundaries" (p. 22). In short, Janzen proposes something like Baxter's "mere Christianity" as the route to escape the logic of division.

As Janzen turns to the fractious debates raging within his own tradition, however, his ecclesiological solution to the problem of division manifests the ecumenical trump that Ratzinger thought characterized the Fries/Rahner proposal. Debates about "women-leadership in the church" need not divide, he argues, as long as both sides submit themselves to "the one God who is revealed in the biblical story." The same holds true for questions of "baptism by immersion or sprinkling," or "divorce and homosexuality." Thus understood, the "mere Christianity" endorsed by Janzen seems to mark a decisive retreat from the Free Church confidence that Scripture enjoins a clear and determinate discipline for ecclesial life. For material division within the church can be embraced only if the account of what unites the church becomes entirely formal. As long as factions manifest a commitment to Scripture, then difference need not divide. The cows are as gray in Janzen's proposal for intra-church unity as they are in the Fries/Rahner proposal for interchurch unity.[23]

The Church of England's decisions about ordaining women threatened to produce the same intra-church divisions that Janzen worries about in his own tradition. In his essay, "Catholicity, Unity and Provin-

23. Not only does this formalism threaten to evacuate Scripture of authoritative content; it also makes Free Church existence untenable. Surely Lutherans and Roman Catholics are committed to Scripture in the minimal sense enjoined by Janzen. Thus, even if they advance all sorts of false conceptions of "artificial unity," their views should no more justify separation than differing assessments of the role of women, divorce, and homosexuality.

cial Autonomy: On Making Decisions Unilaterally," Mark Chapman sets out to explain how the apparently divisive practice of making unilateral provincial decisions does not, in fact, undermine the unity of the Anglican Communion.[24] His explanation testifies to the debilitations imposed by a commitment to unity in the context of division.

For Chapman, unity must be understood eschatologically. It is what the church seeks, but it cannot function as a material test for true doctrine. Indeed, in a reversal only an Anglican could make, Chapman assumes that unity has exactly the opposite role; it is a sign of false doctrine. Surveying the history of the church, he writes, "The unity of Christ functioned both as the eschatological goal where all human division would be overcome and at the same time it served to relativise all historical expression of Christian truth" (p. 323). With such an understanding of unity, Chapman is then able to advance the usual claim that Anglicanism has a providential role in Western Christianity. "Diversity within Christianity is a necessary expression of a vision of the fulness of truth which relativises all historical attempts to express the gospel" (p. 325). Without diversity, we might imagine that a particular form of doctrine is authoritative, and this makes doctrine into an idol. Thus, the great achievement of Anglicanism is to visibly manifest diversity without breaking apart. "Christianity is received in a particular place in a particular tradition at a particular time, and the ecumenical vocation of Anglicanism is to emphasize the positive aspects of such particularity" (p. 325). By willfully making autonomous decisions (Chapman makes this very nearly a positive duty), and by insisting that such decisions in no way impair the unity of the church, the Church of England bears a crucial witness to the world: that agreement of doctrine and practice is not necessary for unity. Unity alone is sufficient for unity.

Chapman may be massively mistaken about the actual function of unity in the history of the church, and he may be hopelessly smug in his assumptions about the special role of Anglicanism, but his formulations accurately capture the consequences, for the truth of doctrine, of affirming both the necessity of unity and the visible division all around us. We can either treat questions of doctrine as decisive, and then make them points upon which to draw the boundaries of the church, or we can insist

24. *Anglican Theological Review* 76, no. 3 (Summer 1994): 313-28. Citations follow in parentheses.

that unity exists even when elements in the church hold opposite views, thereby either implicitly or explicitly denying that such matters are decisive. Something like the ecumenical trump and consequent epistemological minimalism of the Fries/Rahner proposal reemerges yet again as the *terminus ad quem* of the search for unity in the context of division. Again, that minimalism weakens our ability to be articulate about any ecclesiologial commitment, including the commitment to unity. Thus, the more sensible we are of the reality of division and imperative of unity — both key features of the modern ecumenical movement — the less articulate we are as ecumenical agents.

I hope these digressions have not been too tedious and that I have amassed at least fragmentary evidence that when divided churches seek unity, or even coexistence without polemic, they cannot sustain a conceptually developed and precise account of their own identities as churches. This is a debilitation that has repercussions throughout ecclesial reflection and practice.[25] Not by accident, then, the churches are unable to play the roles assigned to them by modern ecumenism. They cannot give a cogent account of their status as churches committed to unity. Given this logic, it would simply seem impossible (to chose one example) for a Roman Catholic dialogue team to come to an effective and ecclesially relevant consensus with a Lutheran dialogue team on the question of the church. Either (1) the consensus would transcend the differences between Roman Catholic and Lutheran, and therefore lose credibility and, just as importantly, effectively fail to identify an actual, existent church. Or (2) the consensus would retain credibility and groundedness in present ecclesial reality, and therefore reiterate, however irenically, the principles that divide the churches. Or (3) with the rhetoric of diversity and complementarity, the consensus would say, in effect, that agreement on the nature of the church is not necessary for unity.

Moreover, this debilitation extends beyond ecclesiology. Insofar as theology is a church discipline, it tends to rise and fall with the ability of the churches to sustain clarity about their identities. Absent that clarity, the ambiguities and uncertainties of "mere Christianity" afflict theology.

25. In an essay drawing on this research, I have elaborated on the ways in which the imperative of unity amidst division has debilitated theological practice. See "Theology in the Ruins of the Church," *Pro Ecclesia* 12, no. 1 (2003): 13-36.

What, after all, is "mere Christianity"? Where are the constraints and realities that would govern thought and practice? As the confessional traditions in the West become less and less plausible — and I have suggested that this stems as much from the pressures of unity as the pressures of modernity — modern theologians have tended to fall back upon other sources for intellectual discipline and guidance. For some, a moral vision suffices (Kaufmann). For others, the tools of philosophy or social science fill the gap (Troeltsch). Still others are able to use personal piety to sustain a pastiche of traditional elements unsustained by any particular ecclesial tradition (Moltmann). In each case, the doctrine that had superseded Scripture as the decisive tool for identifying the church and its determinate form of life is, in turn, superseded by something else, now one step further removed from the apostolic tradition.[26]

I would like to suggest that modern theologians have been neither fools nor knaves. To appeal to "mere Christianity" seems a necessary outcome of the imperative of unity amidst division. For surely that which all share is the only reliable basis for overcoming division. Yet, "mere Christianity" has no crystal-clear boundary and manifests no transparent logic. The difficulty, illustrated so aptly by the Fries/Rahner proposal, is that what weakens the powers of division seems also to weaken our grasp of the apostolic tradition and its power to unify. The more we "know" about the ecumenical imperative of unity, the less we "know" about the proper form of apostolic teaching and practice. An epistemological minimalism seems to be forced upon us by the failure of our ecclesial self-understandings. The more clearly we see the scandal of Christian division, the more clouded is our vision of the gospel. Not surprisingly, then, modern theologians have sought other, non-theological sources to discipline and shape their minds — or they have been forced to trust the inner voices of their own piety.

In their own ways, each of the figures I have analyzed recognized

26. Schleiermacher is again a harbinger. In the notes to his *Reden*, added in later years, he comments on the "decay of religion," manifest not least in the "low stand-point" of many clergy. To combat this ill condition, Schleiermacher does not advocate a *ressourcement*, or at least not in a straightforward fashion. He is aware that the doctrinal traditions are not functional on their own. Instead, to overcome the debilitations of the churches in his own time, Schleiermacher writes, "A deeper speculative discipline would best remove this evil" (*On Religion: Speeches to Its Cultured Despisers,* [New York: Harper & Row, 1958], p. 22).

this obscured vision, and either resisted or affirmed it. Brunsmann, like most nineteenth-century Roman Catholic theologians, assumed that ecumenism would lead to "indifferentism," with the debilitating consequences Tromp anticipated on the eve of the Second Vatican Council. With his keen sense of the communal constraints upon theological reflection, Schleiermacher saw how the actual unity of Reformed and Lutheran blurred centuries-old theological distinctions, and how the very existence of Protestant theology required a reaffirmation of the antithesis between Protestant and Catholic. The Rahner/Fries proposal and its notorious epistemological minimalism would seem to vindicate Tromp's worry, but that proposal simply extends to all of Western Christianity the assumptions Schleiermacher makes about historical differences between Reformed and Lutheran churches. What once divided can no longer be understood as essential, and the orienting judgments of post-Reformation theology can no longer function to structure theological reflection and ecclesial self-understanding.

What are we to make of this great cloud of witnesses? At the very least, we need to be clear-minded about the ways in which any progress toward Christian unity will undermine and diminish the sophisticated theological systems born in the polemical centuries that followed the Reformation. This is especially the case in ecclesiology. What it means to be "church" is a largely post-Reformation question, forced upon the churches by the scandalous fact of division. It should not surprise us that past answers will seem increasingly implausible as the context for questions about the nature of the church changes with even the smallest steps toward unity. But more importantly, we should recognize that these weakened traditions and the consequent inarticulateness about ecclesiology are spiritual challenges. Accepting the clouded vision that unity brings upon churches defined by division may be a necessary penitential discipline.

The notion that unity will require repentance is neither novel nor controversial. Penitence involves accepting the disciplines and renunciations necessary to weaken and remove that which is contrary to God's will. Christian division, born of many complex factors and sustained by equally complex social, political, and theological forces, has long been recognized as fraught with human sinfulness.[27] To repent of this sin and

27. See, for example, Richard Baxter's extensive discussion of the vices that lead to

its consequences would seem a necessary and non-controversial condition for progress toward unity. Since God wills that we be one, divided churches must accept the penitential path necessary to follow the imperative of unity. As such, many ecumenical documents evoke sentiments of repentance necessary for reconciliation.[28]

Certainly pride and sloth, greed and envy play great roles in the history of Christian division. However, the penitential dimension of unity expands beyond sinfulness of the sort that may be identified and assigned to specific agents. In fact, the weight of spiritual sacrifice may fall upon those least "guilty." Consider St. Paul's advice to the Romans. Faced with division over the proper form of holiness and honor of the Lord, St. Paul exhorts those who agree with him to accept submission to the limitations of others. However accurate in knowledge of that which is clean and unclean, none are "to put a stumbling block or hindrance in the way of a brother" (14:13). For if we do so, then we "are no longer walking in love" (14:15). At issue is not a renunciation of sin and falsehood. Quite the contrary, those "who are strong ought to bear with the failings of the weak" (15:1). In the context of division, the imperative of unity requires even those who least need penitence to take on the disciplines and renunciations necessary to weaken and overcome that which divides.

We should not forget that St. Paul's exhortations function against the background of the one who knew not sin, but who suffered the diminishing afflictions due others: "For Christ did not please himself; but, as it is written, 'The reproaches of those who reproached thee fell on me'" (15:3). Christ bore the penitential burden, and in so doing, removed the wall that divided us from God, and from each other. If this reading of Romans 14 and its christological background is correct, then we ought to expect that a desire for unity amidst division will weaken, humiliate, and diminish, not just the sin that impedes, but also those with the clearest vision of communion, those with the most intense and purest desire for fel-

---

division in his tract, "The True Catholic, and Catholic Church Described," in *The Practical Works of Richard Baxter*, vol. 16 (London: James Duncan, 1830). Baxter's career spanned the most fractious century of English Protestantism, and although a proponent of Puritan theology, he ardently resisted the impulse toward separation. He rued the divisive spirit of his age, a spirit often clothed in the rhetoric of unity: "Of the many that are for peace and unity, there are few that have any great skill to promote it . . ." (p. 342).

28. See *Facing Unity*, para. 51-52, for examples relevant to the Lutheran–Roman Catholic division.

lowship, those with the strongest faith. The strong must bear the failings of the weak, and as the passion of Christ makes very clear, such "bearing" will debilitate to a point of silence (cf. the parallel between Matt. 27:14 and Rom. 14:22) and suspension of judgment (cf. the parallel between Luke 23:34 and Rom. 14:13).

St. Paul's exhortation should sober us. One need not be a denominational patriot or an anti-ecumenical traditionalist to admire and enjoy the powerful theological traditions that emerged out of Reformation controversies. Any yet, if my analysis is correct, and as so many theologians who have reflected upon the nature of the church have recognized, divided churches cannot acknowledge the *need* for unity without bearing a "silencing" and "suspension of judgment." Yet, against the Fries/Rahner proposal, this debilitation is not a historical-intellectual phenomenon of epistemological minimalism. Rather, it is a spiritual discipline imposed by a desire for unity. The debilitating logic of a love and desire for unity in churches defined by division is providential: it reforms even those who have long since shed the enmity of division into ones "humiliated" and "burdened" by the weight of a sin not their own. The clouded vision and bankrupt ecclesiologies of the present — burdens that will fall upon all who accept and embrace the ecumenical imperative — form a weakness assigned to the strong.

Our historical moment, shaped by the collapsing plausibility of post-Reformation structures and theologies, may be unique, but the spiritual burdens it imposes are not. Origen developed an ambitious theological synthesis at a time when the identity of Christianity lacked doctrinal and juridical clarity. The apostolic writings had yet to achieve fixed, canonical status. Trinitarian thought had yet to receive the guidance of councils. Not surprisingly, then, Origen was acutely aware of the need to discipline ourselves to see and grasp the truth of the gospel. The carnal letter reveals its spiritual truth to those who have eyes trained to see, and that training is by no means doctrinal or theological in the modern sense of the term. It involves an ascetical discipline that, in the West, came to be known as "spiritual poverty." *This* debilitation opens the way toward fullness of vision.[29]

---

29. For a detailed and compelling account of the properly spiritual nature of Origen's Christian vision, see John David Dawson, *Christian Figural Reading and the Fashioning of Identity* (Berkeley: University of California Press, 2002).

What form the ascetical life must take in our time is unclear to me. To echo Alasdair MacIntyre, the needed St. Benedict will, no doubt, be "new" and not "old." Nonetheless, I offer this observation. In the ecumenical context, spiritual poverty might take the form of accepting the debilitation of our churches, enduring their "silence" and "suspension of judgment." This kind of loyalty to our denominations, a loyalty to that which, however, is "weak," constitutes the reality of our fellowship in Christ at this time and in this place, and it imposes a penitential discipline. We must endure the church's obscured condition, and the consequent penumbral state of her teaching. For it is written: "There is nothing hid, except to be disclosed; nor is anything secret, except to come to light" (Mark 4:22).

Rebuilding the Structure of Love: The Quest for Visible Unity among the Churches

BRIAN E. DALEY, S.J.

We, too, receive the Holy Spirit, if we love the Church, if we are formed into a single structure by love, if we rejoice in both the catholic name and the catholic faith. Let us believe this, my brothers and sisters: to the degree that a person loves the Church of Christ, he or she possesses the Holy Spirit. . . . We have the Holy Spirit, then, if we love the Church; but we love her, if we find our lasting home in her structure, and in love.

> Augustine of Hippo, *Tractate on*
> *the Gospel of John* 32.8 [CCL 36.304]

When Christians — whatever their particular form of Christianity — speak of "the church," they mean a human community of believers that is, of its very nature, *one*. The most universally used of Christian confessions, for instance — the Creed of Constantinople (381) — includes as an object of faith, among the works of the Holy Spirit in history, a church that is "one, holy, catholic, and apostolic": a group of people called by God's grace into unity through the apostolic witness to the risen Jesus, and made holy in accepting that witness; a group of people universal in its composition, its ultimate scope, and the integrity of the faith it has received. In other words, to the degree we are imperfectly one, or lack holiness, or are focused only on some aspect of the gospel message, neglect the long tradition of apostolic faith, or are composed simply of people from one particular ethnic or social group, we are only imperfectly the church of Jesus Christ.

The Epistle to the Ephesians, which offers us the New Testament's most extensive vision of the church, presents it as a fundamental dimension of God's mysterious "plan for the fullness of time" (Eph. 1:10): a community that brings former pagans into the extended, reconciled unity of "the commonwealth of Israel" (2:12), as part of a living, social "body" whose ultimate destiny is to "attain to the unity of the faith and of the knowledge of the Son of God, to mature manhood, to the measure of the stature of the fullness of Christ . . ." (4:13). At the start of his magisterial survey of the aims and fruits of the twentieth-century Christian ecumenical movement, *That All May Be One,* Harding Meyer observes that in Ephesians and other New Testament writings, the unity of the church, as a gift of God in Christ, "is a matter of Christian faith and confession, and not something subject to our disposition or a matter of considerations of mere utility."[1] Meyer continues:

> Here soteriology and ecclesiology, the understanding of salvation and of church, mesh together. Like the salvation of human beings, so also is the church a deed and a gift of God. Both are characterized by the indicative, by the "once and for all" (cf. Heb. 7:27; 9:12; 10:10), and both are antecedent to all human action. All ecumenical "activity" also presupposes this indicative of the present, obtaining unity of the church. . . . The unity of the church is a "God-given" unity; it is God's "gift," his "present."[2]

The aim of what we call ecumenism, Meyer is suggesting, is not to create a unity among Christians where none presently exists, or to re-create it where it has been lost, but to allow the unity that already exists among us as God's gift, and is hindered or clouded by our sinfulness and "slow[ness] of heart" (Luke 24:25), to become more fully evident in the way Christians look upon each other, articulate their faith, carry out their worship, and act in the world. As Meyer puts it:

> The language of "visible unity" corresponds to what is generally true for Christian existence. The new life, which we have received in faith,

1. Harding Meyer, *That All May Be One: Perceptions and Models of Ecumenicity,* trans. William G. Rusch (Grand Rapids/Cambridge, U.K.: Eerdmans, 1999), p. 8.

2. Meyer, *That All May Be One,* p. 9.

seeks to find expression in the renewal of our life-style. The indicative pushes toward the imperative: "If we live in the Spirit, let us also walk in the Spirit" (Gal. 5:25). The promise of salvation leads to exhortations, and the exhortations point to the concrete, visible formation of our life and action. In the same sense, the unity that is a gift to us also becomes a unity that is a task for us. The ecumenical indicative gives rise to the ecumenical imperative.[3]

This "imperative" dimension of the present reality of Christian community life challenges much that all of our churches, divided as they are, currently take for granted. In an important essay on the possibilities of ecumenical union first published in 1977, Cardinal Joseph Ratzinger argued that the task of those engaged in ecumenical dialogue is not only to discern what kind of agreement between the various Christian churches is "theologically possible," but also to prepare their own communities spiritually to accept such agreement in practice, and to question the reasons we continue to give for holding ourselves apart from each other.

> We must learn [he writes] that unity, for its part, is a Christian truth, an essentially Christian concept, of so high a rank that it can be sacrificed only to safeguard what is most fundamental. . . . It is the task of every responsible Christian and, in a particular way, of theologians and leaders of the church to create a spiritual climate for the theologically possible; under the compelling mandate of a unity without sameness, to see and experience the antithetical at all times without specious superficiality; to inquire always not just about the defensibility of union, of mutual recognition, but even more urgently about the defensibility of remaining separate, for it is not unity that requires justification but the absence of it.[4]

The "default position" for Christians with regard to the church, in other words, must not be to accept mutual opposition, or even diversity of theological traditions and plurality of community form, as perennially given, but to suppose, on the basis of faith in a single Savior, that the

3. Meyer, *That All May Be One*, p. 12.

4. Joseph Ratzinger, "The Ecumenical Situation — Orthodoxy, Catholicism and Protestantism," in *Principles of Catholic Theology: Building Stones for a Fundamental Theology*, trans. Mary Frances McCarthy (San Francisco: Ignatius Press, 1987), pp. 199-200.

church that proclaims him is intended by God to be genuinely and concretely one social body, in its own eyes and in the eyes of the world.

In this brief paper, I would like to do three things: to look at the various ways our churches today, on the basis of their own particular approach to the Christian faith, tend to conceive of the unity that belongs to the church as a whole; then to consider, in a summary way, some of the distinctive features of the way Christians thought of the church and experienced its unity during the first millennium — a period that is often held up as an ideal for the reconstructed unity ecumenists seek; and finally, even more briefly, to reflect on the challenges and possibilities of moving closer to a "visible" and universal unity of Christians today.

Conceptions of the Church's Unity

Unity, we have said, characterizes the whole body of Christian believers, as one of the effects of redemption. What this "given" unity means in practice, however, is not easy to discern, precisely because our view of it is inseparable from the way each of us understands and imagines the reality of what we call the church: what we imagine the church to be, in other words, determines the degree to which we do or do not see it as already unified, in principle and in fact. One might think of a number of ways in which Christians imagine the unity of the church:

The Spiritual Oneness of Those Who Call Jesus "Savior"

For many Christians, "the church" means those who genuinely accept the Christian Bible as the word of God, who confess faith in Jesus as Lord and Christ, and who accept and respect each other as fellow disciples. In this view, "the church" is simply another word for "all Christians." Its unity is spiritual; it comes from our sense of "all being in this together."

Agreement on the Fundamental Content of Christian Faith

Others would define the one church in more exacting detail, in terms of agreement on the basic content of the Christian profession: the distinctive and normative character of the Christian Scripture as the word of

God; the trinitarian understanding of God, and the full divinity and full humanity of Jesus, as formulated in the classical ancient creeds and conciliar formulas; the central role of baptism and the Eucharist in shaping and sustaining the Christian community; the central moral obligations imposed by the Bible and Christian tradition. Such doctrinal agreement could be understood, of course, in a variety of ways: as emphasizing an "ascending" or a "descending" Christology, for example, or a modalist or a subordinationist conception of the Trinity; as emphasizing a quite traditional understanding of Christian moral teaching, or as remaining open to an ethical message shaped more by the social and political agenda of modern liberal society. Still, this second approach sees the "one church" of Christians to be defined by agreement on the basic doctrinal and moral teaching assumed to lie at the heart of Christianity.[5]

Unity Expressed in Sacramental Structure and Practice

Others would see the unity of the church as based not only on such agreement concerning basic doctrines, but also on the sacramental acts and offices that define the church's life of proclamation and worship: agreement on the role and efficacy of baptism, on the central ecclesial meaning of the eucharist, on the necessity of a ministry grounded in the historic episcopate; the mutual recognition of these basic sacramental realities — despite historic variations in rite and theological interpretation — by particular communities; and the consequent possibility for members of one community to share in the sacraments and ministries of the other.

Unity of Theological and Spiritual Emphasis

Still others would define the unity of Christ's church, for practical purposes at least, in terms of the particular theological, spiritual, and pastoral tradition in which their own reception of the basic Christian message is

---

5. This is the unity of faith that Karl Rahner and Heinrich Fries, in their controversial book *Unity of the Churches: An Actual Possibility* (Philadelphia: Fortress, 1985), hold out as one of the necessary conditions for the "reconciled diversity" that they consider a real possibility among the main Christian churches and denominations.

articulated. Such traditions are often strongly identified with the figure of a charismatic Christian founder or leader. These would include the various smaller "sects" and denominations of Christianity — the Anabaptist communities, the Adventists, many of the Free Churches — and correspond, in a number of ways, to the theological schools and religious orders that exist within the communion of the Roman Catholic Church: they are lenses through which the unity of the wider Christian body is given the distinctive shape and color that form an integral part of the individual believer's religious identity.

Unity as an Exclusive Possession

Perhaps the most closely integrated vision of Christian unity is that of groups which consider themselves, with their own distinctive doctrines, practices, and structures, to be the only faithful "remnant" of the original community of believers, the one and only "true church." It would include the Donatists of ancient Roman Africa, who considered all other Christian communities to be cut off, by the presumed apostasies of earlier generations, from the single body of Christ. One finds it today among some conservative Orthodox and Roman Catholic groups, and perhaps among those "fundamentalist" Protestants who restrict their use of the word "Christian" to those who have undergone a conversion experience similar to their own. As a distortion of genuine commitment and loyalty, it lurks as a possible attitude within most Christian churches and communities.

One could probably think of other ways in which Christians actually understand and imagine the unity of the church proclaimed and promised in the Scriptures. But these are descriptive rather than theological groupings. From a theological point of view, the actual models or patterns of church unity that dominate the thinking of the mainstream Christian churches today could perhaps be classified, at the risk of oversimplification, in three general categories:[6]

6. Meyer, *That All May Be One*, pp. 15-36, develops a similar typology of five different understandings of church unity, which he associates with the Protestant churches of the Reformation, the Anglican Communion, the Free Church tradition, the Orthodox Churches, and the Roman Catholic Church. It seems to me, however, that the Anglican, Orthodox, and Catholic approaches, as he describes them, are similar enough in their main features to be seen as a single ecclesiological "model."

1. Sacramental-eucharistic unity, characteristic of Orthodox, Roman Catholic, Anglican, and some Lutheran approaches to ecclesiology. In this understanding of the church, unity is grounded in a common apostolic faith, based on the normative Christian canon of Scripture and on the "rule of faith" articulated in the classical creeds and conciliar definitions of the ancient "undivided" church.[7] But that same unity is brought to life, in a normative and determining way, by the sacrament of baptism, which creates the church as the community of those "in Christ," and maintained by the sharing of the eucharist, in which the church's reality as Christ's "Body" is represented and constructed. Individual, local communities, gathered to hear the preached word of God and to share the eucharist at the same table, are united to each other by their mutual recognition as communities of apostolic faith and valid sacraments, and by their common intercessory prayer for each other and for the needs of the world. Further, local communities are united by sharing a common structure of ministerial leadership: the "threefold office" of bishop, presbyter, and deacon, conferred from generation to generation by historical succession and custom. Through these ordained leaders — specifically, through their bishops — local communities are united to each other by ascending structures of decision-making and responsibility that have some degree of real institutional "bite" — by some form or other of what are usually called synodality and primacy.

2. Confessional unity, characteristic of the churches of the Reformation. In this understanding, the church's unity is grounded in a more limited range of essentials; in the famous phrase of the *Augsburg Confession,* "it is sufficient for the true unity of the Christian church that the Gospel is harmoniously preached and the sacraments administered according to the Word of God."[8] The early confessional documents of the Lutheran and

7. Anglican theology has tended to see only the first four ecumenically received councils of the church — Nicea I (325), Constantinople I (381), Ephesus (431), and Chalcedon (451) — as normative for later Christian faith. The reasons for this may be the traditional shape of the divinity curriculum in English universities, along with a cultural distaste — inherited, perhaps, from Gibbon — for later "Byzantine" controversies, as much as any particular theological issue identified with the later "ecumenical" councils — Constantinople II (553), Constantinople III (680-681), for the Orthodox churches the "Quinisext" or Council "in Trullo" (691-692), and finally Nicea II (787).

8. *Augsburg Confession* 7, quoted in Meyer, p. 16. The *Second Helvetic Confession* of

Reformed traditions both expressly distinguish these essentials from the "ceremonies" or "outward rites" of the Christian tradition — including, presumably, devotional and ascetical practices, liturgical actions, and most church offices — which are not attested by the Scriptures as established by Christ and are therefore presumed to be of human institution. Christians and Christian communities, in the mind of the sixteenth-century confessional documents, are to be free to use or to avoid such practices, without thereby weakening "the true unity of the church."[9] The ministry of preaching and of celebrating the sacraments is, of course, presupposed in some way as essential by this vision of church unity, but there is no clear consensus on whether such ministry requires formal ordination by those already so ordained — requires, in other words, a "historic succession" of orders — or whether such a succession is itself one of the optional practices that are of human institution.

The difficult question in assessing the understanding of unity shared by these traditions today is the degree to which the particular theological and spiritual positions of their founders remain a formative hermeneutical characteristic of their community life; Ratzinger asks, for instance, in another article, "To what extent are Luther's writings to be regarded as the real foundation of the Reformation, as the normative basis for interpretation, in terms of which we are to decide the true meaning of the confessional writings?"[10] In his view, the main hope for "visible union" between the Roman Catholic Church and the Lutheran Churches lies, from the Catholic perspective, in the possibility that the Roman Church could receive such documents as the *Augsburg Confession* as expressing the essentials of the Catholic tradition. But it is not always clear, in discussions with contemporary Protestant theologians, which confessional documents from the Reformation period are to be regarded as dogmatically foundational, and how normative a role the writings of Luther or Melanchthon or Calvin are to play in discovering the original intent and meaning of those documents. Ratzinger observes:

the Reformed Church makes the same point, emphasizing more sharply the doctrinal content of gospel preaching: "We teach that the true harmony of the Church consists in doctrines *(dogmatibus)* and in the true and harmonious preaching of the Gospel of Christ and in rites that have been expressly delivered by the Lord" (sec. 17, quoted in Meyer, p. 17).

9. *Augsburg Confession* 7; *Second Helvetic Confession* 17 (Meyer, pp. 16-17).

10. "Elucidations of the Question of a 'Recognition' of the *Confessio Augustana* by the Catholic Church," in *Principles of Catholic Theology*, p. 220.

The distinction between theology and statements of church doctrine cannot be so clearly drawn in the sphere of the Lutheran Reformation as it can in Catholic theology. In fact, the Reformation rests, to a large extent, on the fact that that distinction has been eliminated and that, in consequence, statements of church doctrine can have no higher or different rank in principle than the findings of scientific theology.[11]

One of the main aims of the sixteenth-century Reformation, surely, was to relativize the value of documents and traditions outside the explicit content of Scripture as ways of grounding the church's continuing unity of faith and practice. This makes the achievement of "visible unity" either a simpler task or a much more difficult one, depending in the end on how such unity is conceived: Does it depend simply on accepting the same Bible, or does it require the agreement to live by Luther's or Calvin's reading of the Bible?

3. Unity through individual faith in Jesus, characteristic of the "Free Churches." This family of churches, which includes communities in the Baptist and many other Evangelical traditions, tends to understand the unity of the church as the spiritual and personal bond that unites those who have accepted Jesus as their Savior and have expressed this conversion publicly by allowing themselves to be baptized. The local assembly of believers is the most concrete manifestation of this community of faith, and it finds and expresses its unity in worship (which usually includes occasional eucharistic celebration), in mutual support, and in joint witness and missionary activity in the world. Wider unions of local churches — the Southern Baptist Convention, for instance — are groupings that support the life and efforts of local congregations, but have no final authority in regulating their faith, leadership, or practice. Ministry in the local community is understood to be the outgrowth of particular gifts of the Holy Spirit, recognized in individuals by the community; but all particular ministry remains subordinate, in theory and in practice, to the common "priesthood" of all believers. In this understanding of the church, the unity that makes Christian believers one body, one temple, is grounded simply in their common adherence to Christ, and in their common share in the Spirit who sanctifies and empowers all, according to his

11. "Elucidations of the Question," p. 221, citing for support Siegfried Wiedenhofer, *Formalstrukturen humanistischer und reformatorischer Theologie bei Philipp Melanchthon* (Munich: Peter Lang, 1976), pp. 282-347.

will. In these traditions, as Harding Meyer puts it, "the Church is not connected in its essence to any kind of external and visible conditions and signs. These are subordinate to the personal faith that makes human beings members of the body of Christ."[12] Neither confessional documents — of whatever antiquity — nor theological traditions, nor even particular approaches to biblical interpretation, are seen as being identifying marks of the one church of Christ. For that reason, whatever "visible unity" is proper to the church as a whole already exists in the worldwide phenomenon of believing Christian disciples — in the many graced individuals who call Jesus their Lord. Ecumenical efforts only make sense as promoting the renewal of local communities in faith, and making possible greater practical cooperation among them.

The Patristic Moment

Christian efforts at reform, through the centuries, have usually involved a conscious "return to the sources": a judging of the present faith and practice of the church by the standard of the Bible, but also an attempt to find models and parallels in what we know of the life of the early church for the reshaping of contemporary institutions. History can be a liberating as well as a constricting force. This is obvious in the reforms of the sixteenth-century West: in the Reformers' universal focus on Scripture as the first, unparalleled norm for faith and community life, in Luther's revival of central themes from Augustine, in Calvin's constant recourse to Chrysostom and other figures of "primitive Christianity" in his critiques of the Catholic tradition, but also in the scriptural and patristic focus of the documents of Trent and the writings of Roman Catholic controversialists of the time, and in the theological synthesis of the Elizabethan and Jacobean divines of the Church of England, such as Richard Hooker. In more recent times, it is revealing to note how much the theological and pastoral reforms called for in the documents of the Second Vatican Council — its substantially new approach to characterizing the nature and structure of the church, for example, or its liturgical reforms — relied on the reemphasis of scriptural themes and patristic sources for their theological justification. It is hardly surprising, then, that contemporary ecu-

12. Meyer, *That All May Be One,* p. 25.

menical discussion tends to rely heavily on examples from the early church to justify or to mitigate the apparent radicality of suggested steps towards deeper "visible union." As the official preface to the Faith and Order Commission's 1982 "Lima Document," *Baptism, Eucharist and Ministry*, remarks,

> Indeed, as a result of biblical and patristic studies, together with the liturgical revival and the need for common witness, an ecumenical fellowship has come into being which often cuts across confessional boundaries and within which former differences are now seen in a new light.[13]

Bilateral dialogues, too, continue to draw on the practices and theological sources of the early church to underline common traditions and to support proposed new steps towards unity.[14]

Looking to the past for liberating examples is always risky: we tend to project on its surviving monuments images of what we ourselves desire. As Robert Taft remarks, in a characteristically pungent reflection on the romantic nostalgia that animates the modern Western fascination with Eastern liturgy:

> What the West did with the East is what historians do with the past: they interpret it in the light of present aims and needs. In other words,

---

13. *Baptism, Eucharist and Ministry*, Faith and Order Paper 111 (Geneva: WCC, 1982), p. ix. In the body of the statement, frequent references are made to the sacramental practices of the patristic age: e.g., *Baptism* p. 11 (infant baptism) and p. 19 (chrismation); *Eucharist* p. 21 (ministry of deacons and deaconesses at the Eucharist); *Ministry* p. 22 (threefold ministry), p. 41 (rite of ordination).

14. Reliance on patristic as well as biblical sources is not only evident — as one might expect — in most joint statements of Orthodox and Western ecumenical commissions, but is given normative value in the statement of the Lutheran–Roman Catholic Joint Commission, *Facing Unity: Models, Forms and Phases of Catholic–Lutheran Church Fellowship* (1985), precisely on the issue of reaching a common understanding of episcopal ministry in the church: secs. 47, 104-11. Commenting on the Lutheran tradition of episcopal ordination, for instance, the document observes: "The Lutheran Reformation basically affirmed the episcopal office of the Early Church. There was readiness to retain the episcopal office in its traditional form, even though there was criticism of the manner in which the office was exercised at that time. To some extent this criticism was explicitly associated with and legitimated by references to the Early Church. Thus it is clear that also on the Lutheran side the question of episcopal ministry is dealt with in reference to the Early Church." (106) Continuity with early Christian faith and practice is seen here as a standard of ecclesial continuity — of a unity, catholicity, and apostolicity extended through time.

the Western view of Eastern liturgy, the commonplaces of its virtues, are simply a mirror of our own deepest longings. The qualities we identify in Eastern liturgy are those we think the West has lost.[15]

Our human world, at the start of the twenty-first century, is clearly a radically different place from the world of the Fathers. "Community" has a totally different meaning for most people alive today: the local community, as a stable and concretely identifiable group of people with whom one is always "at home," is rapidly vanishing; cultural symbols, values, desires are steadily becoming homogeneous the world over, leaving individuals in the paradoxical position of being less and less different from most other people alive today, and more and more isolated in their own identity. The mediating role of small, manageable groupings with which a person can form identifying bonds — the village, the ethnic group, the church — is becoming, for many contemporaries, less and less effective; the corporate unities that affect our lives tend more and more to be amalgamated into vast, centralized structures with which the individual has little meaningful relationship: the national or international bureaucracy, the multinational corporation, the religious denomination. In response, various new forms of minority consciousness, even of chauvinism, keep emerging to fill the gap, even while our contemporaries seem to find it more and more difficult to make long-term public commitments, to identify themselves as members of any particular group or as adherents to any particular institution. On the level of religious tradition, people living in this culture that so idealizes endless personal choice seem to find it increasingly difficult to accept binding doctrine. Those who feel the need of religious practice, and of some form of spiritual nourishment, to find a meaning and purpose to their lives are often afflicted with a kind of hermeneutical schizophrenia: while accepting, as a given of modern society, the historicism and empirical rationalism of our technocratic culture, they also seek to be in touch, through their own subjective quest, with a less rationally controllable, more "mystical" order of things: the personal promise of the enlightenment of Eastern spiritual disciplines or alternative medicine, the mythical world of Jungian analysis, the allure of "caring for the soul." All of these elements set us at a great distance, in important ways, from the world of "the undivided

---

15. Robert F. Taft, S.J., "'Eastern Presuppositions' and Western Liturgical Renewal," *Antiphon* 5 (2000): 10-22, here p. 13.

church" of the first millennium; we are, as modern believers, often more Gnostic than Christian, more sectaries than members of a universal body.

For, as ecumenical reformers constantly assume, Christian unity did work, for the churches of the first ten and a half centuries of the Christian era, in ways that it has not worked since then. Despite frequent sharp theological disputes, despite the occurrence at times of incurable division, in what came to be called heresy and schism, the great majority of Christians in the first millennium seem simply to have understood themselves as linked with other Christians around the world in a single, complex, but efficacious system of structures, doctrines, and symbols that had a distant but real effect on the everyday life of faith. Even after the formal breakdown of this Christian commonwealth into two mutually excluding bodies, with the exchange of anathemas by representatives of the Pope and Patriarch of Constantinople in 1054, it was several centuries before either East or West was prepared to accept this division as normal or irreversible. Let me point out at least a few main features of this "undivided" universal church, as it was understood in the first Christian millennium.

1. In a variety of ways, it was *the universal family of local churches,* in its historical continuity with the Apostles, that was understood as *the Body of Christ,* the "Bride" espoused to the triumphant Lamb (Rev. 19:7; 21:2, 9; 22:17; cf. 2 Cor. 11:2). Irenaeus saw all the churches of apostolic origin — held in living harmony through their contact with the Church of Rome, where Peter and Paul had given their final witness — as forming a single reliable source of teaching for believers, a single spring of life-giving truth.

> Since, therefore, we have proofs such as this, it is not necessary to seek the truth among others when it is easy to obtain it from the Church, since the Apostles brought most abundantly to her, as to a rich treasury, all things that pertain to the truth, so that everyone — whoever wishes to do so — can draw from her the water of life. For she is the entrance to life; all others are thieves and robbers.[16]

Origen and Gregory of Nyssa took the whole church, as a trans-historical entity, as well as the saved individual believer, to be the referent of the passionate bridal imagery of the Song of Songs. More than any other ancient

---

16. *Against the Heresies* 3.4.1, trans. Alexander Roberts and James Donaldson (*The Ante-Nicene Fathers* 1.416-417); altered in light of Greek fragment: see SChr 211.44-45.

writer, however, Augustine continually speaks of the church as the universal, corporate object of God's salvation in Christ, the *totus Christus* — the third and final mode of existence of the eternal Word of God, by which Christ continues to be personally present in the world and to involve us in that presence.

> We are, all together, the members and the body of Christ — not just those of us who are in this place but people throughout all the world, and not just those living at this time. How shall I put it? From Abel the just until the very end of the world, as long as human beings beget and are begotten, every just person who makes his journey through this life — whether he exists now, not just in this place but in this life, or shall come to exist in the future — all of them together are the one body of Christ, and each of us are the members of Christ.[17]

It is the church scattered throughout the world, Augustine frequently insists, which is the "field" of the parables of the Kingdom, the place where God's promised human "harvest" of holiness and transformed life, sown through the grace of Christ, is growing to maturity. As he puts it, for example, in a homily on Psalm 149, commenting on the phrase, "His praise is in the assembly *(ecclesia)* of the saints":

> This is "the Church of the saints," the Church made up of grain scattered over the whole face of the earth, sown across the field of the Lord, which is this world. . . . Everywhere it is bearing fruit, a hundredfold and sixtyfold and thirtyfold. You must simply reflect on what you aspire to be, when you think of belonging to "the Lord of the harvest."[18] "The Church of the saints," then, is the catholic Church. "The Church of the saints" is not the Church of the heretical sects. "The Church of the saints" is that assembly which God revealed in sign before it became visible, and which he later made public, that it might be seen.[19] "The

---

17. Sermon 341.9.11 [a mature sermon, usually dated 417-419]. For the "three modes of existence" of the Word — his eternal being as God, equal to the Father; his incarnate being "when, having taken on flesh, he is as one single person God and a human being, as one person human and God"; and finally "the whole Christ, in the fullness of the Church, that is, as head and body 'according to the fullness of a mature man'" — see ibid. 1.1.

18. Or, in some manuscripts, "to the harvest of the Lord."

19. Augustine here is referring to the people of God before and after the incarnation of the Word and the coming of the Holy Spirit on the apostles of Jesus.

Church of the saints" existed first in the pages of the Bible, but now in the nations of the earth. Formerly, "the Church of the saints" was simply something to read about; now it is not only read about, but seen. When it was only read about, it was an object of faith; now it is seen, and has become a sign of contradiction![20]

Salvation, for Augustine, is never a question simply of an elect individual's fate before God, but of an individual's membership in the predestined community of salvation.

2. The way in which the church throughout time and space formed a unity was not understood, however, in monolithic terms in the Patristic period. The most fundamental category for understanding the church was that of *communion:* the sharing *(koinonia)* of many individuals in the grace of Christ — in the life that unites and flows from the persons of the Holy Trinity — by virtue of those individuals' share in the life and worship of the believing community, gathered around lectern and altar. Local churches were not conceived of as branch offices of a centralized international corporation, or as provinces of a single (somewhat less effectively centralized) Roman Empire, but being each as the complete Catholic Church in a particular time and place; their catholicity, like their apostolicity and their unity, was achieved through their "communion" with the other churches of the world that professed the same faith and claimed the same apostolic origin. Communion among the churches was expressed and maintained in a number of ways: at Rome, through the sending of fragments of the eucharistic bread from the bishop's church to outlying churches, for inclusion with the consecrated gifts in their own liturgies; more generally, through "eucharistic hospitality" extended to traveling members of other communities who could show proper credentials; through "canonical letters" *(litterae communicatoriae, litterae formatae)* or

---

20. *Enarratio on Psalm 149,3* [delivered in Carthage, probably between 411 and 413]. — In a sermon on John 7:38-39, where Jesus promises to give the Holy Spirit after he is "glorified," Augustine makes the same point in different terms. The church on the day of Pentecost was shown to have received the Holy Spirit, he says, by the fact that the disciples could be understood in many languages; this was a sign of the church of the future, "when, growing through all nations, it would speak in the languages of all. Whoever is not in this church has not yet received the Holy Spirit" (*Tractate 32 on the Gospel of John 7;* CCL 36.304).

"letters of peace" exchanged between bishops, expressing consensus in the fundamental outlines of the apostolic faith and the desire for unity; through the maintenance of lists in certain episcopal centers, recording those bishops throughout the world who were known to profess the apostolic tradition and to be "at peace" or "in charity" with their colleagues.[21] Structurally, this same communion among local churches — the "communion of communions," which formed the universal Christian body — was sustained by the canonically regulated interplay of what we now call "conciliarity" and "primacy": the joint responsibility of bishops, on the one hand, for the articulation and proclamation of the gospel in their own province or region, and even — in periods of momentous dispute, such as those that occasioned the "ecumenical" councils — of the bishops of the whole Christian world, principally exercised through synods and councils; and the supervisory leadership, on the other hand, of the bishops of major cities — the "metropolitan" cities of each province in the Empire, and the capitals of the imperial super-provinces or "dioceses" — to resolve local disputes, and to make sure that local bishops were canonically elected and continued to maintain the apostolic traditions.[22]

3. When divisions among Christians, serious enough to disrupt the communion of the churches, did occur, it was essentially up to local bishops or regional synods to devise *strategies of reconciliation*. Perhaps the most informative ancient sources on such practices, as well as on the flexibility and desire for reconciliation that characterized early Christian ecclesial

21. For a somewhat dated, but still classic brief description of the contours of ecclesial communion in the early church, see Ludwig Hertling, *Communio: Church and Papacy in Early Christianity,* trans. Jared Wicks (Chicago: Loyola University Press, 1972). For more recent, more theologically developed descriptions of communion, see especially Jean-Marie Roger Tillard, *Église d'églises. L'ecclésiologie de communion* (Paris: Cerf, 1987); and *Chair de l'église, chair du Christ: aux sources de l'ecclésiologie de communion* (Paris: Cerf, 1992; English trans.: *Flesh of the Church, Flesh of Christ* [Collegeville, Minn.: Liturgical Press, 2001]).

22. I have attempted to describe the dialectic of synodality and primacy in the early church in a number of places, especially with reference to the historical exercise of the "Petrine ministry" by the bishops of Rome: see "Structures of Charity: Bishops' Gatherings and the See of Rome in the Early Church," in Thomas J. Reese, ed., *Episcopal Conferences: Historical, Canonical and Theological Studies* (Washington, D.C.: Georgetown University Press, 1989), pp. 25-58; and "Position and Patronage in the Early Church: The Original Meaning of 'Primacy of Honour,'" *Journal of Theological Studies* 44 (1993): 529-53.

policy at its best, are the letters of Basil of Caesarea, written during his episcopate in the 370s. In a famous letter written to his friend Amphlochius, bishop of Iconium (Ep. 188, known as the first of his "canonical" letters because of its influence on the later Byzantine tradition of canon law), the metropolitan of Caesarea tries to explain his own policy in dealing with various church "boundary" issues: what crimes and forms of behavior warrant the exclusion of individuals or groups from ecclesial communion, and what conditions are set down for their reconciliation. The first section deals with the recognition of baptisms performed in dissident Christian communities. Basil here distinguishes among three such groups. "Heresies" (αἱρέσεις) or "sects" are groups that are completely alien in faith from the church, because their notion of God is radically different from that of mainstream Christianity;[23] "schismatics," the second group, comprise "those separated from one another for ecclesiastical reasons, and because of questions that can be resolved" — the examples he gives include the "Cathari," rigorists who denied that major sinners could be reconciled with the church by any human rites, and other groups characterized by excessive asceticism or liturgical deviation; the third group, "illegal congregations (παρασυναγωγαί)," are communities separated from the main church by strictly jurisdictional disputes, and therefore led by unauthorized ministers.[24] The baptisms performed by "heretics," Basil insists, are simply invalid, because the God into whose name they baptize their members is not the Christian Trinity; the baptisms of the other two groups of communities, on the other hand, have traditionally been recognized, "because they are still part of the church," since they confess the same Triune God. Members of schismatic groups, provided they have followed the traditional form of baptism, can be incorporated into the church by public anointing; members of "illegal congregations" are to be reconciled by the simpler gesture of a laying-on of hands, and their ministers can even be accepted into the church's ministry in the same rank as they have hitherto possessed.

23. The examples he gives are mainly Gnostic sects, but he also includes the "Pepuzenes" or Montanists, who at this time were understood to baptize candidates "in the name of the Father, the Son, and Montanus," the sect's prophetic founder, from the second century, who in Basil's time was thought by his followers to be an incarnation of the Holy Spirit.

24. See Basil, Ep. 188.1 (Loeb Classical Library edition 3; London: Heinemann, 1930), pp. 6-21.

Basil's approach, as revealed in this letter and elsewhere, seems to have been one of genuine flexibility, following "the customs of the ancients" as his guiding norm, but making his own exceptions and adjustments for pastoral reasons, "for I fear that while we want to make them cautious about how they baptize, we may in the end be an obstacle to those who seek salvation, through the severity of our policy."[25] In Letter 128, dealing more generally with dissident Christian groups, Basil writes:

> It does not seem best to me to estrange ourselves entirely from those who do not accept the faith, but we should show some concern for these people, according to the old laws of charity, and should with one accord write letters to them, offering every exhortation with kindliness; and proffering to them the faith of the Fathers, we should invite them to join us. And if we convince them, we should be united with them in communion; but if we fail, we should, for ourselves, be content with each other, and should remove this present uncertainty from our way of life.[26]

In still other letters, discussing the vexed issue of how to reconcile former Arians and others who have denied the church's trinitarian faith, Basil insists that his policy has always been to ask nothing more from them than that they profess the faith of Nicea and that they not call the Holy Spirit a creature; if they are able to do both of these things, he receives them into communion without further question.[27]

From all of these passages, we can conclude:

a. Basil did not look on eucharistic communion as itself a means for uniting separated Christians within the larger church; it always expressed for him an existing unity in the apostolic faith.

b. The standard for that unity in faith, in his view, is the "faith of Nicea," including (in those years just before 381) what Nicea seemed

---

25. Basil, Ep. 188.1 (Loeb Classical Library edition 3), p. 18.

26. Ep. 128, trans. Roy J. Deferrari (Loeb Classical Library edition 2; London: Heinemann, 1930), pp. 280-83. The earlier part of this letter makes it clear that the group Basil is thinking of is the so-called Spirit-fighters, led by Eustathius of Sebaste, who insisted that the Holy Spirit is a creature.

27. See Ep. 113, to the presbyters of Tarsus; Ep. 114, to Cyrianus; and Ep. 204, to the Church of Neocaesaraea in Pontus. For a discussion of Basil's treatment of heretics, see Paul J. Fedwick, *The Church and the Charisma of Leadership in Basil of Caesaraea* (Toronto: Pontifical Institute of Medieval Studies, 1979), pp. 69-76.

to imply about the Holy Spirit. If someone could profess that faith, Basil seems to have been willing to take his or her profession at face value, and not to insist on a detailed theological agreement as to how the Nicene Creed was to be interpreted. His desire, he insists in Letter 204, was to follow the precedent of earlier great figures like Athanasius, and "to receive the reward promised to peacemakers."[28]

   c. The reconciliation of Christians into a single community, whose unity was expressed by eucharistic sharing, was for him a major pastoral priority, intrinsically connected with the salvation of souls.

4. Basil's understanding of *the central role of the eucharist* in both expressing and achieving the unity of the church is, in fact, the classical understanding shared by theologians of the first millennium in both East and West. Susan K. Wood, explaining Henri de Lubac's modern characterization of that same tradition, writes that De Lubac "sees the eucharist as related to the church as cause is related to effect, means to end, sign to reality."[29] In the context of a thought-world where classical, divinely ordained signs not only represent inexpressible, transcendent reality to the mind, but actually make that reality operative, communicate its life and energy to intelligent creatures, the eucharistic sign of Christ's body was also understood as incorporating the recipient into his ecclesial body, a term understood not simply to be a social metaphor, but to point to the living church as the fullness of Christ's personal involvement in human history. Augustine, in several places, gives classic expression to this interlocking understanding of eucharist and church. In one of his Easter-week sermons to the newly baptized, for instance, he puts it in astonishingly simple terms:

> That bread which you see on the altar, made holy by the word of God, is the body of Christ. That cup — or rather, what that cup contains — made holy by the word of God, is the blood of Christ. Through these things the Lord Christ wished to entrust to us his body, and the blood which he poured out for the remission of sins. If you have received it well, you are what you have received. For the Apostle says, "We, though many, are one bread, one body" (1 Cor. 10:17). This is how he explains

28. Ep. 204 (Loeb Classical Library 3), p. 170.

29. Susan K. Wood, *Spiritual Exegesis and the Church in the Theology of Henri de Lubac* (Grand Rapids: Eerdmans; Edinburgh: T&T Clark, 1998), p. 54.

the mystery of the Lord's Table: "We, though many, are one bread, one body!" In this bread, it is shown to you how you ought to love unity.[30]

In another, similar sermon, delivered to the newly baptized at Pentecost, Augustine sets out to answer the perennial Christian question about Christ's eucharistic presence: "How can this be?"

> These things are called *sacraments,* my brothers and sisters, because in them one thing is seen and another is understood. What is seen has a bodily appearance; what is understood has a spiritual effect. So if you want to understand the body of Christ, hear the Apostle saying to the faithful, "You are the Body of Christ, and his members" (1 Cor. 12:27). If, then, you are the Body of Christ and his members, your own mystery is placed on the table of the Lord. Receive your own Mystery! To what you are, you respond "Amen," and in that response you give your assent. For you hear, "The Body of Christ," and you respond, "Amen." Be a member of the Body of Christ, that your "Amen" may be truthful. . . . Be what you see, and receive what you are![31]

The eucharist, then, in Augustine's view, itself contains an "indicative" and an "imperative" aspect, calling the believers who share it to become, intentionally and in fact, the single, unified body that this shared bread signifies and forms — to become collectively, institutionally, and behaviorally the body formed by the divine "flesh" on which they are nourished.[32]

5. It seems also to have been the general understanding of patristic writers that *the church we experience in this present history* — in its unity and in its divisions — *is not the full reality of the body of Christ,* but only (as Eph. 4:1-16 reminds us) that body in the process of growth towards unity, holiness,

---

30. Augustine, Sermon 227 [dated 416-417].

31. Augustine, Sermon 272 [dated 405-411].

32. See also Augustine, Sermons 227, 229, and 272, where the analogy of bread as a sign of unity is further developed: to make a loaf, first many grains are ground into uniform flour (as the catechumens are "ground down" — *contriti* — by pre-baptismal penance); then the flour is moistened with water (as the catechumens have been moistened in the font); finally, the dough is baked by fire and transformed into bread (as the newly baptized have been transformed by the heavenly "fire" of the Spirit). For the relationship of eucharistic "flesh" to ecclesial "body" in De Lubac's exposition of the pre-Scholastic tradition, see Wood, *Spiritual Exegesis and the Church,* p. 58.

and perfection. The church, in the language of modern ecumenical dialogue, is always a "uniting" rather than a "united" community. Yet the church is not simply a distant shadow of the eschatological kingdom of God; it is itself the means by which God both offers a representation of the Kingdom to the human race, and begins the work of gathering the world into that Kingdom. In the words of the Second Vatican Council — admittedly not a hallowed ecclesiological phrase, yet rooted in patristic ecclesiology — "By her relationship with Christ, *the Church is a kind of sacrament* or sign of intimate union with God, and of the unity of all humanity."[33] The church itself, like the eucharist, is a sign that makes the unifying presence of God real, even as it points to its coming fullness.

This sense that the full reality of the church, including her holiness and her unity, lies in the eschatological future, and that the one holy church will itself be the eschatological realization of salvation for the individual believer, is also a central theme in Augustine's works. Although he himself developed at length the Donatist theme of the "two cities" running through human history, and insisted many times that the present church is not the final form of the "City of God" but a mixed reality, a gathering of saints and sinners, Augustine also took pains to point out that the present church is intrinsically related to the future Kingdom. In his *Breviculus,* or summary of the *acta* of the reunion conference held between the Catholic and Donatist bishops of Africa in 411, for instance, Augustine reports:

> Concerning their (i.e., the Donatists') false assertion of two Churches, the Catholics repeatedly offered the same refutation, to make it all the clearer what they meant: that they never said the Church, which now has wicked people mingled in it, is foreign to the Kingdom of God, where the wicked will not be mingled in; but rather that the very same one and holy Church now exists in one state, but will then exist in another — that she now has wicked people mingled in her, but will not have them then . . . — in the same way that there are not two Christs, because he who once died will not die again.[34]

---

33. Second Vatican Council, *Lumen gentium,* 1; cf. the Council's Constitution on the Sacred Liturgy, *Sacrosanctum Concilium* 26: "Liturgical services are not private functions, but are celebrations of the Church, which is the sacrament of unity — namely, a holy people united and organized under their bishops. Therefore liturgical services pertain to the whole body of the Church; they manifest it and have effects upon it."

34. *Breviculus collationis cum Donatistis* 3.10.20.

In the last of his long series of sermons on the Gospel of John, Augustine develops this same contrast of the present and future church as part of his explanation of the risen Lord's final command to Peter, "Follow me!" Because of his vocation to primacy, Augustine observes, Peter in the Gospels always "plays the role of the church, in a generalized image";[35]

> thus as long as this Church, which Peter stands for, exists in the midst of evils, it is delivered from evil by loving and following Christ. It follows him more closely, of course, in those who struggle unto death for the sake of the truth. But the command, "Follow me!" is meant for us all, since Christ suffered on behalf of all. . . . Now there will be another life, an immortal one, which is not surrounded by evils. There we will see "face to face" what here we see "through a mirror and in mystery" (1 Cor. 13:12), when we have advanced much further in our ability to see the truth. So the Church experiences two modes of life, both of them foretold and promised to her by God. One of them is in faith, the other in vision; one in temporal wandering, the other in eternal abiding; one in labor, the other in rest; one on the road, the other in the homeland . . . ; one comes to the help of the poor, the other is in a place where the poor can no longer be found; one forgives the sins of others so that its own sins may be forgiven, the other neither experiences anything to forgive nor does anything for which it must request forgiveness; one is tried by evils lest it be inflated by good fortune, the other enjoys such fullness of grace that it knows no evil at all, but without any temptation to pride clings to the supreme Goodness; one discerns between good and evil, the other concerns itself exclusively with good; so the one form of life is good, yet still wretched up until now, while the other is better, and is simply bliss.[36]

6. Behind all these aspects of the patristic understanding of the unity of the church stands a complex, characteristic habit of thought that marks the

---

35. *Tractate 124 on John*, 5 (CCL 36.684): "cuius ecclesiae Petrus apostolus, propter apostolatus sui primatum, gerebat figurata generalitate personam." [This sermon is probably from around 418, the immensely fruitful period in his late maturity when Augustine was finishing *De Trinitate* and working on books 11-14 of *The City of God*.]

36. *Tractate 124 on John*, 5 (CCL 36.685). The whole of the lengthy fifth section of this homily interweaves a reflection on the risen Lord's command to Peter — and through him to the church — with phrases from the Lord's Prayer, which is, in Augustine's view, the constant refrain of the church *in via*.

first Christian millennium, and that may strike us, in our very different world, as irremediably strange. The Fathers think and write about the church almost exclusively in the language of *symbol*. Political and social theory and analysis were certainly not unknown in the ancient world. Plato, and after him Cicero, had written their versions of *The Republic;* Aristotle had reflected on the structures and demands of human society in his two sets of *Ethics* and in his *Politics.* Yet strikingly, throughout the first millennium, Christian writers thought about the church not in terms of organization and distributed power, not as a parallel to the state or even as one of the various corporate bodies regulated by Roman law, but as a part of the world of biblical imagery and promise, a stage in the Bible's universal narrative of God's saving history. The church, for the New Testament and for the Fathers, is, like Israel, central to what we might call the sacramental structure of God's communication of himself to the world: a human reality — in this case, a community, a society — which God has chosen to use, both to represent in a temporal image what the fullness of our salvation will be, when history comes to its end in the finally present Christ, and to be the means, even now, of gradually incorporating us into that life of fullness through its preaching and sacraments.[37] In the language of scholastic theology, the church itself is an "efficacious sign" of the presence of God among us in Christ: a sign that both points us to Christ and makes Christ real in our midst as the initiator of a new creation.

37. This understanding of the church and its sacramental actions is the reason Irenaeus, in Book 5 of *Against the Heresies,* stresses the importance of the eucharist for Christian faith: it reveals that the salvation God has already achieved for us in Christ, the fullness of which will only be realized after history and the final millennium have come to an end, already includes our bodies as well as our minds. He writes: "By his own blood he redeemed us, as also his apostle declares, 'In him we have redemption through his blood, the forgiveness of sins' (Col. 1:14). And as we are his members, we are also nourished by means of creation. . . . He has acknowledged the cup, which is a part of creation, as his own blood, from which our blood takes its increase; and the bread, also a part of creation, he has established as his own body, from which he gives increase to our bodies. When, therefore, the mingled cup and the manufactured bread receive the Word of God and become the Eucharist and the body of Christ, from which things the substance of our flesh is increased and supported, how can they [i.e., Gnostic Christians] affirm that the flesh is incapable of receiving the gift of God which is life eternal, since the flesh is nourished from the body and blood of the Lord, and is his member?" (*Adv. Haer.* 5.2.2-3; trans. Alexander Roberts and James Donaldson, *The Ante-Nicene Fathers* 1.528 [alt. in light of Greek fragment: see SChr 153.32-34]).

So the Fathers speak about the church continually in images. The treatises on the church they do write are either commentaries on the Song of Songs — like those of Origen and Gregory of Nyssa, of Ambrose and Apponius and Gregory the Great — in which the church, as well as the individual soul, is the Bride who captivates the heart of God,[38] or else allegorical explanations of the liturgy, like those of Pseudo-Dionysius and Maximus Confessor, in which the church's worship, complete with its ministers, its rites, and its physical surroundings, becomes an elaborate metaphor for a renewed cosmos, in which the church itself is the first-fruits of transformation. Augustine, as we have seen — in the long tradition of Origen, Hilary, and Ambrose — describes the real nature of the church as the "Body" of which Christ is the head, the "Bride" joined to him in "one flesh," the "dove" whose very soul is the Holy Spirit, the "ark" that rides out the flood, the "house of God" built on rock, the "field," now sown with wheat and tares, which in the end will produce God's harvest.[39] As Augustine understands the church, these are not, it seems, simply poetic metaphors for a social reality; they are the kind of image that can never be dispensed with when one is speaking of the mystery of God's involvement in time — biblical images, images of salvation, images pointing to Christ. For the church, in its inner reality, cannot, in the usual Patristic view, be understood separately from Christ himself; in the church, as the church, we become part of his life, and he of ours. The catholic church of the Apostles finds its unity and its holiness in being the *totus Christus.*

In this sense, patristic language about the church rests on the same assumptions and makes the same demands as does patristic biblical exegesis — assumptions which demand that we distance ourselves, in important ways, from our modern way of understanding both our Bible and our Christian communities. Like ancient exegesis, the patristic way of thinking of the church begins with the assumption that the God who has revealed himself to us is the most immediate, the most fundamentally *real* of realities, even though his reality is "veiled" by the present sensible

38. For a survey of the Latin tradition of these commentaries into the Middle Ages, see especially E. Ann Matter, *The Voice of My Beloved: The Song of Songs in Western Medieval Christianity* (Philadelphia: University of Pennsylvania Press, 1990), esp. pp. 86-122.

39. See, for example, *De diversis quaestionibus 83,* q. 69.10; *Enarratio on Psalm 111.1; On Baptism, against the Donatists* 7.51.99. For a full treatment of Augustine's ecclesiology, in terms of these and other images, see Stanislaus J. Grabowski, *The Church: An Introduction to the Theology of St. Augustine* (St. Louis: Herder, 1957).

world. It assumes, too, that the history narrated in the Bible — from the creation of the world, through the call and growth of Israel, until the present age — is a continuous narrative, whose central point, the point that reveals the direction of the whole story, is the coming of Christ. It assumes that the meaning hidden in the various events and characters of the story, including the true nature of the church in which we find ourselves, cannot be exhaustively plumbed by a single idea or expressed in a single term, but that it must be teased out in an almost inexhaustible stream of images and analogies, which release to us new aspects of the one mystery: the overarching mystery of our salvation in Christ. The key to interpreting individual texts, like the key to discovering the meaning of the church itself, is already present to us in the church's baptismal "rule of faith," the formulated summary of the whole narrative that serves as the continuing framework for the church's self-understanding and its understanding of Scripture. And while this way of understanding text and community certainly does not disregard what we moderns would call their "historical" reality — the details of events as they actually happened, the material character of bread and wine, the mundane political features of institutions and the human flaws of their leaders — it rests on the conviction that the "deeper" reality of God's gracious purpose in this history is the only thing that is of real significance for the eye of faith.

In her explanation of De Lubac's "eucharistic" ecclesiology — an understanding of the church based on the early medieval understanding of the eucharist not only as an efficacious sign of the present Christ, but as a sign of the church that is on the way to realizing the fullness of his earthly presence — Susan Wood draws this same parallel between patristic figural exegesis and a sacramental understanding of the church:

> Just as the spiritual sense of Scripture does not eliminate the literal sense or add something else to it, but rather gives it its fullness and reveals its depths, so does the ecclesial sense of the Eucharist depend on the real presence at the same time it reveals its larger signification.[40]

Wood points out that it was at about the same point in history — the latter half of the twelfth century — that Western theologians began to lose interest in the spiritual or figural interpretation of both the Bible and the eucharist, and to take a more literal, self-consciously "scientific" approach

40. Wood, *Spiritual Exegesis and the Church*, p. 68.

97

to them: to focus on the "historical" or plain-sense meaning of Scripture, and to speculate about the metaphysics of Christ's presence in the sacrament.[41] With the new study of canon law in the twelfth-century universities, and the revival of Aristotelian learning — including the translation and study of the *Politics* — in the following century, it was perhaps inevitable that the church, too, came to be thought of more and more exclusively as a human society, and less and less in terms of the mystery of Christ. The unity of the body would become, as a result, increasingly difficult to comprehend or to justify in any but purely practical and political terms. The de-sacramentalization of both Bible and church had begun.

Possibilities for Visible Union Today

The whole direction of the ecumenical movement of the twentieth century has been set, quite obviously, by the growing conviction that all the Christian churches need to take active steps towards understanding more deeply, and realizing more fully than they now do, the unity that is a fundamental dimension of the ecclesial body of Christ. Although the declarations of the Faith and Order Conferences at Lausanne (1927) and Edinburgh (1937) paved the way for a common enunciation of this vision, the classic statement of the modern, ecumenical vision of the church as a comprehensive "communion of communions" remains the "formula of unity" adopted by the Assembly of the World Council of Churches at New Delhi in 1961:

> We believe that the unity which is both God's will and his gift to his Church is being made visible as all in each place, who are baptized into Jesus Christ and confess him as Lord and Savior, are brought by the Holy Spirit into one fully committed fellowship, holding the one apostolic faith, preaching the one Gospel, breaking the one bread, joining in common prayer, and having a corporate life reaching out in witness and service to all; and who, at the same time, are united with the whole Christian fellowship in all places and ages, in such wise that ministry and members are accepted by all, and that all can act and speak together, as occasion requires, for the tasks to which God calls his people. It is for such a unity that we believe we must pray and work.[42]

41. Wood, *Spiritual Exegesis and the Church,* p. 67, n. 60.
42. Quoted from Meyer, *That All May Be One,* p. 42.

This dense, carefully honed statement contains a whole ecclesiology, and deserves (and has received) much more comment than I can hope to give it here. It is sufficient, perhaps, to point out some of its main features:

- the basic "model" by which Christian unity is imagined is that of "one fully committed fellowship": *communio, koinonia,* the sharing of life and possessions that involves both believers and local communities in a kind of permanent covenant;
- this is presented as something to be prayed for and labored for — something not yet present, and something not simply to be achieved by bureaucratic negotiation, but which will be both God's free gift, the gift of the Holy Spirit, and the fruit of human effort;
- the fundamental norm for membership in this one Christian body is that one be "baptized into Jesus Christ and confess him as Lord and Savior";
- the basic elements of the church's unity are a single apostolic faith, the preaching of a single gospel, the sharing in a single eucharist, common prayer, common witness, and common service in the world;
- the "catholicity" of this one church means its unity in the essentials of faith, sacraments, and witness with the whole historical body of Christians, spread through time and space;
- the practical signs of unity today are the mutual recognition of members and ministries by all the particular communities involved, and the ability of all of them to undertake common Christian witness and action.

Clearly this vision of a single Christian communion leaves us a good deal of room for imagining how it might be achieved. It does not necessarily call for a single institutional structure, or postulate uniformity in theology, spirituality, or mode of worship; but it does call for full acceptance by each church of the faith and religious practice of other communities as authentically Christian, and for the integration of each group's religious self-understanding and form of life into the longer and wider Christian tradition. It also calls for sufficiently developed structural features — a sufficient degree of both "conciliarity" and "primacy" — to allow for effective common discernment of what the tradition of faith implies, and for effective common witness in the world.

In fact, a number of different models for the union of formerly separate Christian communions have been developed over the past several decades, in more or less explicit response to the urging of the ecumenical movement, models that we need not rehearse here.[43] It seems likely that for the present, no one model of "fully committed fellowship" fits the desires and capabilities of all churches; a more attainable goal — if still one that is challengingly remote — might be to work to develop increasing dialogue, mutual understanding, and respect among all Christian churches, while working towards deeper union among those particular families of churches that share more fully in the same ecclesiological visions.

From the Roman Catholic perspective, the ideal of "unity without uniformity" among churches that share the same essential conception of faith and sacrament — an ideal first articulated in the "Malines conversations" between representatives of the Catholic and Anglican communions in the 1920s[44] — remains the immediate and primary goal of ecumenical dialogue. Vatican II's Decree on Ecumenism, *Unitatis redintegratio,* expressed this goal in general but hopeful terms:

> While preserving unity in essentials, let all members of the Church, according to the office entrusted to each, preserve a proper freedom in the various forms of spiritual life and discipline, in the variety of liturgical rites, and even in the theological elaborations of revealed truth. In all things let charity be exercised. If the faithful are true to this course of action, they will be giving ever richer expression to the authentic catholicity of the Church, and, at the same time, to her apostolicity.[45]

The difficulty, of course, is to flesh out this ideal in an effective, concrete way. Although Western ecumenical documents sometimes point to the short-lived agreement of East and West at the Council of Florence as an example of a bold attempt to construct such unity in diversity, or to the various unions of Eastern Catholic Churches with Rome since the sixteenth century as examples of its limited success,[46] all these earlier unions

43. For a detailed description and discussion of the chief models, see Meyer, *That All May Be One,* pp. 79-126; more briefly, *Facing Unity,* pp. 11-17.

44. For further references, see Meyer p. 115 and n. 101.

45. *Unitatis redintegratio* 4, trans. Walter M. Abbott and Joseph Gallagher (New York: America Press, 1966), p. 349.

46. See, for example, *Facing Unity,* 35-40 (pp. 17-19); Meyer, *That All May Be One,* pp. 114-15, 130.

are considered by the Orthodox today as simple illustrations of Western ecclesiological imperialism. The Joint International Orthodox–Roman Catholic Commission, in its Balamand Statement of 1993, while recognizing the Eastern Catholic churches' continuing right to exist, formally disowned "uniatism" as a model for the Christian unity of the future, and adopted the vaguer, but presumably more symmetrical notion of "sister churches" as the objective for future dialogue.[47] Central to any progress towards unity in recognized diversity, as Cardinal Ratzinger has observed, is that all sides be willing to relax their historic "maximum demands" on each other, and genuinely search for new ways of conceiving what they hold to be most essential to the church's being, an approach that will not require that individual churches simply give up their identity in order to share a wider communion.[48]

47. "Uniatism, Method of Union of the Past, and the Present Search for Full Communion," in John Borelli and John H. Erickson, eds., *The Quest for Unity: Orthodox and Catholics in Dialogue* (Crestwood, N.Y.: St. Vladimir's; Washington, D.C.: USCC, 1996), pp. 175, 177. The use of the phrase "sister churches," however, has recently been put under prescribed limits by the Roman Catholic side: see "Note on the Expression, 'Sister Church,'" dated June 9, 2000, a letter sent from the Congregation for the Doctrine of the Faith to national bishops' conferences, published in *National Catholic Reporter,* September 5, 2000.

48. Ratzinger's trenchant reflections on this point are worth quoting in full: "The maximum demands on which the search for unity must certainly founder are immediately clear. On the part of the West, the maximum demand would be that the East recognize the primacy of the bishop of Rome in the full scope of the definition of 1870, and in so doing submit in practice to a primacy such as has been accepted by the Uniate churches. On the part of the East, the maximum demand would be that the West declare the 1870 doctrine of primacy erroneous, and along with it, that it dissolve all the binding declarations that are based on it, from the removal of the *Filioque* from the Creed to discarding the Marian dogmas of the nineteenth and twentieth centuries. [The text of the preceding sentence, garbled in the English translation, has been reconstructed from the German original.] As regards Protestantism, the maximum demand of the Catholic Church would be that the Protestant ecclesiological ministries be regarded as totally invalid and that Protestants be converted to Catholicism; the maximum demand of Protestants, on the other hand, would be that the Catholic Church accept, along with the unconditional acknowledgement of all Protestant ministries, the Protestant concept of ministry and their understanding of the Church, and thus, in practice, renounce the apostolic and sacramental structure of the Church — which would mean, in practice, the conversion of Catholics to Protestantism and their acceptance of a multiplicity of distinct community structures as the historical form of the Church. While the first three maximum demands are today rather unanimously rejected by Christian consciousness,

Two dangers seem to face the ecumenical movement today, as it becomes more conscious of the difficulties that stand in the way of realizing the vision of New Delhi. One is the tendency visible among the present leadership of the World Council of Churches — and passionately, if tactfully, decried by Harding Meyer[49] — to reorient the goal of the Christian ecumenical movement away from an "internal" unity in faith and sacraments and towards an "external" unity in political and social engagement, usually following a left-wing agenda. Such a reorientation seems to suggest a kind of spiritual and mental exhaustion in the face of the difficulties that prevent real communion among the churches, and a willingness to settle simply for practical cooperation in external programs; it also may suggest, at a deeper level, the substitution of political causes for the doctrinal and moral content of the Christian tradition in the priorities of some church leaders.

The second danger, it seems to me, is that a realignment of forces may take place (and may well be already under way) which will regroup Christians in theological and ideological layers that cut across present church lines, but which will only make it more difficult for the churches as historic wholes to move towards unity. The direction of this realignment seems to be towards at least three major groupings of Christian believers:

- *Evangelicals:* already largely non-denominational or interdenominational, with a non-sacramental ecclesiology and an individualistic approach to salvation, but with a strong emphasis on evangelization and a sharply critical, at times apocalyptic understanding of modern culture. This movement mainly includes Protestants; but even some Evangelicals who have joined the Catholic or Orthodox communions retain much of the counter-cultural ethos and aggressive missionary style of their Evangelical background.

---

the fourth exercises a kind of fascination for it — as it were, a certain conclusiveness that makes it appear to be the real solution to the problem. This is all the more true since there is joined to it the expectation that a Parliament of Churches, a 'truly ecumenical Council,' could then harmonize this pluralism and promote a Christian unity of action. That no real union would result from this, but that its very impossibility would become a single common dogma, should convince anyone who examines the suggestion closely that such a way would not bring Church unity but only a final renunciation of it" ("The Ecumenical Situation" pp. 197-98).

49. See Meyer, *That All May Be One,* pp. 151-56.

- *liberals:* including members of many "mainline" Protestant churches, as well as a substantial number of educated, left-leaning, mainly middle-aged Catholics, who share a tendency to see the central concerns of Christianity more in terms of the liberal political and social agenda than in terms of traditional doctrine and Christian morality. They tend to be suspicious of central authority, congregational in polity, and vague on ecclesial boundaries, and to set a high value on tolerance and diversity.

- *sacramentalists:* including educated Catholics, Orthodox, and members of many of the "mainline" Protestant churches, who recognize the central place of liturgy and sacraments in the life of the churches, who usually take a more favorable view of authority and the longer Christian theological and spiritual tradition, and who look to the church for a wisdom that is distinctively religious and biblical. People of this cast of mind may be driven by the activities of the two above-mentioned groups to seek greater support from like-minded believers in other churches than from the less like-minded members of their own church, and so may become alienated from their own fellow communicants.

While it is probable that none of these new configurations will end as an actual ecclesial community, it seems possible that tension between them will only weaken the churches that now exist, and lessen their ability to enter into honest, consistent dialogue with each other about the things that have historically held them apart.

To make real progress towards a more organic and comprehensive unity — towards the "fully committed fellowship" or *koinonia* held up by the New Delhi statement as the goal of ecumenism — we clearly will need, as individuals and as historic communities, to undergo the process of conversion and illumination that will allow us to loosen our hold on the power and self-satisfaction that our entrenched positions afford us, in order to be created anew.[50] More specifically, it seems to me, if we do

50. In his encyclical on Christian dialogue, *Ut Unum Sint* (1995), Pope John Paul II emphasizes the central role of the "examination of consciences" and of readiness for conversion in ecumenical relations: "Even after the many sins which have contributed to our historical divisions, Christian unity is possible, provided that we are humbly conscious of having sinned against unity and are convinced of our need for conversion. . . . Dialogue cannot take place merely on a horizontal level, being restricted to meetings, exchanges of points of

hope to recapture, without romantic or antiquarian self-delusion, the "unity without uniformity" that generally characterized the worldwide Christian body of the first millennium, we will need to recover, in appropriately new terms, the sense of sacramental mystery that characterized the Christian understanding of both Scripture and church in the patristic age. We will need to learn again to read both Scripture and the life of the church not just in historical, but also in "anagogical" terms: as pointing beyond the details of our narrative, our worship, and our cherished institutions to the present reality of Christ, incorporating us into his "Mystical Body" and involving us in the rest of his story. As Susan Wood remarks, "Within such a context, 'mystical,' far from being a denial of the 'real' or the 'true,' becomes the ultimate reality or truth spiritually present within the 'figure.'"[51] We need, in other words, to rediscover Christ himself as the living, unifying center of the Scripture we preach in our churches, and as the true eucharistic gift who allows our churches, despite their particularities, to share in the wider communion of his own life.

One of the peculiarities of early Christian language about the church is its tendency to oscillate between the inner-worldly and the spiritual, without giving the impression that its field of reference had changed in the slightest. A striking example of this is the practice of the Fathers, from Ignatius of Antioch[52] to the Latin writers of the fifth century, to refer to the church in the same breath as both a human institution, with officers, members, and functions, and as "love" — ἀγάπη, *caritas*.[53] What

---

view, or even the sharing of gifts proper to each community. It has also a primarily vertical thrust, directed toward the One who, as the redeemer of the world and the Lord of history, is himself our reconciliation. This vertical aspect of dialogue lies in our acknowledgement, jointly and to each other, that we are men and women who have sinned. It is precisely this acknowledgement which creates in brothers and sisters living in communities not in full communion with one another that interior space where Christ, the source of the church's unity, can effectively act, with all the power of his Spirit, the Paraclete" (nos. 34-35).

51. Wood, *Spiritual Exegesis and the Church,* p. 68.

52. This, at least, is one explanation of the mysterious phrase in the inscription of Ignatius's Epistle to the Romans, where, at the end of a list of flattering attributes, he says of the Church of Rome that it "ranks first in love (ἐν ἀγάπῃ), being true to Christ's law and stamped with the Father's name," in *Early Christian Fathers,* trans. Cyril C. Richardson, ed. C. C. Richardson (Library of Christian Classics 1; Philadelphia: Westminster, 1953), p. 103.

53. For further references, see my article "Structures of Charity" (above, n. 22), pp. 54-55.

seems to us an obvious example of metaphor is for them simply reality: the heart of the church's institutional life, the soul that animates the body, *is* the love poured out by the Holy Spirit as the gift of himself, of the life-giving divine substance; the concrete manifestation of that God-given love is not simply feelings of fellowship, but functioning corporate life. One of Augustine's favorite words for this institutional reality of the church is *compages,* "structure," "framework," "organized whole." It is the love of God, in Augustine's view, the gift of love by which alone we can love each other durably and selflessly, that builds the church into a single structure which points to the eschatological Kingdom. Speaking of this rhythm of love, in his tenth *Homily on the First Letter of John,* he writes:

> The sons of God are the Body of God's only Son; because he is head and we are members, the Son of God is still one. Therefore to love the sons of God is to love the Son of God; to love the Son of God is to love the Father; none can love the Father unless he love the Son; and the one that loves the Son, loves also the sons of God. These sons of God are the members of God's Son; and the one that loves them, by loving, becomes himself a member: through love he becomes a part of the structure *(in compage)* of Christ's Body. And thus the end will be the one Christ, loving himself; for the love of the members for one another is the love of the Body for itself.[54]

In the end, the main goal of the ecumenical movement is surely no more, and no less, than to rediscover the structure that is implied in love.

---

54. *Homily 10 on I John* 3, SChr 75.414, trans. John Burnaby (Library of Christian Classics 7; Philadelphia: Westminster, 1955), p. 341.

Essential Unity and Lived Communion: The Interrelation of the Unity We Have and the Unity We Seek

MICHAEL ROOT

The modern ecumenical movement is driven by a contradiction. On the one hand, most Christian churches have come to recognize that they share a basic ecclesial unity with at least some other churches (or significantly church-like bodies) with which they do not share communion. This unity exists despite divisions, and it calls out for expression or realization. On the other hand, the lack of communion among these bodies is non-trivial; a real disunity plagues the churches, which not only burdens mission, but is in itself a scandal. Unity seems to exist and not to exist simultaneously.

How is this apparent contradiction to be understood? If the church, unlike God, is not absolutely simple, then its unity must be a function of some set of relations among some group of elements or aspects of the church. This set of relations constitutes unity. If this statement is true, then a possibility arises that may blunt the apparent contradiction. The contradiction arises from the use of "unity" in distinct senses, referring to different sets of relations. One set of relations does exist, making the churches one in this sense; another set of relations does not exist, making them not one in this second sense. Diverse senses of unity would then refer to different sets of relations that constitute unity in different senses.

In this essay, I will explore the distinction and interrelation of different senses of ecclesial unity in an attempt better to grasp the apparent contradiction at the heart of the ecumenical quest. This paper will be primarily conceptual rather than historical; no attempt will be made to describe the history of the unity of the church or of differing understandings of that unity.

It should be noted at the outset, however, that the ecumenical problem can be avoided entirely if one insists that unity only has one sense. At least two versions of this possibility flit around the edges of the ecumenical discussion. On the one hand, one can deny that any body other than one's own is a church. Other communities are at most bodies of heretics who are objects of persuasion, more like candidates for interfaith dialogue than ecumenical partners. Their existence is then no more a cause of theological scandal than is that of the Buddhist Sangha. If division occurs, one and only one of the remaining bodies is church; the other simply isn't. All division is thus *from* the church, never within it. I will call this view the narrow alternative. As far as I can tell, no major church body adheres consistently to an unqualified version of this position, although it may have been held in the past. The Orthodox and Catholic Churches seem to affirm variants of it, and more conservative members of many traditions may reflectively or unreflectively hold this view.

On the other hand, one might believe that the unity that presently exists among the seemingly divided churches is theologically adequate. That which now exists among the churches — a certain minimal theological agreement, mutual respect and tolerance, an openness to cooperation when such seems appropriate — is all that unity requires. Greater cooperation or communion might be pragmatically desirable, but so might be a greater spirit of self-sacrifice among one's own members. Those who are truly beyond the limits of this unity — Mormons, perhaps, or Christian Scientists — are obviously so and simply are not Christian in an authentic sense. Again, no scandal of division exists. This view can be called the broad alternative. To my knowledge, no major tradition adheres consistently to this understanding, but it can be found among liberal or anti-institutional Protestants of various sorts.

For both of these approaches, ecclesial unity has some single, univocal sense; it refers to one discrete set of relations. There is thus no contradiction between different senses of unity. The perception of contradiction mentioned at the opening of this paper comes both from a use of "unity" in more than one sense and a judgment that these different senses of unity somehow belong together in a way that our present ecclesial reality denies. Herein lies the fundamental ecumenical problem.

The Essential Unity of the Church

That the church possesses a unity it cannot lose and still remain truly church would seem to be a non-controversial assertion.[1] When Paul asks "Has Christ been divided?" (1 Cor. 1:13), he expects the answer to be "No." The church is Christ's body and Christ cannot have multiple bodies. As Vatican II stated: "Christ the Lord founded one church and one church only" (*Unitatis redintegratio,* para. 1). This affirmation is also made on the other side of the Reformation divide, as the Lutheran Peter Brunner made clear: "This church which we confess in our creed is one. It was never divided into multiplicity and can never be so divided. . . . Christ has only one body in which all of His children are members. The unity of the church is unquestionably constantly given."[2]

Unity as an Essential Characteristic of the Church

That unity is a characteristic the church cannot lose and still be the church follows from the common assertion that unity (along with holiness, catholicity, and apostolicity) is an essential characteristic of the church. To say that it is essential is to say that it must be characteristic of anything that might be called church. If no body possesses such unity, then the church has ceased to exist. Similarly, any body that can truly be called church must be within that unity. Otherwise, it would lack an essential characteristic of being church and thus would not truly be church.

This rather elementary assertion has significant consequences. If unity is an essential characteristic of any body we could rightly call

---

1. Assertions that unity is only an ideal, not realized in history, can be found in the ecumenical literature, however. For example, A. C. Headlam, Regius Professor at Oxford, Bishop of Gloucester (Church of England), and influential figure in Faith and Order during in the 1930s, stated: "When we say that the Church is 'one,' we mean that Christ intended it to be 'one,' as He intended it to be 'holy'; that the Apostles founded it as 'one'; that it must be our continuous aim to make it 'one.' We must always have that ideal before us." Arthur C. Headlam, *The Doctrine of the Church and Christian Reunion* (London: John Murray, 1921), p. 217.

2. Peter Brunner, "The Realization of Church Fellowship," in *The Unity of the Church: A Symposium,* Papers presented to the Commission on Theology and Liturgy of the Lutheran World Federation (Rock Island, Ill.: Augustana Press, 1957), pp. 12f.

"church," then any relation a church could lack and still truly be a church cannot be a relation included within this sense of unity. If a community that abandoned baptism by immersion is still truly church, then common participation in baptism by immersion is not an aspect of that unity essential to the church. If a community that abandoned the Lord's Supper has by that action ceased truly to be church, then a common participation in the Lord's Supper is an aspect of the essential unity of the church.

We now can perform a thought experiment. If the church on an isolated Pacific Island were, after a devastating nuclear war, to be cut off from all contact with the outside world for generations, what would it need to preserve to be considered within the unity of the church in the strict sense (and not by a principle of economy or a notion of *ecclesia supplet*)?[3] I assume a Roman Catholic would say that if such a church continued to preach the gospel, celebrate the seven sacraments, including the ordination of bishops in succession, then that community would be church. (I assume the impossibility of active collegiality with bishops beyond the island, including the bishop of Rome, would not be decisive in this judgment, although I could understand the stipulation that such a church must continue to desire such collegiality and to seek it when it again becomes possible.) A Lutheran or Presbyterian might answer the question of what this church needs to do to remain church rather differently, but the general structure of the answer would remain the same: those activities essential to being church — the proclamation of the authentic gospel, baptism, the Lord's Supper — would need to continue.

Catholics, Lutherans, Presbyterians, and others could affirm that such an isolated island community is still church because what constitutes the communion which is the church is a *common* participation in the communion which is the life of the Trinity. "The Church is not the sum of individual believers in communion with God. It is not primarily a communion of believers with each other. It is their common partaking in God's own life whose innermost being is communion."[4] A Methodist and an Orthodox may disagree on what constitutes the means needed for such

---

3. In such a thought experiment, the danger exists of drawing false conclusions from extreme situations. As the saying goes, "hard cases make bad law." Thus, the question must be, what is needed for such a community to be church in the strict sense, and not by a sense modified by the particular extreme situation.

4. Faith and Order Commission, *The Nature and Purpose of the Church: A Stage on the Way to a Common Statement,* Faith and Order Paper 181 (Geneva: WCC, 1998), para. 13.

an isolated community to participate as church in the life of God, but they agree that when such means are present, it does so participate and thus is church. Because it does so in common with all other churches, it is a part of the unity of the one church.

Some Formal Comments on Essential Unity

At a high level of generality, Christians of different traditions can agree that the unity essential to the church is constituted by the relation of a common participation in the life of God. This essential unity is equally synchronic and diachronic. All churches that are, have been, or will be are included within this unity. Disagreement develops when we become more specific and seek to state the means by which that common participation in God is mediated — through the gospel, through the sacraments, through the ordained ministry, through faith, through charismatic gifts. Disagreement on the means probably also brings with it disagreement on a more detailed description of what a common participation in the life of God includes. Whatever these means are, however, we can agree that the means that mediate a common participation in God are also the means that constitute the being of the church as church.

At this same level of generality, we can agree that the being and unity of the church is a gift of grace rather than a human achievement. To say that such unity is a gift of grace is not to deny that a human activity is involved, viz., whatever activity is involved in that which mediates the being and unity of the church. The reality of such human activity in the sacraments does not destroy the character of what is given through them as gifts of grace. Thus, there is no reason to think that the mediation of the being and unity of the church through human actions undermines its character as a gift of grace. We may disagree on the relation between the mediation and the human activity, but that disagreement is compatible with an agreement that, say, the preaching of the gospel mediates grace.

Finally, agreement at this level of generality is neutral on the visible or invisible character of this unity. Most would probably agree that unity has both visible and invisible aspects.[5] Again, the visibility and invisibility

---

5. With the substitution of "ministry" for "hierarchical order," the following quo-

of unity would be a function primarily of which activities one sees as mediating unity and the relation one sees between the activity and the unity mediated.

The Unity a Church Can Lose While Remaining Church

If some concept of a unity that cannot be lost while a community is still church seems to follow directly from the confession of the church as one, holy, catholic, and apostolic and thus seems necessary, the need for an understanding of a unity a church can lose while remaining church is less obvious. The referent of such an understanding of unity is relatively clear: unity in this sense is the unity that has been lost in our divisions. It is the unity that does not now exist between Catholic and Anglican, Presbyterian and Baptist, Methodist and Pentecostal, Lutheran and Orthodox. It is the unity which is the goal of the ecumenical movement.

There may be good reasons, however, to be suspicious of such a concept of unity. On the one hand, if this conception of unity is not clearly differentiated from the essential unity of the church, then some might worry that the existence of this essential unity is being seen as compromised, that the actual existence of the unity of the church is being denied, that unity is being made merely an ideal to be sought. Such a view would overestimate the significance of present divisions.

On the other hand, if this conception of unity is too sharply differentiated from the church's essential unity, others would conclude that

---

tation is probably general enough to elicit widespread agreement: "Ecclesial communion is at the same time both invisible and visible. As an invisible reality, it is the communion of each human being with the Father through Christ in the Holy Spirit, and with the others who are fellow sharers in the divine nature, in the passion of Christ, in the same faith, in the same spirit. In the Church on earth, there is an intimate relationship between this invisible communion and the visible communion in the teaching of the Apostles, in the sacraments and in the hierarchical order. By means of these divine gifts, which are very visible realities, Christ carries out in different ways in history his prophetical, priestly and kingly function for the salvation of mankind." Congregation for the Doctrine of the Faith, "Letter to the Bishops of the Catholic Church on Some Aspects of the Church Understood as Communion," *L'Osservatore Romano* (English Weekly Edition), 17 June 1992, para. 4.

the significance of present divisions is being underestimated, reduced to a merely accidental phenomenon that does not touch the church's true unity, made merely regrettable rather than scandalous. If unity in the previous sense is essential, is unity in this second sense then only accidental?[6]

Both of these suspicions point to misunderstandings we must avoid. Nevertheless, some understanding of a unity a church can gain and lose seems necessary.

The Need for an Understanding of a Unity That Can Be Gained and Lost

Even if one insists that the one church must always remain, it is difficult to deny that "Even in the beginnings of this one and only church of God there arose certain rifts [*scissurae*]" (*Unitatis redintegratio,* para. 3).[7] These rifts on occasion have touched those activities that various churches have believed mediate unity: the proclamation of the gospel, the celebration of the sacraments, the ordering of ministry. The rifts have meant that churches could not together proclaim the gospel, could not celebrate the sacraments together, could not exercise ministry together. The rift thus touches in some sense the essential unity of the church.

If each side of this rift viewed the other as having simply left the church, then no problem would arise for the understanding of unity. The "narrow alternative" noted above would then be taken. Striking in twentieth-century ecumenical documents, however, has been the reluctance to draw that conclusion. While the Church of England and the Evangelical Church in Germany cannot at present enter into full commu-

---

6. A forceful presentation of such a worry can be found in Bruce D. Marshall, "The Disunity of the Church and the Credibility of the Gospel," *Theology Today* 50 (1993): 83-86.

7. Similarly, "Throughout centuries Christ's commandment of unity has been repeatedly violated. Contrary to the catholic unanimity enjoined by God, differences and divisions have arisen in Christianity." Jubilee Bishops' Council of the Russian Orthodox Church, "Basic Principles of the Attitude of the Russian Orthodox Church toward the Other Christian Confessions" (2000), para. 1.12., which can be found at http://www.russian-orthodox-church.org.ru/s2000e13.htm. I thank John Erickson for alerting me to this important document.

nion because of their continuing disagreement on episcopacy, they nevertheless affirm each other as "churches belonging to the One, Holy, Catholic and Apostolic Church of Jesus Christ and truly participating in the apostolic mission of the whole people of God."[8] Similarly, while the nine American churches that make up the Churches Uniting in Christ have not yet reached full communion among themselves, they nevertheless extend to one another "mutual recognition of each other as authentic expressions of the one church of Jesus Christ."[9]

Nor do the Roman Catholic and the Orthodox Churches affirm the narrow alternative without decisive qualification. While the Roman Catholic Church does not affirm the full ecclesial status of the Western non-Roman churches, it does affirm that the Orthodox Churches are in fact churches (*Unitatis redintegratio,* paras. 13-18), even if recent Vatican statements have asserted that Orthodoxy's lack of communion with the Roman See "means that their existence as particular Churches is *wounded*"[10] and even that the church of Christ "continues to exist fully only in the Catholic Church."[11] The Catholic Church approaches the narrow alternative in its assertion that "the unity of the one and only church . . . subsists in the Catholic Church as something she can never lose" (*Unitatis redintegratio,* para. 4). Nevertheless, the existence of bodies that are truly churches outside communion with the Bishop of Rome "also injures the Catholic Church . . . in that it hinders the complete fulfilment of its universality in history."[12] Beyond the unity which the Catholic Church states it can never lose, there is a unity which is painfully lacking with other bodies which are also church.

The Orthodox seem a bit less clear. On the one hand, the Russian Orthodox "Basic Principles" state: "The ecclesial status of those who have

---

8. *The Meissen Agreement: Texts,* Council for Christian Unity Occasional Paper, no. 2 (London: Council for Christian Unity, General Synod, Church of England, 1992), p. 20, para. 17A.

9. Executive Committee of the Consultation on Church Union, "Recommendation for a New Relationship: Churches Uniting in Christ," *Mid-Stream* 41 (2002): 32.

10. Congregation for the Doctrine of the Faith, "Church Understood as Communion," para. 17.

11. Congregation for the Doctrine of the Faith, "Dominus Jesus: On the Unicity and Salvific Universality of Jesus Christ and the Church," *Origins* 30 (2000): para. 16.

12. Congregation for the Doctrine of the Faith, "Church Understood as Communion," para. 18.

separated themselves from the Church [which would seem to include all non-Orthodox, including Catholics] does not lend itself to simple definition. . . . By establishing various rites of reception, however, the Orthodox Church does not assess the extent to which grace-filled life has either been preserved intact or distorted in a non-Orthodox confession, considering this to be a mystery of God's providence and judgment."[13]

On the other hand, joint Catholic-Orthodox texts regularly refer to "our churches" in a way that would seem to imply some sort of mutual recognition.[14] Communications from the Ecumenical Patriarch to the Pope regularly refer to "the holy Church of Rome."[15] At least one Catholic-Orthodox dialogue has taken the position that churches cannot avoid a mutual recognition of "an ecclesial reality in the other," which would provide a "certain basis" for referring to each other as "sister churches."[16]

Similarly, the dialogue between the Chalcedonian and non-Chalcedonian Orthodox, divided far longer than East and West, seems to have proceeded on the assumption that both are churches.[17] The official

13. Jubilee Bishops' Council of the Russian Orthodox Church, "Basic Principles," para. 1.16-17.

14. See, e.g., the Joint Declaration by Pope John Paul II and Patriarch Dimitrios I establishing the Catholic-Orthodox Theological Dialogue, which states that the dialogue envisages "an advance towards the reestablishment of full communion between the Catholic and Orthodox sister Churches." E. J. Stormon, ed., *Towards the Healing of Schism: The Sees of Rome and Constantinople: Public Statements and Correspondence Between the Holy See and the Ecumenical Patriarchate 1958-1984*, Ecumenical Documents (New York: Paulist, 1987), p. 367. More recently, the Common Declaration signed by John Paul II and Catholicos Karekin I of the Armenian Apostolic Church extensively speaks of "our Churches" in a way that makes no sense apart from mutual ecclesial recognition ("Common Declaration Signed by Pope John Paul II and Catholicos Karekin I," *L'Osservatore Romano* [English Weekly Edition], 1925, 18 December 1996, p. 2). Such language can be compared with footnote 9 in the Catholic-Lutheran *Joint Declaration on the Doctrine of Justification,* which explicitly disavows any mutual recognition that might be implied by the use of the word "church" in the document. This footnote was inserted at the insistence of the Catholic authorities.

15. See, e.g., Stormon, *Healing of Schism,* pp. 36, 145, 256, 382, 471.

16. North American Orthodox-Catholic Theological Consultation, "Baptism and 'Sacramental Economy'" (1999), I.C, http://www.nccbuscc.org/seia/agreed.htm.

17. On this dialogue, see John H. Erickson, "Eastern Orthodox–Oriental Orthodox Dialogue and Its Implications for Christian Unity," *Eastern Churches Journal* 5 (1998): esp. 26f.

statements from the dialogue refer consistently to "our two families of Orthodox churches"[18] or to "our two families of churches."[19]

Thus, it would appear that the Orthodox also to some extent are willing to grant that some body outside their own limits can rightly be called "church."

It should be stressed that the conceptual problem is raised for Catholics and Orthodox more sharply by their mutual separation from each other than by their common separation from the Western non-Roman churches. The latter have, in their view, to some degree left the essential unity of the church, even if not entirely. They are, to use the Roman phrase, ecclesial communities and not churches in the proper sense.[20] That some limitation of communion exists with such communities is understandable, even if the very notion of such semi-churches is inherently odd. Nevertheless, that Catholics and Orthodox or Chalcedonian and non-Chalcedonian Orthodox can each recognize the other as churches and yet remain separated "is contrary to the nature of the Church," as the international Catholic-Orthodox Theological Dialogue puts it.[21]

No major tradition today seems willing to make the somewhat implausible claim that it and it alone is church and that thus it and it alone belongs to the essential unity of the church. Thus, every tradition faces the problem of understanding the relation between the unity that essentially belongs to the church and the unity that has been lost with communities — even though they may still be recognized as church.

---

18. Joint Commission of the Theological Dialogue between the Orthodox Church and the Oriental Orthodox Churches, "Communiqué, Anba Bishoy Monastery, Egypt, 24 June 1989," in *Growth in Agreement II: Reports and Agreed Statements of Ecumenical Conversations on a World Level, 1982-1998,* ed. Jeffrey Gros, Harding Meyer, and William G. Rusch (Grand Rapids: Eerdmans, 2000), p. 192.

19. Joint Commission of the Theological Dialogue between the Orthodox Church and the Oriental Orthodox Churches, "Second Agreed Statement and Recommendations to the Churches," in *Growth in Agreement II,* ed. Gros, Meyer, and Rusch, p. 197.

20. Congregation for the Doctrine of the Faith, "Dominus Jesus," para. 17.

21. Joint Commission for Theological Dialogue between the Roman Catholic Church and the Orthodox Church, "Uniatism, Method of Union of the Past, and the Present Search for Full Communion," *Information Service (PCPCU)* 83 (1993): para. 6.

The Distinction between the Two Senses of Unity

How do we understand the difference between these two senses of unity? The way I have developed the analysis so far, one sense of unity refers to that unity which is essential to the church's being, without which a body is not church in the theological sense. The other is not essential in the same sense, since it can be lacking between churches that nevertheless recognize each other as churches. Can the difference be further specified? I would suggest (and the word "suggest" is meant to communicate a certain tentativeness in this assertion) the following:

The essential unity of the church, the unity a community cannot fall out of and still be church, is a function of a *common* participation in the life of God through a *common* participation in the means that mediate this participation. As the churches exercise the same means and receive the same Spirit, they are taken into the unity of the one church. "The identity of one eucharistic assembly with another comes from the fact that all with the same faith celebrate the same memorial, that all by eating the same bread and sharing the same cup become the same unique body of Christ into which they have been integrated by the same baptism."[22]

Such a focus on common participation was suggested by the thought experiment carried out above (p. 109). The essential unity that continues to encompass the church on the isolated, post-nuclear-war Pacific Island is a function of its continued participation in those means through which the gift of the church is mediated and which it exercises in common with all other bodies that are truly church. This common participation communicates the common life in God which is the foundation of the unity of the church.

The unity of the church that can be gained and lost without immediately destroying the essential unity of the church is a function of a *joint* participation in the life of God through a *joint* participation in the means that mediate this participation. Catholics and Orthodox (or Lutherans and Catholics or English Anglicans and German *Evangelische*) can recognize that the other has in common with themselves the means by which a body is church. What they cannot do is exercise the full range of those

---

22. Joint Commission for Theological Dialogue between the Roman Catholic Church and the Orthodox Church, "Mystery of the Church and the Eucharist," III, 1, p. 195.

means jointly, i.e., together. A Catholic and an Orthodox might each recognize (with some qualifications) that the eucharist in the other church is truly the eucharist through which the one church gathers. Nevertheless, a Catholic and an Orthodox cannot celebrate the eucharist together, i.e., jointly. They have lost the unity that would permit such a joint celebration. Similarly, in the *Meissen Agreement,* the Church of England and the Evangelical Church in Germany both "acknowledge one another's ordained ministries as given by God and instruments of his grace," yet they cannot together carry out ordinations jointly because of a continuing disagreement over episcopacy.[23] This second form of unity is thus the unity that is realized through some joint participation in those means that mediate the being of the church. Ecumenical efforts are often focused on the realization of unity in this sense, under the names "full communion" or "full visible unity."[24] Here I will refer to unity in this sense as lived communion.

The Pacific Island thought experiment would indicate that such joint participation cannot be essential to the being of the church. If it were, then the church on such an island would either cease to be church or would be church only by some principle of economy or *ecclesia supplet.* (And, while such a total isolation for generations may seem extreme, less extreme but comparable cases have occurred. German Lutheran communities along the Volga, already under great government pressure in the 1930s, were banished to Central Asia and Siberia at the time of the German invasion of the USSR in 1941. These communities survived, organizing congregations where they could, without contact with the outside world in some cases for over thirty years. The one respect in which this example does not match the thought experiment is that these communities for the most part did not explicitly continue the office of ordained ministry that most Lutherans would say is essential to the church. The office disappeared because most pastors were executed by the Soviets and the remaining communities apparently did not know Luther's advice that in such a situation a lay community could rightly ordain one of its own to carry out the office of ministry. They did continue forms of pastoral lay

---

23. *The Meissen Agreement: Texts,* paras. 17A(iii), B(vii), pp. 20, 24.

24. *Ut unum sint,* for example, refers to the unity ecumenically sought as "full communion" (§§3, 4, 36, 56), as "full visible unity" (§§77, 78), and as "full and visible communion" (§84).

ministry, however, which arguably were a realization of the ministerial office.)[25] Of course, the loss of such joint participation through the accidents and evils of history, but through no action of the church itself, is different from its loss through dispute within the church. Nevertheless, the difference between the unity that goes with being church and the unity that can be gained or lost without immediately ceasing to be church would seem to be that between a *common* participation in the means that mediate the church's being and a *joint* participation in such.

Two analytic points need to be noted. First, unlike the church's essential unity, lived communion defined in this way is primarily synchronic. It is a unity among churches that are contemporary to each other. Joint participation with churches of the past or future is not possible in the same way. Similarly, churches of different ages cannot be "out of communion" or in only partial communion in the same way that contemporary churches can be. The unity of the church across time may call for forms of continuity that will witness to the solidarity of the churches across the ages (e.g., the use of the same creeds, or practices of succession in ministry), but such forms cannot function in the same way as do forms of lived communion.

Second, this distinction between common and joint participation may only hold when the topic is unity among communities each of which is church, not when the topic is the unity of the local church as fundamental unit of the church. Especially if the local church is understood as a eucharistic assembly or as a community gathered around word and sacrament, the unity of the local church may depend on joint participation in the means that mediate the being of the church. The unity that exists among churches may be different from the unity of each such church. Such a difference was suggested by the Roman Catholic Congregation for the Doctrine of the Faith when it stated that the concept "communion," which applies univocally to the unity of the local church and to the unity of the universal church as the communion of saints, applies only analogically to "the union existing among particular churches."[26]

25. Jens Holger Schjørring, Prasanna Kumari, and Norman A. Hjelm, eds., *From Federation to Communion: The History of the Lutheran World Federation* (Minneapolis: Fortress, 1997), pp. 170f.

26. Congregation for the Doctrine of the Faith, "Church Understood as Communion," para. 8.

The Interrelation of the Two Senses of Unity

If these two senses of unity are distinct, how do they interrelate? How one answers this question will determine the validity of the suspicion that the concept of a unity that can be gained and lost over- or underestimates the significance of present church division. A beginning point for a discussion of this question is the nature of the local church and its relations to the wider church.

It has become an ecumenical commonplace to say that the local church (whether understood to be the congregation or the diocese) is fully church, i.e., it realizes all the essential characteristics of the church, but is not the whole church.[27] As church, every local church has a communion with all other churches. In a case such as our isolated Pacific Island church, that communion may not result in any joint activities with any contemporary church — no joint celebration of the sacraments, no collegiality of ministry, no joint witness, no joint decision-making. Nevertheless, when possible, some form of joint life is not optional among local churches. "Communion with other local churches is essential to the integrity of the self-understanding of each local church, precisely because of its catholicity. Life in self-sufficient isolation . . . is the denial of its very being."[28] A local church that refused such a joint life with other churches when such was possible would call into question its own ecclesial status. The eucharist, as an anticipation of the one great eschatological feast, always has reference to all other eucharistic celebrations. So, "it is precisely the eucharist that renders all self-sufficiency on the part of the particular churches impossible. . . . From the eucharistic center arises the necessary openness of every celebrating community, of every particular church; by allowing itself to be drawn into the open arms of the Lord, it achieves insertion into his one and undivided Body."[29]

One can speak of a trajectory of the unifying work of the Holy Spirit. The Spirit comes to us in those means we identify as mediating the being of the church. Through these means the Spirit unites us with Christ

27. See, e.g., Faith and Order Commission, *Nature and Purpose of the Church,* para. 66.

28. Anglican–Roman Catholic International Commission, *Church as Communion* (London: Church House Publishing, 1991), para. 39.

29. Congregation for the Doctrine of the Faith, "Church Understood as Communion," para. 11.

and with one another. There is "one body and one Spirit," which then implies that we are called "to lead a life worthy of the calling to which you have been called, . . . bearing with one another in love, making every effort to maintain the unity of the Spirit in the bond of peace" (Eph. 4:1-4). The Spirit moves through the means into the hearts of those who receive him in faith, and then out into a joint life, as is appropriate in the historical conditions of the time. As Peter Brunner puts it: "That which is valid for the Holy Spirit drives to realize itself in concrete existence. The Spirit yearns for corporeality. Therefore, the given spiritual unity of the *sancta catholica ecclesia* works with the necessity of a *dynamis* of the Holy Spirit on the form and corporate life of the local *ecclesiae*."[30] The movement is thus from common participation to joint participation, from the essential unity of the church to the unity of a joint life.[31]

This image of a trajectory from essential unity to lived communion may suggest a similar trajectory from baptism to the eucharist. While baptism is entry into the unity of the church, the eucharist is often presented as the focal celebration of the church's unity. One might think that the two trajectories are identical, so that the church's essential unity is its baptismal unity and its lived communion is its eucharistic unity. The distinction made here between common and joint participation in the means that mediate the church does not, however, perfectly coincide with unity related to these two sacraments. Lived communion does focus more on joint celebrations of the eucharist than on joint baptisms; but the church's essential unity involves a common participation in the Lord's Supper, and lived communion should imply the possibility of communities together celebrating a baptism.[32]

To speak of a trajectory of the unifying work of the Spirit avoids the possible misinterpretation that the essential unity of the church is a gift of grace while lived communion is a human achievement.[33] That the church

---

30. Brunner, "The Realization of Church Fellowship," p. 17.

31. I have tried to develop the idea of such a trajectory of the Spirit in Gabriel Fackre and Michael Root, *Affirmations and Admonitions: Lutheran Decisions and Dialogue with Reformed, Episcopal, and Roman Catholic Churches* (Grand Rapids: Eerdmans, 1998), pp. 66-80.

32. On the relation between baptismal unity and the unity of the church, see Michael Root and Risto Saarinen, eds., *Baptism and the Unity of the Church* (Grand Rapids: Eerdmans, 1998).

33. Such a misunderstanding is expressed by the recent statement on church fellow-

is held in existence — and thus in its essential unity — is a work of the Spirit; that churches are able jointly to live out their life in Christ is also a work of the Spirit. Our common participation in God is mediated through our common participation in word and sacrament, in which unity in Christ is a gift; our joint participation in God is mediated through our joint participation in word and sacrament, in which unity is again a gift.

Terms for This Interrelation

Various terms might be used for the relation between these two senses of unity. Often the language of "making visible" is used. The unity we seek will "make visible" the unity we have in Christ.[34] A major drawback of such language is that it seems to imply that an independently existing invisible unity is now becoming visible. A joint eucharist is certainly more visible as joint and shared than the commonality of distinct eucharists, but the distinct eucharists are not invisible. In addition, to the degree that our unity is invisible (in that the faith of our hearts that unites us to Christ is not straightforwardly visible), it remains invisible in a joint life.[35] Alternatively, one can find language of "expressing" or "making manifest" our unity in Christ. "For the Catholic Church, then, the communion of Christians is none other than the manifestation in them of the grace by which God makes them sharers in his own communion, which is his eternal life."[36] A difficulty with the language of manifestation or ex-

---

ship or communion [*Kirchengemeinschaft*] from the *Kammer für Theologie* of the Protestant Church in Germany, according to which such fellowship or communion is strictly a "human work," *Kirchengemeinschaft nach evangelischen Verständnis: Ein Votum zum geordneten Miteinander bekenntnisverscheidener Kirchen*, EKD Texte, 69 (Hannover: Kirchenamt der EKD, 2001), II, 1, p. 9.

34. For example, this passage from the Encyclical Letter of the 1920 Lambeth Conference: "The unity we seek exists. It is in God, Who is the perfection of unity, the one Father, the one Lord, the one Spirit, Who gives life to the one Body. Again, the one Body exists. It needs not to be made, nor to be remade, but to become organic and visible." Randall Davidson, comp., *The Six Lambeth Conferences, 1867-1920* (London: SPCK, 1929), App., p. 12.

35. This latter argument against the language of visibility is stressed by Brunner, "The Realization of Church Fellowship," p. 13.

36. John Paul II, *Ut Unum Sint: On Commitment to Ecumenism* (Vatican City:

pression is again that it can give the impression that our joint life (or lack thereof) expresses or fails to express a reality that exists simply independently of such an expression.[37] The suspicion that the significance of our present divisions is being underestimated is hard to avoid. Our failure becomes only one of not adequately expressing what is the case despite our failure.

It is more adequate to say that our joint life historically realizes or lives out the unity we have through our common participation in God. The Lutheran–Roman Catholic document *Facing Unity* thus opens: "The full realization of unity given in Christ and promised by him calls for concrete forms of ecclesial life in common."[38] Similarly, the Leuenberg Agreement distinguished "the declaration of fellowship" achieved in the affirmation of the agreement with "the realization of church fellowship" achieved in actually living out the new relation.[39] The advantage of such language as "realization" or "living out" is that the close interrelation of the two senses of unity is thus enunciated. Our joint life does more than merely express an independent and prior reality. It rather constitutes the focus of our historical living out of that reality, the realization of that reality within our history.

Such language also better expresses the anomaly of two churches being within the essential unity of the church (which must be the case if they are both churches), but not able to live out that unity. What is a unity that remains unrealized or unlived? At the very least, the understanding that two churches share a common participation in that which constitutes the church is called into question by the inability of those churches jointly to participate in that reality. If this inability persists for

---

Libreria Editrice Vaticana, 1995), para. 9. Similarly: "We believe that it is God's purpose to manifest this fellowship, so far as this world is concerned, in an outward, visible, and united society." Lambeth Conference 1920, "An Appeal to All Christian People," in *The Six Lambeth Conferences, 1867-1920,* comp. Davidson, App., p. 27.

37. The preferred language of the statement of the German Protestant Kammer für Theologie, that "full visible unity" *witnesses* to the unity of the body of Christ, has the same problem, *Kirchengemeinschaft nach evangelischen Verständnis,* I,2,2, p. 8.

38. Roman Catholic–Lutheran Joint Commission, *Facing Unity: Models, Forms and Phases of Catholic–Lutheran Church Fellowship* (Geneva: Lutheran World Federation, 1985), para. 1.

39. *Agreement Between Reformation Churches in Europe* (Leuenberg Agreement). Trilingual Edition with an Introduction (Frankfurt am Main: Otto Lembeck, 1993), IV.2, p. 42.

decades or centuries, then the question must be raised whether they both (or either?) in fact are within that unity which is essential to the church's being. More apt is the language of *Communionis notio,* the letter of the Roman Catholic Congregation for the Doctrine of the Faith (CDF) on the church as communion. While not denying that the Orthodox Churches remain churches despite their lack of full communion with the bishop of Rome, the text states that this lack of communion means "that their existence as particular churches is *wounded. . . .* This in turn also injures [the term in the Latin original is the same as that translated by "wounded"] the Catholic Church . . . in that it hinders the complete fulfillment of her universality in history."[40] Non-Catholics may not wish to follow the CDF in the way it distinguishes the wound to the Orthodox Churches from the wound to itself, but the image of a wound being inflicted on our essential unity by our lack of lived communion is powerful and, I believe, fitting.[41] Our lived communion does not constitute our essential unity, and the absence of communion does not immediately destroy that unity; but a unity that remains historically unrealized or not lived out is a unity that is itself impoverished or wounded, even if it continues to exist. This impoverishment inevitably has effects on the wider life of the church, as is well demonstrated in R. R. Reno's essay in this volume.[42]

Terms such as "wounded" or "impoverished" are, of course, analogical or metaphorical, but herein lies some of their usefulness in this context. They leave the anomalous situation of essential unity without lived communion not fully explained, not rationalized in a way that allows conceptual comfort. If the movement from essential unity to lived communion is not a movement that we undertake on our own, but a trajectory of the work of the Spirit, then our failure to live out the unity we are given is nothing less than a frustration of the Spirit's work.[43] An analysis

40. Congregation for the Doctrine of the Faith, "Church Understood as Communion," para. 17.

41. The Russian Orthodox "Basic Principles" use similar language: "Christian division has become an open and bleeding wound on the Body of Christ. The tragedy of divisions has become a serious visible distortion of Christian universality. . . ." Jubilee Bishops' Council of the Russian Orthodox Church, "Basic Principles," para. 1.20.

42. See "The Debilitation of the Churches," Chapter 4 above.

43. In his last book (an English translation of which is forthcoming), the late Jean-Marie Tillard was willing at least to entertain the proposition that a refusal to work to end

of the relation between essential unity and lived communion should not presume to judge how the Spirit reacts to such a frustration. Thus, the imprecision of "wound" is appropriate.[44]

In summary, the essential unity of the church has within it an inherent impulse toward lived communion. Common participation in the life of God impels us to a joint and mutual participation in the life of God. Lived communion is thus the historical realization or living out of essential unity. Historical accidents and evils can hinder, limit, or even block the possibility of such lived communion, but they cannot destroy the church's essential unity, if the churches remain faithful. Truly anomalous is the situation in which churches that cannot deny that they are in essential unity nevertheless find that theological conviction blocks the full realization of lived communion. While this loss of fully lived communion does not itself destroy essential unity, it calls it into question and wounds or impoverishes that unity. As the Anglican–Roman Catholic International Commission puts it: "Christians can never acquiesce with complacency in disunity without impairing further their communion with God."[45]

Conclusion

The unity that the church cannot lose while remaining church, on the one hand, and the unity that can be lost and gained by churches, on the other, are realities that can be distinguished, but not permanently sepa-

---

Christian division is a sin against the Holy Spirit. See Jean-Marie R. Tillard, *Je crois en dépuit de tout* (Paris: Cerf, 2000), pp. 72f.

44. Much of the power of Ephraim Radner's *The End of the Church: A Pneumatology of Christian Division in the West* derives from the way he portrays the threat that lack of lived communion (to use my language) represents to the essential unity (and thus the essence) of the church. Unfortunately, he fails to elaborate in what he believes the unity of the church to consist and thus his pathos remains open to the accusation that it is a function of unclarity rather than insight. (I believe the problem becomes even clearer in his more recent essay "Bad Bishops: A Key to Anglican Ecclesiology," *Anglican Theological Review* 82 [2000]: 321-41.) The analysis I have offered here I believe preserves the core of his concern, but in a more carefully specified form. He might judge, of course, that I have eviscerated his critique.

45. Anglican–Roman Catholic International Commission, *Church as Communion*, para. 47.

rated. Churches that share the church's essential unity can almost always in fact jointly carry out many activities of the faith: prayer, evangelism, various forms of worship. Rarely is every form of this lived communion rejected between churches that can regard each other as churches or church-like communities. The difficulty is that something blocks the churches from together carrying out some activity they must be able to carry out together to live out their reality as one church truly and fully.[46]

As Bruce Marshall has argued (although in a significantly different fashion),[47] the division of the church is "a genuine aporia." It is a difficulty we can neither think through, nor, in my opinion, dissolve in favor of the narrow or broad alternatives suggested at the outset. We can, however, seek to become clearer about the nature of this aporia and precisely where the conceptual difficulty lies. A test of an adequate understanding is precisely that it does not make the division of the church easily bearable. Thought should not try to solve a problem that can be solved only by conversion.

46. I have argued elsewhere that the existence or non-existence of such an inability constitutes a test for whether a conceptual difference is or is not church-dividing. Michael Root, "Identity and Difference: The Ecumenical Problem," in *Theology and Dialogue: Essays in Conversation with George Lindbeck,* ed. Bruce Marshall (Notre Dame: University of Notre Dame Press, 1990).

47. Marshall, "Disunity of the Church," p. 86.

Issues and Perspectives in
Roman Catholic Ecclesiology Today

SUSAN K. WOOD

The assigned tasks are to describe briefly the current state of ecclesiology in the Roman Catholic tradition and then to indicate how systematic theology may contribute to it. I will do so by sketching the broad outlines of the first and by discussing the category of the sacramentality of the church for the second.

Roman Catholic ecclesiology takes its charter from the Second Vatican Council, which has properly been called an ecclesiological council. Its major contributions to ecclesiology lie in its self-definition, in its advances in the theology of governance, and in its relationships to those outside its visible structures. It defined the nature of the church, describing it as the people of God, sacrament, mystical body of Christ, and temple of the Spirit. In these documents the church appears to be less triumphalistic as it looks less to itself and its own prerogatives and more to Christ. The conciliar documents note that the church, although holy, is "always in need of purification," and "follows constantly the path of penance and renewal."[1] They describe the church not primarily as an institution or a visible society, but in theological terms as a mystery and in historical terms as a pilgrim people who have yet to reach their eschatological destination.

The Council developed a theology of the episcopacy and the local church and situated the governance of the church within the collegiality of

---

1. *Catechism of the Catholic Church*, The Profession of the Christian Faith, art. 3, no. 827.

the communion of bishops with each other and the Bishop of Rome. It taught that the bishops possess the fullness of the sacrament of Orders[2] and that their power is "proper, ordinary, and immediate."[3] Consequently, bishops are not legates of the pope, nor is the local church a branch office of the Vatican. Although the exercise of authority in the Roman Catholic Church derives from a combination of sacramental empowerment and jurisdictional delegation, the teaching on the sacramental nature of episcopal consecration strengthened the sacramental foundations of episcopal authority by situating pastoral leadership and governance within the threefold office of priest, prophet, and shepherd conferred in ordination. Consequently, any statement that there is trickle-down authority in the Roman Catholic Church is not theologically accurate.

An emphasis on the local church necessitates an ecclesiology of communion. In 1985 the Synod of Bishops identified communion as the most important image of the church in the documents of Vatican II. However, this theme seems to be more indirect than the other themes and a way of approaching ecclesiological issues rather than a model that stands on its own. Communion ecclesiology is operative in the theology of the local church wherein each local church is wholly church even though no local church is the whole church. The relationship among particular churches is represented by the relationship among bishops. Bishops serve the communion of the church by personally representing their particular church within the communion of churches through their participation in the college of bishops. This view of the church underscores the personal, communal, and collegial nature of authority in the church although there is room for further development. Structures and processes of synodality remain rather underdeveloped, as is provision for the participation of the laity in governance.

A third contribution of the Council was to promote dialogue with the modern world. The First Vatican Council in 1870 had been a council responding to what it perceived to be the dangers of modernism and liberalism. It refuted error and defined doctrine, notably the doctrine of papal infallibility. By contrast, the Second Vatican Council was not convened to refute error, but to engage the contemporary world in dialogue. In comparison with Vatican I, the documents of Vatican II reveal the

2. *Lumen gentium*, 21.
3. *Lumen gentium*, 27.

church to be less defensive and more open to modern culture as well as to other religions. This is not only evident in the Pastoral Constitution on the Church in the Modern World, but also in *Lumen gentium's* acknowledgment of elements of sanctification and truth outside the church's visible structure,[4] the decrees on Religious Liberty and Ecumenism, and the Declaration on the Relations of the Church to Non-Christian Religions.

These three contributions to ecclesiology — self-definition, advances in the theology of governance, and relationships to those outside its visible structures — result in a more decentralized church. The church is more decentralized in the shift from Roman primacy to universal episcopacy, from an exclusive hierarchical ministry to the apostolate of the laity grounded in baptism and confirmation as a sharing in the salvific mission of the church, from identifying itself as coextensive with the church of Christ to recognition of the ecclesial character of other Christian churches, from Rome to the church worldwide.[5]

Now, thirty-five years after the close of the Council, we are still in a process of reception of the Council and are experiencing a conflict within the church over the interpretation of the conciliar documents. The results of the Council will be "received" when they pass into the life of the church. In terms of theology, the two major tensions today lie in the relationship between a more centrist universalism versus the diversity that accompanies a focus on the local churches[6] and the relationship between a theology of ordained priesthood and a theology of lay ministry.[7] This theological tension, which bears to no small extent on a division between the sacred and the secular in the documents of Vatican II, is accompanying a practical crisis in the number of ordained priests in the church. Also within the practical life of the church, the major challenge to the Western church is that of cultural secularism. Where atheism was the denial of religious truths and value, secularism today is indifference to them. Ironically, this seems to coexist with a widespread interest in spirituality.

---

4. *Lumen gentium,* 8.

5. See Edward Schillebeeckx, *L'Église du Christ de l'homme d'aujourd'jui selon Vatican II* (Paris: Mappus, 1965).

6. See John R. Quinn, *The Reform of the Papacy: The Costly Call to Christian Unity* (New York: Crossroad, 1999).

7. This tension is apparent in the document "Some Questions Regarding Collaboration of Nonordained Faithful in Priests' Sacred Ministry," issued by eight Vatican offices. *Origins* 27, no. 24 (November 1997): 398-409.

The spirituality is often very eclectic, individualistic, and is often perceived as being in contrast to organized religion rather than as flowing from it.

Church as Sacrament

One of the most important contributions of systematic theology in Roman Catholic ecclesiology is the concept of the sacramentality of the church. The category of sacramentality has generally not been considered to be a very fruitful category from an ecumenical perspective. Thus the Faith and Order document, *The Nature and Purpose of the Church,* lists it as one of the disputed areas in ecclesiology from an ecumenical perspective.[8] Apart from differing views as to what constitutes a sacrament, the two main reasons that some churches do not apply the concept of sacrament to the church are:

1. there should be a clear distinction between church and sacraments. The latter are means of salvation through which Christ sustains the church, not actions by which the church realizes or actualizes itself; and
2. using the term "sacrament" for the church might obscure the fact that, for them, the church is sign and instrument of God's design as the communion of Christians who, though being redeemed believers, are still liable to sin.[9]

Nevertheless, I hold that the category of sacramentality can be helpful ecumenically by helping to maintain a distinction between Christ and the church. The sacramentality of the church also provides a theological foundation for a participatory church within Roman Catholicism. I will develop these themes in the rest of the paper.

Three different articles in *Lumen gentium* identify the church as a sacrament, each with a slightly different nuance:[10] intimate union with

8. World Council of Churches/Faith and Order, *The Nature and Purpose of the Church,* Faith and Order Paper 181 (Geneva: WCC, 1998), p. 23.

9. Faith and Order Paper 181, p. 23.

10. *Lumen gentium,* 1, 9, 48.

God and the unity of humanity, salvation, and saving unity. In addition, three instances of identification of the church as sign occur in the Constitution on the Sacred Liturgy.[11] The references in articles 2 and 26 stress the church as a sacrament or sign of unity. Article 5 associates the church with the blood and water issuing from the side of Jesus, which are also symbols of baptism and eucharist.

The identification of the church as a sacrament occurs within a chain of sacramentality in the theological writings of Edward Schillebeeckx and Karl Rahner.[12] Christ is a sacrament of the Father. The church is a sacrament of Christ, and the seven sacraments are sacraments of the church.

This model can be diagramed thus:

$$\text{God} \rightarrow \text{Christ} \rightarrow \text{Church} \rightarrow \text{Sacraments}$$

The sign or sacrament is the actualization in the world of that which is signified, namely, God, Christ, and the church, respectively. This, of course, is precisely the disputed ecumenical issue. However, the point is that the church is most visibly fulfilling its mission and ministry when it is engaged in those acts of salvation through which Christ sustains the church. When the church is engaged in the acts of Christ, it is most authentically being itself, the church of Christ.

The nature of the church is evident through each of the sacraments. In the eucharist we know the church to be the body of Christ. We are incorporated into that body, both the church and the body of Christ, in baptism. We are reconciled to both Christ and the church in the sacrament of penance. Marriage, the covenant between two human beings, is a sign of the relationship between Christ and the church. So, too, what is "ordered" in the Sacrament of Order is the church. In this sacrament the ordained person is ordered to both Christ and the church in such a way that the ordained is representative of both.

11. Yves Congar, *Un peuple messianique: L'Église: sacrement du salut, salut et libéra-tion* (Paris: Cerf, 1975), p. 31.

12. Karl Rahner, *The Church and the Sacraments* (New York: Herder, 1963); Edward Schillebeeckx, O.P., *Christ the Sacrament of the Encounter with God* (Kansas City: Sheed and Ward, 1963). See also Avery Dulles, *Models of the Church* (New York: Doubleday, 1974); P. Smulders, "L'Église sacrement du salut," in G. Barauna, ed., *L'Église de Vatican II,* vol. 2 (Paris: Cerf, 1967), pp. 313-38; Jan Groot, "The Church as Sacrament of the World," *Concilium* 1, no. 4 (London: Burns & Oates, January 1968).

The idea of the church as sacrament is closely related to the image of the body of Christ. In the concept of sacrament, there is unity and difference: unity between the sign of the sacrament and what is signified; difference, because what is signified is not absolutely identical with the sign that makes it present. Historical presence and sacramental presence are two different modalities. The church as the body of Christ is the sacramental presence of Christ in the world in an analogous way in which Christ is the sacrament of the Father. Christ is the image of and self-expression of the Father. The one who sees the Son sees the Father (John 14:9). In Karl Rahner's theology the Son is a real symbol, which means real presence under sign, of the Father. He shares the same divine nature as the Father (unity) and yet is distinct from the Father as the Father's object of self-knowledge (difference). The identity between Father and Son lies in the identity of their divine nature, and their difference lies in their relationship. The Father generates the Son and the Son is begotten of the Father. The Son does not generate and the Father is not begotten. They are so close, however, that in Edward Schillebeeckx's theology, we encounter God when we encounter Christ.

In a similar way there is both a unity and a difference between the church, under the aspect of the biblical image of the body of Christ, and Christ. The guiding principle is that you can have as high an ecclesiology as you want as long as your Christology is higher. Strictly speaking, the church is not a prolongation of the incarnation, but is that which enables Christ to act sacramentally in the world. This distinction allows the church's members to be frail human beings liable to sin. In the case of the church, the visible sign includes the institutional and social aspect of the church, that is, all that is manifest in history and located in space and time. The referent of the sign is the resurrected Christ. It is important not to confuse the sign with its referent. As with the incarnation, in the church there is the union of the divine and the human, the human being the manifestation and revelation of the divine.

Even though the concept of the church as the sacrament of Christ is closely related to the image of the church as the mystical body of Christ, it avoids a major weakness of this image of being too close an identification between Christ and the church. The concept of sacrament is able to express the unity between the sign and the referent of that sign at the same time that it maintains the distinction between sign and referent. This unity and distinction are analogous to the relationship between the

divine and human natures in Christ: "as with Christ the distinction between his Godhead and his humanity remains without confusion though
they are inseparable signs and reality, manifest historical form and Holy
Spirit are not the same in the church, but as in Christ, are not separable
any more either."[13]

The Sacramental Basis of Authority in the Church

The church is not only a sacramental sign of the union of God and humanity; its governance reflects the principles of unity and communion
proper to the eucharist. Additionally, as the church is a sacrament, so also
is authority in the church circumscribed sacramentally even though there
is also a jurisdictional dimension to the exercise of authority. The sacramental basis of authority has far-reaching implications for both a theology of the laity and for a description of ecclesial relationships and structures. The point is that the sacraments confer an authority that is proper
to the sacrament received and not dependent upon a delegation of authority from another source. Furthermore, as Donald J. Keefe has noted,
"authority in the church is totally ordered to the worship of the Church
and totally measured by what that worship is. . . ." This is easily seen since
the bishop is head of a particular church defined as "an altar community
under the sacred ministry of the bishop."[14] Presbyters are ordained to
"preach the Gospel, shepherd the faithful, and celebrate divine worship as
true priests of the New Testament."[15] All the baptized are "consecrated by
their baptismal character to the exercise of the cult of the Christian religion," that is, to the public worship of the church.[16]

This authority, however, is not unlimited. The Petrine ministry for
the universal church and the local bishop for the particular church retain
the responsibility for testing the authenticity of the charisms and their use
for the good order of the church, but are themselves limited by the content of revelation and their apostolic heritage. The exercise of the "proper,

13. Karl Rahner, *Studies in Modern Theology* (London: Burns & Oates, 1964),
p. 201.

14. See Donald J. Keefe, "Authority in the Church: An Essay in Historical Theology," *Communio* 7 (1980): 343-63.

15. *Lumen gentium*, 26.

16. *Lumen gentium*, 11.

ordinary and immediate" authority of the bishop is "ultimately controlled by the supreme authority of the Church and can be confined within certain limits should the usefulness of the Church and the faithful require that."[17] One limit of the episcopal office of teaching and governing is that the bishop remain in hierarchical communion with the head and members of the college.[18] With regard to the priesthood, the priest's authority to forgive sin and celebrate the eucharist is regulated by his bishop even though he has been empowered to do so by virtue of his ordination.

Frequently overlooked is the fact that the laity, too, possess rights and responsibilities that are sacramentally grounded in their baptism and confirmation. A baptized couple, for example, possesses the power to confer the sacrament of marriage on each other. They have a right, not merely the privilege, to participate in the sacraments and receive the word of God.[19] Through baptism and confirmation the laity are appointed to the apostolate of sharing in the mission of the church.[20]

For both the episcopacy and the baptized, their rights and responsibilities are grounded in the sacramental character proper to the sacrament. In either case this character constitutes a specific ecclesial relationship.[21] These relations constitute and hierarchically structure the people of God. Rights and responsibilities related to sanctifying, governing, and teaching accrue to the episcopacy under the direction of the Petrine ministry, by virtue of episcopal consecration identified as a sacrament in *Lumen gentium*.[22] The rights and responsibilities of the laity, also identified with a priestly, prophetic, and kingly role, are theirs by membership in the church effected through baptism. In both cases, the ecclesial relationship governing the rights and responsibilities is constituted sacramentally, thus giving authority its sacramental identification.

17. *Lumen gentium*, 27.
18. *Lumen gentium*, 21.
19. *Lumen gentium*, 37.
20. *Lumen gentium*, 32.
21. See Eliseo Ruffini, "Character as a Concrete Visible Element of the Sacrament in Relation to the Church," in *The Sacraments in General: A New Perspective,* ed. Edward Schillebeeckx and Boniface Willems, *Concilium* 31 (1968): 101-14. He cites a number of authors who identify the sacramental character as a real relation with the church in note 8, p. 103.
22. *Lumen gentium*, 26. The trifold *munera* is mentioned in the consecratory prayer of ordination to the priesthood.

Collegiality within a Eucharistic Ecclesiology

The sacramentality of the church is closely related to the notion of the communion of bishops in the episcopal college and the relationship between the local and universal church. The Roman Catholic Church identifies the basic unit of the church as the altar community under the sacred ministry of the bishop.[23] Thus the local church is defined as a eucharistic community even though the only time the people usually experience themselves as gathered around the eucharistic table of the local bishop, unless they happen to reside in the cathedral parish, is for special occasions like confirmation in their local parish. The local church as a eucharistic community cannot exist alone as church all by itself, but must be united to its bishop and through the bishop to all the other eucharistic communities within the church. The local church, although wholly church, is not the whole church. The universal church is the communion of these altar communities.

We might represent this conceptualization of the church thus:

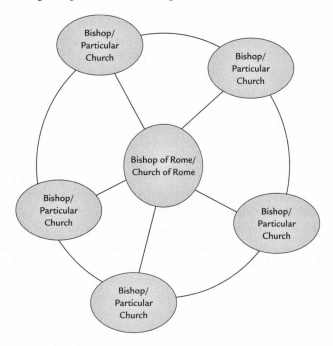

23. *Lumen gentium,* 26.

In this model each particular church is in communion with every other particular church and the Bishop of Rome, who exercises the ministry of safeguarding the unity and communion of the particular churches. This communion is personalized and objectively sacramentalized in the college of bishops to which each bishop is admitted upon consecration. The bishops in their persons represent their churches.

Elements of a eucharistic model of the church as the mystical body of Christ within the documents of Vatican II include: the definition of the local church as an altar community, the episcopal collegiality described in Chapter III of *Lumen gentium,* and the relationship between the one universal church and the many local churches. The statement in *Sacrosanctum concilium* that the church is most manifestly itself when it celebrates the eucharist could not be clearer: "The church is displayed with special clarity when the holy People of God, all of them, are actively and fully sharing in the same liturgical celebrations — especially when it is the same Eucharist — sharing one prayer at one altar, at which the bishop is presiding, surrounded by his presbyterate and his ministers."[24]

Consequences Flowing from the Sacramentality of the Church

A number of consequences flow from the sacramentality of the church:

1. The basis for authority in the church is the Lordship of Christ and his continuing presence in the power of the Spirit. As Giuseppe Alberigo comments, ". . . in the church the source of all responsibility and all mandates to service lies in Christ and these can be participated in only by means of a sacramental act."[25] The authority of the ordained minister is conferred sacramentally and exercised within a eucharistic community. The ordained minister represents the person of Christ as representative of the community which is the body of Christ. The authority of the ordained minister is the authority of the Head, whose authority does not suppress the authority of the

24. *Sacrosanctum concilium,* 41.

25. Giuseppe Alberigo, "Ecclesiology and Democracy: Convergences and Divergences," in *The Tabu of Democracy within the Church,* ed. James Provost and Knut Walf (London: SCM, 1992), p. 21.

Body, but establishes it on the Cross. "Clericalism," understood as the identification of authority in the church with the preponderant influence of the clergy, lacks foundation in the church's worship, particularly in the sacrament of baptism that empowers the laity for liturgical worship in the eucharist and also empowers them to mutually confer the sacrament of marriage, and to exercise an apostolate that is properly theirs.

2. Through its sacramentality, the church is the corporate presence of God in Christ in the unity of the Spirit. The church's missionary obligation is to manifest what it embodies. As a sign it must manifest in its external structure the values it professes. One consequence of this obligation is that the church, which speaks to others about justice, must be just itself in its own institution and in its dealings with its members and with others. Not to do so prevents the church from being a clear and unambiguous sign of the presence of Christ in the world.

3. The church as sacrament is inseparable from its baptismal and eucharistic practices, for the unity of the church is sacramentally realized in its communion with its Lord (1 Cor. 10:16-17). The principles of good worship therefore are also the principles of life in the church more generally since the nature of church is manifested through the liturgy.[26] Specifically this means that insofar as the nature of the liturgy requires the "full, conscious, and active participation" of the faithful in liturgical celebrations,[27] so also must the faithful participate in the church fully, consciously, and actively. This does not mean turning the church into a political democracy, however, although it does mean incorporating liturgical principles into the governance of the church.

4. The sacramentality of the church requires that pastoral leadership and liturgical presidency be united in the normal practice of the church. The minister who presides over the unity of the community generally should preside over the sacrament of unity, the eucharist. Presidency refers to the ecclesial life of the community before it refers to a liturgical action.[28] Ministry is first a pastoral charge before

---

26. *Sacrosanctum concilium*, 2.

27. *Sacrosanctum concilium*, 14.

28. See Paul Bradshaw, *Liturgical Presidency in the Early Church*, Grove Liturgical

it is a liturgical function. This practice emphasizes the intrinsic connection between the nature of the church and its liturgical worship, as well as the relationship between a pastoral liturgical minister and the church.

5. When the sacramentality of the church is viewed from the perspective of the eucharist with all its implications for unity and communion within the church, it becomes evident that governance is personal, collegial, and communal. In the Roman Catholic Church, even though it is very clear that the ultimate authority for a parish rests with the pastor, the diocese with its bishop, and the universal church with the pope, in reality there is a rich network of relationships within which each of these authorities operates. Pastors govern in communion with and under the authority of their bishop. Bishops govern in communion with the college of bishops and the Bishop of Rome. The Bishop of Rome, even when acting alone, is acting implicitly as the head of the college of bishops. Structures for the participation of the laity in collegial structures have not developed, partly because governance has been restricted to clerics. However, the fact that more of the laity are involved in professional church ministry and some being pastoral associates is raising new questions about structures of governance.

Study no. 36 (Cambridge: Grove Books, 1983), pp. 7-8: "[In the New Testament] . . . no one was ordained or appointed to an office which consisted primarily of saying the eucharistic prayer, but whoever said it did so as the natural expression of what they already were within the community."

The Possible Contribution of
Papal Authority to Church Unity:
An Anglican/Episcopalian Perspective

J. ROBERT WRIGHT

The Princeton Proposal is appropriately optimistic about the possible contribution that papal authority can make to church unity. It acknowledges that the Roman Catholic Church, including as it does about half of the world's Christians, has a special ecumenical place to play simply because the Bishop of Rome is "the only historically plausible candidate to exercise an effective worldwide ministry of unity" (para. 65). At the same time, the Proposal agrees that "the bishop of Rome should recognize the special responsibility for unity implied in the claim to primacy and universal pastoral jurisdiction and should discharge the papal office in the spirit of sacrificial service to separated sisters and brothers in Christ" (para. 66). The signatories of the Proposal, nonetheless, make these statements in full awareness that they "come from various churches and have varying convictions about the shape that full visible unity should take," including differing judgments about the role of the Bishop of Rome (para. 45). What does unite the signatories is their common commitment to the biblical vision of visible Christian unity, of all in each place one, as it received special articulation at New Delhi in 1961, and their conviction that this unity "must appear more fully in our worship, our mission, and the structures of our religious life" (para. 1, 4). In particular, they agree, this necessitates "sustained attention to the structures and forms of communion, and to their foundation in a common faith and discipleship" (para. 10). Can papal authority assist this process?

In contrast to the theological agreement that was signaled by the

Joint Declaration on the Doctrine of Justification between the Roman Catholic Church and the Lutheran World Federation, which the convenors of the Princeton Proposal appropriately highlight in their preface, the most prominent international agreement about the actually visible role of the papacy in facilitating church unity to appear in recent years has been *The Gift of Authority* (hereafter GA), released by the Anglican–Roman Catholic International Commission (hereafter ARCIC) on May 12, 1999.[1] It will be the subject of the present essay and should be of interest to the general readership of this volume because, so far, it is the only viable scheme on the ecumenical table that would actually produce a visible international unity of churches of the sort that the Princeton Proposal envisions. This is not to say, however, that GA has received an overwhelming endorsement from either of the two churches heretofore involved with it, or that it would necessarily have much appeal to other churches, although there are some positive things that can indeed be said about its implications. Obviously, therefore, the comments that follow can be written from only one perspective, that of the author himself, who is an Anglican/Episcopalian, although such comments may be of assistance in enabling other readers of other churches to reflect upon possible contributions that papal authority might make to visible church unity in the light of the Princeton Proposal itself.

This essay therefore presents a brief survey of the actual contents of GA as well as my own appreciation and critique of it, offered from the perspective of one Anglican/Episcopalian who has been intimately involved in dialogues about papal authority for many years. I believe that what I say will resonate with the thoughts of many within the Episcopal Church, although it remains to be seen how far my observations may be shared in other churches as they reflect upon GA especially in the light of the Princeton Proposal.

Now it happens that GA, itself the product of some five years of dialogue, is also the third statement on "authority" that has so far been issued over the years by ARCIC (although the same membership did not issue each statement).[2] Among the many reasons why this statement is impor-

---

1. Published 1999 by Anglican Book Centre, Toronto, Catholic Truth Society, London, and Church Publishing Incorporated, New York. The commission consists of about twenty members from both churches.

2. The present author was a member of it at an earlier time.

tant and should be given careful attention, the following are noteworthy: (1) Religious authority, especially that of the papacy, was a key element in the division that occurred at the time of the Reformation in most countries. (2) Questions of truth and its relationship to teaching authority in the church are raised and then answered by this new statement in a radical way that could have profound implications for all the churches if its proposals meet with acceptance. (3) Pope John Paul II and George Carey, then archbishop of Canterbury, agreed at their joint meeting in 1996 that unless these two churches, Anglican and Roman Catholic, can reach sufficient agreement about authority, they will "not reach the full, visible unity to which we are both committed." It seems likely to me that the Vatican proposed this assertion, and that the Anglican side consented to it as an obvious statement of the papal claim (cf. Princeton Proposal pars. 9, 63), and therefore that it is reasonable to assume that the expectations demanded in GA of Anglicans for visible unity with the Bishop of Rome will also be proposed by the Vatican as a standard for other churches as well. (4) Authority is certainly a topic that has come to the front page of Anglican interest for many reasons, both internationally and especially in this country, and if Anglicans have been concerned with a problem of insufficient central authority in leadership, the problem with the Roman Catholic Church has to many seemed to be just the reverse. The present Presiding Bishop and Primate of the Episcopal Church, Frank T. Griswold, in his own final paper prepared for the Anglican–Roman Catholic dialogue in the U.S.A. — which he had chaired as Bishop of Chicago, called for an intentional dialogue on the question of universal authority in the church, and GA speaks directly to his appeal.

So what does GA actually say? Here I do not intend to rehearse in the limited space available the many generalized ingredients of the GA statement that are unexceptionable and should be welcomed by all persons of good will. Rather I shall summarize the "bottom line" contents of GA as it pertains to truth and teaching authority and visible unity and then afterwards offer a different sort of appreciation followed by some hard questions in critique. Quoting as closely as possible from the original document so as not to distort it by either favorable or unfavorable embellishment, and giving "para" numbers for reference, the following is my summary:

ARCIC in this statement says that it is unanimously convinced that there is now "sufficient agreement on universal primacy as a gift to be shared" that such a primacy can "be offered and received even before our churches are in full communion" (para. 60), and that "such a universal primate will exercise leadership in the world and also in both communions" (para. 61). The commission further agrees that one expression of such universal primacy is the particular ministry of the Bishop of Rome "concerning the discernment of truth," and that "reception of the primacy of the Bishop of Rome entails the recognition of this specific ministry of the universal primate" (para. 47). This, ARCIC believes, "is a gift to be received by all the churches." "Such infallible teaching," moreover, "is at the service of the Church's indefectibility" (para. 42), which means that "with confidence in the promise of Christ" the church "will persevere and be maintained in the truth" (para. 41). The church's faith is to be found, first of all, in the faith of "all the baptized" (para. 47), although it is the entire college of bishops that is charged collectively with "the ministry of memory" (paras. 41, 43), "to teach and affirm the faith" (para. 47), "to determine what is to be taught as faithful to the apostolic tradition" (para. 38). And "in specific circumstances, moreover, those with this ministry of oversight *(episcope),* assisted by the Holy Spirit, may together come to a judgement which, being faithful to Scripture and consistent with apostolic Tradition, is preserved from error." And "this is what is meant when it is affirmed that the Church may teach infallibly" (para. 42). Finally, it is this "wholly reliable teaching of the whole Church that is operative in the judgement of the universal primate" (para. 47). Such teaching, infallible as it is, should be seen as a renewed expression of God's "yes" to humankind in Jesus Christ, so that humanity may offer its response of "Amen" to God's glory. Thus the commission rests the overall theme of its message (paras. 8, 42, 50, etc.) in Paul's words at 2 Corinthians 1:18-20: "As surely as God is faithful, our word to you has not been Yes and No. For the Son of God, Jesus Christ, whom we preached among you, Silvanus and Timothy and I, was not Yes and No; but in him it is always Yes. For all the promises of God find their Yes in him. That is why we utter the Amen through him, to the glory of God." This ends my summary.

GA has provoked much discussion among Anglicans the world over, including no small disagreement especially in this country, but before offering my own critique I want first to sketch out an appreciation of some of its positive affirmations that I think many Episcopalians would endorse even while leaving its particulars of implementation for further debate. These positive affirmations, all voted by ARCIC unanimously, include the following: (1) that the unity of the church is visible and must be made even more clearly visible (in resonance with the Princeton Proposal); (2) that the church's unity should be visibly structured, and that this structure must include the Historic Episcopate and can even include some sort of worldwide central and personal authority in leadership for the sake of mission and evangelization; and (3) that this worldwide central authority can indeed be the papacy, if the parameters of its authority are agreed by all parties and not imposed by force. In the worldwide ecumenical picture, I think a majority of Anglicans would stand on these points.

Now I proceed to some questions, hard questions, that are also part of the debate and do indicate that Anglicans are certainly not ready to accept the authority of the papacy by means of a blank check: (1) Is authority really a "gift," or would it have been more honest for the statement to admit that "authority" is at best a responsibility and at worst a problem? (2) Does not the statement clearly say that papal infallibility is one expression of universal papal primacy (para. 47), and does it not clearly imply that the Anglican members of the commission have joined their Roman Catholic colleagues in urging the Anglican Communion to accept such a primacy now, even before full communion is reached (para. 60)? (3) Since the commission states that it is convinced that the Anglican Communion should go ahead with such recognition of papal primacy now, how would the Anglican members propose to reconcile the "discernment of truth" (para. 47) that the Bishop of Rome has already made against the ordination of women, on the one hand, with the increasing Anglican tendency to authorize and welcome such ordinations, on the other? Are the statements of the Bishops of Rome against the ordination of women part of the "truth" that he has discerned, or not? (4) Is the device from 2 Corinthians perhaps too facile, where it asserts that "the aim of the exercise of authority and of its reception is to enable the Church to say 'Amen' to God's 'Yes' in the Gospel" (para. 50)? Doesn't this rather easily provide a rationale for so-called teaching authority in the church to suppress free thought and speech, as such persons "enable" us to say "Amen" to God's "Yes" because they collectively have "discerned" it, or because the Pope has primatially "discerned" it (cf. para. 43)?

(5) The statement says that "the bishops" (not, we may observe, "the historians") are charged with "the ministry of memory" (paras. 41, 43). So what would the commission think to be the role of historians in the church? And is there documented evidence that "the bishops" have always

been accurate in what they have "remembered" (para. 42), or that the Pope has always exercised his primatial ministry of "discernment" either for the benefit of the whole church or at least for the benefit of a particular local church (para. 46)? Is this really the case, or is too much being claimed here? Why did the commission not qualify these assertions by an adverb such as "generally" or a phrase like "in consultation with historians"? (6) Which are the specific papal judgments that the commission, including the Anglican members, has actually agreed upon as being "preserved from error" (para. 42)? Are such papal judgments seen by the commission to be verbally infallible or merely conceptually infallible? If they merely intended to say that papal judgments are conceptually infallible, then whom would the commission propose as the authority to enunciate the infallible concept that is alleged to exist behind or beneath the words themselves (para. 42)? (7) Would the commission conceive the GA as being a document the truth of which is so obvious and appealing that a great many other churches will rush to endorse it? Or will they even do so after a few years of careful reflection?

(8) And finally, although the widespread toleration of sexual abuse by clergy did not seem so apparent back in the days when GA was being written, the growing impression that so many of these cases have been condoned or downplayed in some 161 dioceses in the USA by bishops, all of whom are directly appointed by the Pope,[3] has given rise to further doubts as to whether the Pope's discernment or judgment really can be "preserved from error" and "wholly reliable" as GA seems to assert. Is the ascription to the Bishop of Rome of "supreme, full, immediate, and universal ordinary power in the Church, which he can always freely exercise" (canons 331, 333 of the 1983 *Code of Canon Law,* which he himself revised and promulgated as its "legislator") really the sort of papal authority for the sake of church unity that ARCIC wants to commend — now — to the Anglican Communion and to other churches?

All these questions, I hasten to conclude, are not uttered against the good intentions of the GA. But they do show that it has problems as well as possibilities. It is truly a "mixed bag" as regards its implications for the possible contributions that papal authority could make to church unity. On the positive side GA has certainly provided a stimulus for discussion, not least about the possibility or need for a worldwide center of visible

---

3. *New York Times,* 12 January 2003.

unity, and the Princeton Proposal in one sense can be seen as a further contribution to that debate across a spectrum that is broader than merely the Episcopal Church and the Anglican Communion. GA with its calls for conciliarity, collegiality, synodality, shared decision-making, and a greater role for the laity does open up possibilities of a renewed papacy for a brighter future, but of course that is not exactly what it says, since it is actually calling for Anglican acceptance of papal primacy, perhaps even infallibility, not at some vague time of the future but right now! (See its paras. 47, 60.) With due respect for the commission's amazingly unanimous vote in support of this call, a clear indication that the commission did not regard its proposals as premature, I myself am not convinced that GA has made a sufficiently compelling case on its own for the acceptance of universal primacy "now," by Anglicans or by any other church. But, as I have already intimated, the fact that an international commission of very diverse and prestigious Anglicans could all vote for it unanimously, does give a clear signal that, at least for their church and mine, the future of unity lies not in further fragmentation or merely warm feelings or the absence of visible structures or the paralysis of any authority to get things decided.

The promotion of an international church unity that is visible and viable is a particular gift that the see of Rome tries to offer to the renewal of the worldwide church. Can this be a positive contribution to the longing for visible unity that is clearly present, but in broader strokes, within the Princeton Proposal? I myself believe so. If GA is not exactly the way forward to achieve this goal, if the present papacy is not perfect and if no human system ever can be, then we must all seek for better ways, and continue to strive towards the goal of the high prize of our calling.

The One True Church: Thoughts concerning an Ecumenical Conundrum

JOHN H. ERICKSON

We believe that the church is one. As God is one, Christ is one, the Spirit is one, so also the church is one. To this basic Christian conviction both Scriptures and the historic Creeds bear ample testimony. As Michael Root has observed, "the church possesses a unity it cannot lose and still remain truly church." It has what Root has referred to as an "essential unity," as distinct from all the accidental unities (or disunities) that human ingenuity or other circumstances may devise.[1]

We also believe that the church is holy, catholic, and apostolic — to continue with the attributes enumerated in the Nicene-Constantinopolitan Creed. Most Christians, whether or not they use this or any other creed, believe that the church has an essential holiness, an essential catholicity, an essential apostolicity, just as it has an essential unity; and they regard themselves as belonging to this one, holy, catholic, and apostolic church. They believe that the community of faith to which they belong (the ecclesial family, the denomination, the local congregation . . .) is — here and now — an expression of that church, that it participates in the reality of that church, that it is wholly church though not necessarily the whole church.

We "believe in one, holy, catholic and apostolic church," just as we "believe in one God, the Father almighty . . . and in one Lord Jesus Christ . . . and in the Holy Spirit." Belief in this church forms part of our confes-

---

1. See Chapter 6, p. 108 above.

145

sion of faith. But while these marks of the church may be perceived by the eyes of faith, they do not readily lend themselves to empirical demonstration. Anyone who reflects on church life in the time and space of this present age cannot but be aware of division where there should be unity; sinfulness where there should be holiness; partiality where there should be catholicity, wholeness, and universality; and deviation where there should be faithfulness to the apostolic preaching of the gospel. We are aware of this, first of all, within our several communities of faith, and the perplexity that we face is hardly new. Perplexity of this sort is evident in the Corinthian church at the time of Paul and in the Roman church at the time of Hermas, not to mention the African church at the time of Cyprian or again in the time of Augustine. The crucial problem of ecclesiology has always been what Florovsky referred to as the "double condition" of the church, its "dual life," its existence "at once in two different dimensions," the historical and the eschatological.[2]

This problem has taken on a new form in modern times, particularly over the past century with the rise of the ecumenical movement. It may be, of course, that the self-understanding of whatever one might regard as the "true church" has always been formed in the context of disagreement and division — that the self-understanding of the emerging great church in the second century, and particularly its understanding of apostolicity, was formed in the context of its conflict with gnosticism; that the self-understanding of the church catholic in the third to fifth centuries, and particularly its understanding of the relationship between the holiness of the church and the unity of the church, was formed in the context of a succession of conflicts over penitential discipline (Novatianist schism, Donatist schism . . .); that the self-understanding of the orthodox churches, whether Chalcedonian or non-Chalcedonian, was formed in the context of christological controversy, etc. Even so, at least through the Middle Ages, the range of ecclesiological issues under discussion and debate remained rather broad. As the examples just given suggest, the issue of unity was practically inseparable from issues of holiness, catholicity, and apostolicity. In addition, expressions of ecclesiological reflection remained remarkably rich and varied, albeit (from a modern perspective) rather dif-

---

2. G. Florovsky, "The Historical Problem of a Definition of the Church," in *Collected Works* 14 (Belmont, Mass.: Nordland, 1989), p. 30. The article in question originally appeared in *The Unity We Seek* (New York and Oxford: Oxford University Press, 1963).

fuse. What is the relationship between the church on earth and the church in heaven, between the ecclesiastical hierarchy and the celestial hierarchy, between the church militant and the church triumphant, between the church as a visible historic community and the church as the body of Christ, between the church as a hospital for sinners, a company of frail human beings *in via,* always in travail, and the church as a glorious *koinonia* with God, with the saints of all ages, and with all the hosts of heaven? Such questions were less often addressed in systematic treatises *de ecclesia* than in treatises on mystical theology. But they *were* addressed, and in ways that might be termed holistic. Concern for church structures was never separated from christological and eschatological reflection and from the sacramental and ascetical experience of church life. In more recent times, however, the ecclesiological problem has contracted, as it were, to the problem of how to explain and possibly overcome present divisions.

With this contraction have come certain gains and losses. On the one hand, ecclesiology has become the central theological preoccupation of our time, and no doubt we are all the richer for the reflection, discussion, and debate that have taken place both within and between our churches. On the other hand, the issue of unity all too often has been treated without much regard for wider theological issues. The "vertical," trans-historical concerns evident in earlier reflection have given way to a rather limited range of "horizontal" concerns. Above all, we are preoccupied with determining what structures are necessary for "visible unity" (whatever that may mean) here and now.

Others have surveyed the course of modern ecumenical reflection on "visible unity" and the principal forums within which this reflection has taken place, giving special attention to the privileged position the World Council of Churches has enjoyed within the "one ecumenical movement."[3] At the risk of some repetition, I should like to review some of the same material, and indeed to push back this review by a couple centuries, to the age of the Protestant Reformation. I shall do so, however, from the perspective of the (Chalcedonian) Orthodox Church, noting (among other things) the impact of Western ecclesiological reflection on that church; and — if only for lack of time — I shall do so in the broadest possible strokes, in generalizations and assertions that certainly could be qualified and refined in various ways.

3. See Chapters 1 and 2 in this volume.

As suggested earlier, one could argue that disagreement and division have always and necessarily been the context in which the church's (or a church's) sense of identity has been formed. One could point to at least two ways in which this has happened:

- by emulation, i.e., by imitation or appropriation for oneself of the claims, institutions, or practices of another;
- by contradiction, i.e., by rejection of the claims, institutions, or practices of another and concurrent development of claims, institutions, or practices more or less directly opposed to them.

And one could find examples of the formation of ecclesial identity by emulation and contradiction in practically every period of church history. Consider, for example, relations between Chalcedonians and non-Chalcedonians in late antiquity and the Byzantine Middle Ages. Particularly in the later fifth and early sixth centuries, both sides vied for the designation "orthodox" and in various ways sought to demonstrate their own perfect fidelity to the faith of Nicea (e.g., by introducing the Creed into the eucharistic liturgy). But emulation of this sort often enough was accompanied by contradiction. We can see this at its simplest in the Byzantine *Triodion's* rubric for Cheesefare Sunday: "During this week the accursed Armenians fast from eggs and cheese, but we, to refute their damnable heresy, do eat both eggs and cheese for the entire week." What one side does is enough to prompt the other to do the opposite!

One *could* construct an argument along these lines. But in fact, for many centuries ecclesiological reflection remained diffuse, with prayer and poetry contributing to it at least as much as polemics. Disagreements and divisions were certainly present. It is altogether illusory to speak of "the undivided church of the first millennium" or of any other early period. But the kinds of direct, sustained challenges that led to conciliar "limits" *(horoi)* in triadology and Christology were largely absent in the sphere of ecclesiology. The closest would be the challenge of Donatism in North Africa, but controversy in this and other cases that could be mentioned focused more on the problem of the church's holiness than on the problem of its synchronic and diachronic unity. Certainly disagreements of various sorts might lead to breaches in communion and even to mutual anathemas. Sometimes these breaches were healed (e.g., between the Armenian Church and the Syrian Church — both non-Chalcedonian but not always in perfect unanimity); sometimes they were not (as eventually would be the case between the Oriental and the Eastern Orthodox churches and, still later, between the Eastern churches and the Latin West). But virtually all parties operated with a common, shared ecclesiology. At least there was sufficient commonality that emerging ecclesiological differences (e.g., between Rome and the East) could be neglected in favor of properly dogmatic issues. When the churches fought, it was about christological terminology, the procession of the Holy Spirit, etc.; and when anathemas were pronounced, it was against those holding deviant christological or triadological positions, not against those holding a deviant position on the church.

All this changed with the Reformation. Tensions relating to a host of issues within the late medieval Latin church exploded into open conflict. Conflict over justification led swiftly to conflict over authority and a multitude of related ecclesiological issues. Catholics and Protestants of various persuasions developed mutually exclusive positions concerning the nature of the church's diachronic and synchronic unity and the institutional structures appropriate or necessary for maintaining this unity. Reformers taxed papists for deforming the church's apostolic faith; papists taxed reformers for rebelling against the apostolic see. Quickly enough historical scholarship was pressed into the service of controversial theology. The Magdeburg Centuriators found the true continuity and identity of the church in those faithful few who, *in* every century, rightly understood the gospel message of justification by faith alone. In response Cesare Cardinal Baronius found the true principle of the church's unity and continuity in the see of Peter. And so the debate proceeded. As various self-understandings and identities developed by way of contradiction, ecclesiology emerged as a central issue — perhaps even as *the* central issue — for debate. It is hardly an accident that denominational labels from this period — episcopal, congregational, presbyterian, and of course also papist — so often reflect distinctive ecclesiological positions. And these labels (along with many of the ecclesiological differences behind them) survive more or less intact until our own day, even though differences over issues like justification and the mode of Christ's presence in the eucharist have now been largely overcome. With the Reformation, disagreement in Faith led to differences in Order. By the closing decades of the twentieth century, that century of remarkable ecumenical advances, differences in Order would continue to divide, even though disagreement in Faith had lost much of its divisive power.

The Orthodox, of course, were not immediately or directly involved in struggles of the Reformation, and when they did become involved, their contribution was most often derivative, reactive, and negative. Nevertheless, ecclesiological developments in the West in this period did have a significant impact on the formation of the modern Orthodox sense of ecclesial identity.[4]

Initial episodes of this story can be summarized fairly quickly. In response to the challenge of the Protestant reformers, with their tendency to regard the true unity and continuity of the church as virtually invisible to human observation, Roman Catholic theologians from Trent onward developed what has been called "soteriological and ecclesiological exclusivism," i.e., the idea that no salvation is possible outside the visible institutional structures of the (Roman) Catholic Church.[5] An earlier sacramental approach to ecclesiology, which even as late as the Council of Florence could envision reunion above all as the restoration of communion between sister churches, gave way to a predominantly institutional ecclesiology aimed at the "conversion" of individual "schismatics" to the Roman Church and their "submission" to the Roman pontiff, its very visible head. This new ecclesiology expressed itself, among other ways, in the phenomenon that has been called "uniatism," beginning with the Union of Brest (1596). Such unions, of course, did nothing to advance the wider reunion of the churches. Rather, they sharpened their division, as each side insisted ever more strongly that it and it alone was the exclusive bearer of salvation. Symptomatic on the Roman Catholic side was a 1729 order of the Propaganda Fide forbidding any *communicatio in sacris* with the "dissident orientals." Symptomatic on the Orthodox side was the *Definition of the Holy Great Church of Christ Defending the Holy Baptism Given from God and Spitting Upon the Baptisms of the Heretics Which Are Otherwise Administered*, which was issued by Patriarch Cyril V of Constantinople in 1755. Just as for Roman Catholics, the "dissident orientals" were outside the one true church, so also for the Orthodox, the Latins

---

4. See my paper on "The Formation of Orthodox Ecclesial Identity," *St. Vladimir's Theological Quarterly* 42 (1998): 301-14.

5. See W. Hryniewicz, "Der 'Uniatismus' und die Zukunft des katholisch-orthodoxen Dialogs," *Ostkirchliche Studien* 40 (1991): 210-21 and elsewhere for the expression in question.

were "outside" — so much so that (re)baptism was required for their admission to the fold.

The exclusive view of the church expressed in this *Definition* was developed with somewhat greater refinement especially in the *Pedalion* of Nicodemus the Haghiorite (Leipzig 1800) and thereafter by his spiritual heirs. These would argue that in principle any "convert" to Orthodoxy should be received by baptism, and that if some other mode of reception is used, this is simply a matter of "economy" and implies nothing whatsoever about the prior ecclesial status of the one being received (i.e., the existence of "grace" or the validity of the sacraments in the group from which that person is coming). This approach, "Cyprianic" as opposed to the "Augustinian" approach of the Latins and the Latin-influenced Russians, to this day is widely regarded as representative of "traditional" Orthodoxy, particularly in Greek circles. It has never been formally rejected by the Orthodox Church as a whole, even by the Patriarchate of Constantinople (which has been in the vanguard of Orthodox involvement in the ecumenical movement). In fact, as I have argued elsewhere, this approach marks a seismic shift in Orthodox practice and reflection with regard to Christians outside the institutional limits of the Orthodox Church.[6] Continuing practice and reflection in earlier centuries, as revealed in numerous canonical and liturgical texts, distinguished between the forms that separation from the church could take and therefore between modes of reception for those baptized "outside." It is enough here to cite Basil the Great (canon 1), who indicates with approval that "the ancients" distinguished between heresies, schisms, and illegal congregations. Only those coming from heresies in the strict and narrow sense of the word (e.g., Gnostics), "who are completely broken off and, as regards the faith itself, alienated," were to be received by baptism. Those coming from groups whose separation arose from "questions that admit of a remedy" (and for Basil this included many groups that later would be labeled heretical) were to be received by anointing with chrism or simply by profession of faith (as would eventually be the case with the non-Chalcedonians). What invalidated was heresy in the strict and narrow sense of the word, not simply the fact of separation, as Cyprian

6. In "Formation . . ." and "On the Cusp of Modernity: The Canonical Hermeneutic of St. Nikodemos the Haghiorite (1748-1809)," *St. Vladimir's Theological Quarterly* 42 (1998): 45-66. For further background see my "Reception of Non-Orthodox into the Orthodox Church: Contemporary Practice," *St. Vladimir's Theological Quarterly* 41 (1997): 1-17.

had maintained. Now, however, all outside the Orthodox Church — Roman Catholics, Protestants, and even non-Chalcedonians — were in principle to be regarded as no different than Jews and pagans — at least as long as they continued in their separation.

In the nineteenth century and long into the twentieth, relations between the Orthodox Church and the Roman Catholic Church remained hostile. Catholics might regard the Orthodox as having valid sacraments, but these were inefficacious. Their bishops, having been ordained in apostolic succession, might possess the power of orders, but they did not possess jurisdiction. Pius IX's *Letter to the Easterners* and Leo XIII's encyclical *Satis cognitum* might speak of such personages as "excelling others in ecclesiastical honors," but they stu*diously avoid referring to them as bishops, much less as brother bishops heading sister churches in which Christ's body is being built up even now. The easterners are "aliens from the holy throne of the apostle Peter," "scattered sheep" wandering in "pathless and rough places." They must be sought out and brought into the one sheepfold, under one shepherd.[7] For their part, in response to such initiatives, the Orthodox taxed Rome for its myriad innovations, which departed from the undivided faith and practice of the church of the ancient councils, the true church, the Orthodox Church.

In taxing Rome for its innovations, the Orthodox were not alone in the nineteenth century. Protestants did so as well. If nothing else, its proclamation of new dogmas demonstrated clearly that Rome and not they were the real innovators, that Rome in fact had abandoned the faith and practice of the early church. (The church of the New Testament? The pre-Constantinian church? The church of the *consensus quinquesaecularis?* The church of the seven ecumenical councils? The "undivided church of the first millennium"? — that was not always clear in polemics of the period.) This mutual antipathy to Rome (along with a host of geopolitical factors, such as the formidable presence of the British navy in the Eastern Mediterranean) helped bring Orthodox and Protestants, and especially Orthodox and Anglicans, closer together.

---

7. Quoted in the introduction to *Encyclical Epistle of the One Holy Catholic and Apostolic Church to the Faithful Everywhere, Being a Reply to the Epistle of Pius IX to the Easterners* (reprint South Canaan, Pa., 1958), pp. 3-4. This *Reply* and related controversial texts can also be found online at a major "traditionalist" Orthodox website, Orthodoxinfo.com.

The story of Orthodox ecumenism in the nineteenth century, already told so well by Florovsky, need not be repeated here.[8] Several points should be noted, however. The "soteriological and ecclesiological exclusivism" so evident in the 1755 *Definition* on heretic baptism had little practical impact, whether in Russian circles, where it was generally regarded as a regrettable aberration, or even in Greek circles, where the principle of "economy" could be invoked to justify acceptance not only of Anglican baptism but also of Anglican orders. But this did not mean that the Orthodox had a fully thought-out, clearly articulated, and consistent alternative to this position — one capable of explaining how the church can be one when Christians are so palpably divided. The Orthodox (but perhaps also the Anglicans) seem to have entered upon this remarkable first stage in the ecumenical movement full of naïve optimism but with little firsthand knowledge of their counterparts. The mood on both sides was well expressed in the words of a Greek churchman to a group of Anglicans: "With the Romans we know everything and expect nothing; with you we know nothing and expect everything." In general the Orthodox seem to have taken for granted that at least Anglicans and Old Catholics had sufficient ecclesial status to permit negotiation with them concerning the possibility of corporate (re)union. Here negotiations between the Orthodox and the Old Catholics are revealing. These began in the 1870s, but only at a relatively late stage, in the 1890s, was the doctrine of the church mentioned. Until then discussion had centered on the *Filioque* and other classic dogmatic issues.

But what precisely was this ecclesial status? What was the relationship of such groups to the one, holy, catholic and apostolic church spoken of in the Creed? Negotiations with Old Catholics and Anglicans during this period revealed a serious divergence of opinion among the Orthodox themselves. A few adopted what Michael Root has referred to as the "narrow alternative" to the ecclesiological dilemma posed by the fact of Christian divisions: Communities outside one's own, outside the "one true church," are "at most bodies of heretics who are objects of persuasion, more like candidates for interfaith dialogue than ecumenical partners. . . .

8. "The Orthodox Churches and the Ecumenical Movement Prior to 1910," in R. Rouse and S. C. Neil, eds., *A History of the Ecumenical Movement* (London, 1954), pp. 171-215, reprinted in *Collected Works* 2, pp. 161-231. The same history is recounted in somewhat more detailed fashion in "Russian Orthodox Ecumenism in the Nineteenth Century," *Collected Works* 14, pp. 110-63.

All division is thus *from* the church, never within it." A few came close to adopting what Root has referred to as the "broad alternative," according to which "the unity that presently exists among the seemingly divided churches," or at least some of them, "is theologically adequate."[9] For Svetlov (a late-nineteenth-century professor of religion at the University of Kiev), for example, the church was "an invisible or spiritual unity of believers scattered in all Christian churches," of which the Old Catholic Church is, in its own right, as much a part as the Orthodox.[10] But most seem not to have been seriously troubled by such questions — a vestige, perhaps, of pre-Reformation attitudes. Frequently they held to a kind of ecclesiological agnosticism: "We know where the church is; we do not know where it is not." In any case their principal concern was with Faith, with establishing unity in doctrine. They had less to say about Order. That they took for granted.

We come — at long last — to the story of the modern ecumenical movement as this is usually presented, from the 1910 World Missionary Conference in Edinburgh on through the Faith and Order and the Life and Work Movements to the formation of the World Council of Churches and its subsequent activities. As the Orthodox have sometimes complained, the ecumenical movement (thus understood) was essentially Protestant in its origins and inspiration, but its inspiration came from Protestantism of a particular kind and period. Who around the turn of the last century had a lively sense of the scandal of Christian division? Not, by and large, the churches — meaning here the more or less established Protestant churches of northern Europe and North America or for that matter the equally established Orthodox churches of the East. The main impulse for unity came from what we would call parachurch groups and organizations, often transdenominational in their composition, whose leaders — often lay men and women at some remove from the centers of church/denominational power — were deeply committed to the task of evangelization, mission, and the establishment of a better society on the basis of (Protestant) Christian principles. They were convinced of their own fundamental unity — and indeed of their churches' fundamental unity — in matters of Faith, or possibly they just took this for granted. But they were scandalized by the churches' manifest disunity in matters of Order.

9. See Chapter 6 in this volume.
10. Cited by Florovsky, "Russian Orthodox Ecumenism," p. 141.

Clearly all parties — Orthodox, Anglicans, and other Protestants of various sorts — worked with different operative assumptions at this point in the emerging ecumenical movement. What is amazing today is not that the Orthodox (among others) should now be raising questions about the ecumenical movement in general, and more specifically about Orthodox participation in the World Council of Churches, but that they (and others) were willing "to stay together" so long. That this has happened is due, on the Orthodox side, in large part to the work of Fr. Georges Florovsky, an early participant in Faith and Order, one of the founding fathers of the World Council of Churches, and a major — perhaps *the* major — contributor to the 1950 Toronto Statement on "The Church, the Churches, and the World Council of Churches" and its principle of "ecclesiological neutrality." At this point it is difficult to distinguish Florovsky's personal contribution from what has become the received Orthodox position on ecumenical involvement and its ecclesiological significance. This becomes evident if one reads Florovsky's own essays on ecumenical issues and the various statements and separate reports presented by the Orthodox on such occasions as the Evanston Assembly of the WCC (1954), the Oberlin Faith and Order Conference (1957), and the New Delhi Assembly of the WCC (1961). That there is little difference between them should come as no surprise, since Florovsky was the principal drafter of the statements and reports in question. But many of the same affirmations and concerns are expressed in much more recent texts, such as the contributions of the Patriarchate of Constantinople, the Russian Orthodox Church, and the Romanian Orthodox Church to the Common Understanding and Vision (CUV) process (1996 and 1997)[11] and in the "Basic Principles of the Attitude of the Russian Orthodox Church Toward the Other Christian Confessions" (2000).[12] Indeed, even in this last document there are verbal echoes of some of Florovsky's essays.

In any case, before Florovsky most Orthodox engaged in ecumenical activity had not given serious consideration to the ecclesiological implications of Christian division or to the basis for their own ecumenical involvement. Florovsky provided a necessary theological grounding for

---

11. Available most conveniently in *Turn to God, Rejoice in Hope: Orthodox Reflections on the Way to Harare,* ed. T. FitzGerald and P. Bouteneff (Geneva: WCC, 1998), pp. 62-78.

12. Available, among other places, in English translation on the website of the Russian Orthodox Church, www.russian-orthodox-church.org.ru/s2000e13.htm.

Orthodox ecumenical involvement, a way of explaining why the one true church could be involved in a council of churches distinguished by their lack of unity. His ecumenical theology is coherent but complex, and therefore difficult to summarize. Aspects of it also have sometimes been taken out of context, giving a mistaken notion not only of his own thought but also of the nature of Orthodox ecclesiology in general. The following brief quotations and observations are simply an attempt to summarize some of the main themes that emerge throughout his many essays on ecumenical issues.

(1) For Florovsky, first of all, the Orthodox Church "is in very truth *the Church,* i.e., *the true Church* and the only true Church."[13] "The Orthodox Church is conscious and aware of her identity through the ages, in spite of all perplexities and changes. She has kept intact and immaculate the sacred heritage of the Early Church, of the Apostles and the Fathers, 'the faith which was once delivered unto the saints.' She is aware of the identity of her teaching with the apostolic message and the tradition of the Ancient Church."[14] Florovsky therefore is "compelled to regard all other Christian churches as deficient." Basically, in his view, "Christian reunion is simply universal conversion to Orthodoxy."[15] But here no triumphalism is intended. "The Church is still in pilgrimage, still in travail, *in via.* She has her historic failures and losses, she has her own unfinished tasks and problems."[16] For "the *true* church is not yet the *perfect* Church."[17] Neither does Florovsky advocate "soteriological and ecclesiological exclusivism" or the "narrow alternative" mentioned earlier. For him Orthodoxy did not mean simply the faith and practice of one contemporary church among many but rather the faith and practice of the

13. Florovsky, "The True Church," *Collected Works* 13, p. 134. The text in question originally appeared as part of the collective essay "Confessional Loyalty in the Ecumenical Movement," *The Student World* 43 (1950): 57-70.

14. Florovsky, "The Quest for Christian Unity and the Orthodox Church," *Collected Works* 13, pp. 139-40. The article in question was originally published in *Theology and Life* 4 (1961): 197-208.

15. Florovsky, "The True Church," p. 134.

16. Florovsky, "The Quest," p. 140.

17. Florovsky, "The True Church," p. 134. Florovsky uses the same formulation on several other occasions. On its significance for his thought, see C. Kunkel, "The true church is not yet the perfect church": Oekumenisches Denken und Handeln bei Georges Florovsky," in *Tausend Jahre Christentum in Russland,* ed. K. C. Felmy et al. (Göttingen, 1988), pp. 583-90.

early church, which (in his view) was undivided, the church of East and West. The Orthodox Church in a sense was "a continuation, a 'survival' of Ancient Christianity."[18] Her task and unique vocation in the ecumenical movement therefore was not to "impose her own claims" but rather to "remind all Christians of their common heritage and their common background."[19]

(2) With some regularity Florovsky distinguishes between the unity of the *church,* which is realized on earth even now in the Orthodox Church, even though it will be fully manifested only on the Last Day, and the unity of *Christians* or of *Christendom* or of the *Christian* world, which has been tragically shattered. Florovsky's choice of words here may suggest that he wishes quietly to unchurch, if not to unbaptize, the non-Orthodox, that he regards them (oh so politely!) as "separated brethren." But this is not his point. Florovsky takes very seriously the idea that they really are Christians and that God really is quietly at work among them. He is able to do so because of his insistence on the need for a "neo-patristic synthesis," which would be based on the fathers of both East and West. Specifically, Florovsky appreciated Augustine's recognition of the "validity" of the sacraments even outside the visible canonical limits of the church. Indeed, Florovsky goes rather farther than his Roman Catholic contemporaries in this regard. Catholic exclusivism in this period might recognize the validity of the sacraments administered "outside" the one true church, but it also regarded them as inefficacious. Florovsky is more optimistic at this point:

> For Augustine it was not so important that the sacraments of schismatics are "unlawful" or "illicit" . . . ; much more important was the fact that the schism is a dissipation of love. But the love of God overlaps and surmounts the failure of love in man. In the sects themselves and even among heretics the Church continues to perform her saving and sanctifying work. It may not follow, perhaps, that we should say, the schismatics are *still in the Church;* at all events this would not be very precise. It would be more accurate to say that the Church continues to

18. Florovsky, "The Quest," p. 140.

19. Florovsky, "The Testimony of the Church Universal," *Collected Works* 13, p. 165. The text in question is excerpted from "The Eastern Orthodox Church and the Ecumenical Movement," *Theology Today* 7 (1950). See also "The Greek and Latin Mind in the Early Ages of the Church," *Collected Works* 14, pp. 40-47, excerpted from the same article.

work in the schisms in expectation of the mysterious hour when the stubborn heart will be melted in the warmth of "preparatory grace," when the will and thirst for communality and unity will burst into flame and burn. The "validity" of the sacraments among schismatics is the mysterious guarantee of their return to Catholic plenitude and unity.[20]

(3) Florovsky's understanding of the sacraments and their relationship to the church is closely related to his understanding of unity. Unity is God's gracious gift, given in and through the sacraments, and not a human achievement. It is precisely a gift, not a given — i.e., it is not something to be taken for granted. Florovsky therefore was quick to criticize any suggestion that Christians already now, in their visibly divided state, possess a fundamental though invisible unity that now needs only to be manifested. Put slightly differently, Florovsky was quick to criticize any attempt to diminish the seriousness and tragedy of Christian division by substituting union for unity, merger for unanimity. He was especially critical of horizontal adjustments undertaken for various tactical reasons without sufficient concern for doctrinal agreement and historical consistency. Florovsky therefore expressed appreciation for a phrase that appears in a 1960 Faith and Order report and subsequently in the 1961 New Delhi description of "the unity we seek."[21] "The unity which is both God's will and His Gift to His Church is one which brings all in each place . . . into fully committed fellowship with one another . . . and which at the same time unites them with the whole Christian fellowship in all places *and in all ages*. . . ."[22] In general, Florovsky believed, "current ecumenical discussion has been, as it were, excessively and exclusively *planimetrical,* without the third dimension, without depth, both historical and theological. It

20. Florovsky, "The Boundaries of the Church," *Collected Works* 13, p. 43. This important article originally appeared as "The Limits of the Church," *Church Quarterly Review* (October 1933): 117-31. Florovsky treats the relationship between the thought of Cyprian and Augustine even more trenchantly in "St. Cyprian and St. Augustine," *Collected Works* 14, pp. 48-51, excerpted from "The Doctrine of the Church and the Ecumenical Problem." Verbal echoes of Florovsky's words quoted here can be found (along with echoes of *Lumen gentium*) in the "Basic Principles . . ." of the Russian Orthodox Church, 1.15.

21. The New Delhi text is discussed at length in Geoffrey Wainwright's paper (see Chapter 2) and many other places in this volume.

22. Discussed in "The Quest," pp. 138-39.

was a kind of *ecumenism in space,* concerned with the adjustments of the existing denominations as they are at the present."[23] The phrase singled out for attention, however, at least began to answer Florovsky's long-standing plea for an "ecumenism in time."

It would be hard to overestimate the importance of Florovsky's contribution to modern Orthodox ecclesiology. But is the solution to the problem of Christian disunity really as simple as Florovsky seems to think? Florovsky writes, "I would suggest that the way out of the present confusion and into a better future is, unexpectedly, through the past. Divisions can be overcome only by a return to the common mind of the early Church. *There was no uniformity, but there was a common mind.*"[24] Is that really true? Florovsky was pleased when "divided Christians" undertook the "pilgrimage into Christian antiquity."[25] But would they really discover there the one true church? Is the shape of early church history, the thought of the Fathers, the pattern of early church practice, polity, and worship really as consistent as he assumed? The picture that emerges from modern scholarship in these fields suggests much greater diversity, whether in doctrinal articulation or in church order and practice, than Florovsky allows for. And is modern Orthodoxy in fact a readily recognizable "continuation" or "survival" of ancient Christianity, effectively unscathed by its own historical path? Many Orthodox, and indeed many non-Orthodox, like to believe that this is so. Even if "the true church is not yet the perfect church," they like to claim that it is the unchanged and the unchanging church. Here we may have another case of self-definition by way of contradiction: All those other churches have changed, but the Orthodox Church, the one true church, hasn't and never will.

Comments of this sort could be multiplied. One wonders whether Florovsky took seriously enough the historical aspect of the church's life. During the twentieth century, as most others were pursuing an "ecumenism in space," dialoguing with their contemporaries from other churches and traditions, Florovsky was calling for "ecumenism in time," a dialogue with the past. The modern ecumenical movement and the rise of modern historical scholarship made such a twofold dialogue possible. But Florovsky's will-

---

23. Florovsky, "The Quest," p. 139.

24. Florovsky, "Theological Tensions among Christians," *Collected Works* 13, p. 13. The essay in question originally appeared in *The Christian Leader* 5 (1950).

25. Florovsky, "The Quest," p. 143.

ingness to pursue "ecumenism in time" was, in effect, compromised by some of the presuppositions he brought to "ecumenism in space." He expected non-Orthodox Christians to "undertake the pilgrimage into Christian antiquity" in the confidence that they would find there the one true church, the Orthodox Church. But he himself seems to have been unwilling or unprepared to enter fully into such a pilgrimage or to acknowledge all the risks and perplexities that such a pilgrimage might involve. In principle, dialogue with the past should involve a serious effort to accept and understand that past on its own terms, to recognize the possibility of its differentness from our own situation, not just its similarity. Only this allows the possibility of spiritual growth, of deeper self-understanding, of deeper understanding of the many factors that impinge on our relations with others. We cannot hope to understand the answers given by our own tradition or any other (e.g., the Nicene-Constantinopolitan Creed) unless we first take the trouble really to understand the questions that gave rise to these answers in the first place. So also, we cannot hope to apply these answers to our own situation unless we first take the trouble to understand what questions people really are asking today. Florovsky — and to an even greater degree some of his less sensitive heirs — looked to the past mainly to confirm present-day Orthodoxy's essential identity and unity with that past. He tended to evaluate the past on the basis of present-day Orthodoxy (or possibly his own personal vision of what present-day Orthodoxy should be) rather than vice versa. This was not an approach conducive to real engagement and unity.

Serious engagement with the past can be unsettling. Certainly since Walter Bauer's *Orthodoxy and Heresy in Earliest Christianity,* the discoveries at Nag Hammadi, and more recently various postmodern reconstructions of early "alternative Christianities," many have become rather cynical about the very possibility of a normative orthodox — catholic — Christianity. It no longer is possible to view the history of the true church and its relationship to heresy and schism simply as the history of the latter's innovations and secessions from the pure and unchanging former. And this has had serious consequences for the ecumenical movement. Theologies and practices inspired by various ancient "alternative Christianities" (usually Gnostic), which once would have been roundly condemned as heretical, now are presented as legitimate and appropriate manifestations of diversity. As Metropolitan Kyril of Smolensk has remarked, "The World Council of Churches prefers not to use the word 'heresy' and replaces it with a vague notion of 'pluralism.' As far as I remember, the word 'heresy' was used only once in the early 70s in connection with a debate on racism which was called heresy at that time. I do not recall any other occasions."[26]

Yet without such an engagement with the past, it is hard to see how any authentic "ecumenism in time" will be possible. As the Orthodox know very well, for many the experience of modern "ecumenism in space" has been unsettling. But it also has been exhilarating and in fact liberating, and through it all, participants — even the Orthodox — have managed to stay together. Perhaps our experience of "ecumenism in time" will prove to be equally exhilarating and equally liberating. Perhaps we will be able to affirm our past, and recognize even in its differentness the same Holy Spirit at work forming the one body of Christ. In any case, renewed attention to the question of the church's continuity, and not just to its planimetric unity, is long overdue.[27]

---

26. "Orthodox Relations with the World Council of Churches," in Georges Lemopoulos, ed., *The Ecumenical Movement, the Churches, and the World Council of Churches: An Orthodox Contribution to the Reflection Process on "the Common Understanding and Vision of the WCC"* (Geneva: WCC, 1997).

27. For the beginnings of such an effort, from an Orthodox perspective, see J. Behr, *The Formation of Christian Theology,* vol. 1: *The Way to Nicaea* (Crestwood, N.Y.: St. Vladimir's, 2001).

The Crisis of Orthodox Ecclesiology

VIGEN GUROIAN

At the Third Assembly of the World Council of Churches held in New Delhi in 1961, the Orthodox representatives of the Section on Unity submitted a response to the advance report of the Commission on Faith and Order. They praised Faith and Order's pronouncement that "'ecumenism in faith with all ages' [is] one of the normative prerequisites of unity."[1] New Delhi made this kernel of ecclesiological wisdom the heart of its famous prescription for church unity, as it adopted with just small revisions the full statement that Faith and Order submitted to the Assembly. New Delhi affirmed that genuine unity, "which is both God's will and his gift to his church," must necessarily be a fellowship "made visible as all in each place who are baptized in Jesus Christ and confess him as Lord and Savior." It went on to say this fellowship is both spatial and across time. It is "in all places and in all ages." In a memorable address to the Assembly, the Greek Orthodox theologian Nikos Nissiotis summarized the Orthodox position and what I take to be the spirit of New Delhi. Nissiotis stated:

> In Orthodox thinking Church Union is an absolute reality pre-established by God. It is not a "spiritualized," sentimental, humanistic expression, of good will. It is not the result of a human agreement or of the acceptance of a particular confessional position. Unity among

1. Gennadios Limouris, ed., *Orthodox Visions of Ecumenism: Statements, Messages and Reports on the Ecumenical Movement, 1902-1992* (Geneva: WCC, 1994), p. 30.

Christians is to be identified with the union of the Father and the Son — "that they may be one, even as we are one" (John 17:22-23). Unity among men in the Church is the result, the reflection, of the event of the Father's union with Christ by his Spirit realized in the historical Church on the day of Pentecost. The One undivided historical Church is the outcome of God's revelation and his real Presence which is realistically affected in his Communion with men. Unity is not an *attribute* of the Church, but its very *life*. It is the divine-human interpenetration realized once and for all in the Communion between Word and Flesh in Christ. It includes the act of Creation of man by the Logos; and the reality of the Incarnation of this same Logos in man; man's redemption and regeneration through him, and the participation and consummation of all history in the event of Pentecost — when the Holy Spirit accomplished the communion of mankind in Christ.

Therefore, the Church does not move toward unity through comparison of conceptions of unity, but lives out the union between God and man realized in the communion of the Church as union of men in the Son of Man. We are not here to create unity, but to recapture its vast universal dimensions.[2]

Over the past forty years, Orthodox have steadfastly argued for this christological and trinitarian vision of unity — just as they have consistently rejected every form of incrementalism that denies implicitly or explicitly that unity is the church's very essence and reason for being. They have objected vociferously to recent suggestions that by shared witness and service a spiritual and invisible unity exists, despite visible divisions of Christians into confessions and denominations. On the one hand, unity is not a goal that human organization or schemes of denominational merger can achieve, and on the other hand, neither is it some vague spirituality that can exist apart from visible concord. Rather, unity is God's gift in Jesus Christ bestowed upon all who call upon Him as Lord and are committed to living out that unity in a love that binds them together as one mystical and sacramental body in Christ. New Delhi was brutally realistic about what the churches must do to enjoy this unity. It declared that "Nothing less than a death and rebirth of many forms of church life as we have known them" is required. I intend to return to this

---

2. Constantin G. Patelos, ed., *The Orthodox Church in the Ecumenical Movement: Documents and Statements, 1902-1975* (Geneva: WCC, 1978), pp. 231-32.

stipulation of "death and rebirth" further on because if Orthodox Christians are to be a really credible witness to others as regards true unity, they too must take to heart this imperative to let go of old forms of ecclesial existence and be reborn in a renewed pentecostal spirit. Thus far, they have not shown a willingness to do so.

Orthodox Criticism, Orthodox Responsibility

Yet in many ecumenical contexts, Orthodox spokesmen have condemned denominationalism and called upon Protestants to reform themselves according to the model of unity expounded at New Delhi. In their New Delhi report the Orthodox members fired an initial salvo in the direction of Protestants on this matter. They rejected any and all notions that unity might be constructed out of existing confessions and denominations, as if denominations could be used as building blocks to construct a single structure. They opined that Protestant bureaucratic and organizational approaches to unity are not adequate. They stated that "the Orthodox cannot accept the idea of a 'parity of denomination' and cannot visualize Christian Reunion just as an interdenominational adjustment." They went on to say:

> The Orthodox Church is not a confession, one of many, one among many. For the Orthodox, the Orthodox Church is just the Church. The Orthodox Church is aware and conscious of the identity of her inner structure and of her teaching with the Apostolic message (kerygma) and the tradition of the ancient undivided Church. She finds herself in an unbroken and continuous succession of ministry, sacramental life, and faith. . . . The Orthodox Church, by her inner conviction and consciousness, has a special and exceptional position in the divided Christendom, as bearer of, and witness to, the tradition of the ancient undivided Church, from which all existing denominations stem, by the way of reduction and separation.[3]

Perhaps the key passage from this report is, however, the following: "For the Orthodox the basic ecumenical problem is that of schism. . . . The unity has been broken and must be recovered."[4] From the Orthodox

---

3. Limouris, ed., *Orthodox Visions of Ecumenism,* p. 30.
4. Limouris, ed., *Orthodox Visions of Ecumenism,* p. 30.

standpoint, as injurious as denominationalism is to unity, it is a secondary problem, caused by schism in the one holy, catholic, and apostolic body of Christ. Today, most Protestants, even those that are active within the ecumenical movement, implicitly if not explicitly accept the legitimacy, or the normalcy, of this state of schism (although they do not name this fundamental division as schism).

I affirm the Orthodox position that schism is at the heart and center of the problem of unity, not merely confessionalism or denominationalism. And I agree that schism needs to be named so that it can be healed with the help of the Spirit. This stance, however, entails also a responsibility to seek strenuously to live in accord with the high standard of unity. In traditional Orthodox lands, much exists and persists that puts a lie to the Orthodox position. Old forms of ethnocentrism, nationalism, and establishmentarianism prevail and divide Orthodox churches against one another and against other churches, viciously in some instances. Orthodoxy needs to let old forms die and give birth to new forms of church life that are truly catholic, apostolic, and evangelical. In America, Orthodox Christians need to face and address with complete honesty the fact that, however much their church condemns denominationalism, they have joined the denominational fold *de facto*. This has harmed the ability of the Orthodox churches to persuade others of the imperative of genuine unity. Both here in America and in traditional Orthodox lands, Orthodox must cease pointing out the speck in the other's eye until they are serious about removing the speck from their own.

Here is my contention: If Protestants are guilty of dividing the one body of Christ into confessions and denominations and not being truly willing to let go of those separate and divisive identities, then the Orthodox are guilty of a comparable sin of dividing the one body of Christ into exclusivist national and ethnic churches that they will not let die even when the opportunity arises, as it has in America.

The Sin of Phyletism

There is precedent in Orthodox history for treating this matter with as much severity as my formulation suggests. In 1872 an Orthodox Council was held in Constantinople that condemned the so-called Bulgarian Schism. The Council was not without blemish. It got nasty with its self-righteous invective against "the Bulgarians," as if they alone were guilty of ecclesiastical nationalism. Nevertheless, as John Meyendorff points out, the Council's actions are still worth recalling. For it named and condemned a heresy, "phyletism,"[5] that has weakened Orthodoxy severely in its modern history, and has undermined the high calling of church unity. Phyletism is both a description of conditions under which an ecclesial body exists and its behavior in that environment. Phyletism is a heresy because, at core, these conditions and this behavior deeply contradict the unity of the church. Phyletism arises in situations where several Orthodox national churches exist simultaneously in the same place and claim independent existence from one another premised on racial or nationalist ideology. Phyletism in the American context is the Orthodox version of denominationalism.

The pill that is most bitter for Orthodox to swallow is the idea that they have been complicit in that reduction and separation of the undivided church of which they accuse Protestants and others. But one must be clear about this. The issue is not mere localism or regionalism. Regionalism is not incompatible with the essential unity of the church, as New Delhi made clear. As far back as at least "the fifth century, beyond the borders of the empire, there were independent [Orthodox] churches," for example, the Armenian and Georgian churches, each headed by a primate who often carried the title of *catholicos*. Very early, the identity of these churches was defined primarily along cultural or ethnic lines, and was not tied to Byzantine universalism. In fact their identity was forged over and against real and imagined threats of national and ecclesial absorption by the Byzantines. Issues of regionalism versus the unity of the church certainly were raised by these early occurrences. But these alone did not bring phyletism into being. Later still, independent Orthodox patriarchal sees grew up among Bulgarians, Serbs, and others. "The original ideology of these churches was Byzantine and therefore accepted the principle of a united universal Christian empire," observes John Meyendorff. "The failure of Bulgarian and Serbian leaders, [however], to secure the imperial throne for themselves led in practice to the creation of monarchies and regional patriarchates." Yet, as Meyendorff adds, even in these instances "there were no canonical obstacles to the existence of . . . patriarchal plural-

---

5. John Meyendorff, *The Byzantine Legacy in the Orthodox Church* (Crestwood, N.Y.: St. Vladimir's, 1982), p. 228.

ism. To the contrary, the ancient canons of Nicea and subsequent councils were still serving as the backbone of Orthodox canon law, and these ancient rules sanctioned ecclesiastical regionalism in the framework of a universal faith."[6] But social, cultural, and ideological forces ultimately intervened that created environments much less hospitable to unity.

The Origin and Fate of the
Orthodox National Churches

These forces included the dissolution of the Byzantine Empire, the invasion of the Turks, the creation and ultimate demise of the Ottoman Empire, the birth of imperial Russia, and the rise of nationalism and the modern nation state. It is reasonable to say that, at the start, the Orthodox national churches were not phyletistic. They consciously sought to cultivate Orthodox peoplehood and in this process arose the idea of a Christian nation. Alexander Schmemann argues that the self-identified national Orthodox church is in itself "justifiable, . . . especially in light of the steady decline of the empire and its universalistic ideology." In the history of the Orthodox East, "the 'Orthodox nation' is not only a reality, but in many ways a 'success'; for in spite of all their deficiencies, tragedies and betrayals, there indeed were such realities as 'Holy Serbia' or 'Holy Russia,' there took place a national birth in Christ, there appeared a national church." The Orthodox national church became the bearer of ethnic and national identity, Schmemann continues, and "there is no need to think of this as a 'deviation' — in merely negative and disparaging terms."[7]

The trouble is that the rise of secular nationalisms and other modern intellectual and social movements transformed virtually all of these national churches into *nationalistic* churches. In sociological terms, this transformation imitates the compromise of the Christian church's identity after the Roman Empire embraced Christianity. The church rightly accepted the call to mission and conversion, but (1) it was overtaken by the empire's powerful universalistic ideology and claim to be the kingdom

---

6. Meyendorff, *The Byzantine Legacy*, pp. 224-25.

7. Alexander Schmemann, *Church, World, Mission* (Crestwood, N.Y.: St. Vladimir's, 1979), p. 99.

of God realized on earth, and (2) it succumbed to a self-definition as mere sacral instrument and legitimizer of the empire's civil religion. In this a profound lesson may be learned about Christian realism and the need for it whenever and wherever the church is navigating political waters. But that is a matter for another occasion.[8]

While Schmemann argues that the historical development of the national Orthodox churches can be justified in the relative terms, he also makes clear that this has had a cost. The norm of universality and the missionary character of the church were compromised. More strident Orthodox apologists see things differently. They insist that the development of the national church was entirely compatible with the essential ecclesiology of the church. This claim, however, ignores the actual historical forces that successfully competed against and subverted that truly catholic and apostolic understanding of the church. In virtually all instances, whether among Russians or Serbians, Greeks or Armenians, religio-nationalist myths and secular ideologies came into play that justified the subservience of the national church to the secular goal of nation statehood. Ottoman rule already had narrowed severely the church's vision, but this later combination of forces and influences verily gutted and displaced all the rest that was left of a sense of freedom and independent ecclesial identity in these churches. They succumbed to the intoxicating and enthralling influence of modern nationalism.

In recent times, some Orthodox leaders have tried to draw a distinction between national identity and nationalism in order to make a latter-day defense of the national church model. The late Armenian Patriarch Karekin I was one. In an address he delivered in 1964 entitled "Church and Nation," His Holiness argued that "Christianity becomes the living religion of the nations, and inversely, through which the nations become the people of God, as revealed in and through Christ. Therefore we must conclude that the national element in the Christian church is a natural one, fully justifiable and in no way contradictory to the universal character of Christ's message and mission" if it is "kept in its proper place and within its proper limits."[9] Thirty years later, in 1994, just one year preced-

8. See Vigen Guroian, *Incarnate Love: Essays in Orthodox Ethics,* 2nd edition (Notre Dame: University of Notre Dame Press, 2002), ch. 7.

9. Karekin I, *Challenge to Renewal: Essays for a New Era in the Armenian Church,* ed. Christopher Hagop Zakian (New York: St. Vartan Press, 1996), pp. 31, 37.

ing his enthronement as Catholicos of All Armenians, Karekin I explained to an interviewer: "We need to be able to explain to our people the fact that nationhood *(azkootyune)* is not opposed to religion. It is *nationalism* that repudiates Christian faith — nationalism that is exclusivist, i.e., that does not recognize anything beyond itself, that absolutizes itself. [Whereas] the national character of our church is a unique character and we should not ignore it."[10]

On several occasions I had the opportunity to discuss, even to argue, this distinction that His Holiness drew between the national character of the Armenian Church and nationalism. I challenged that distinction as overly simplified. For it seems to me that this language about nations becoming the people of God, which is so commonly expressed within the Orthodox churches, is fraught with difficulty and danger. If the meaning is limited to the biblical sense that the gentiles are offered the gospel and some, even dominant portions of an ethnic and national group, are converted, that is a legitimate use of the expression. But, unfortunately, this terminology has been employed rather more loosely and broadly. Like so many other Orthodox churchmen, Karekin I was prone to describe the ethnic people as a whole as a Christian people, even though he showed moments of real breakthrough, as in the interview cited above, when His Holiness admitted boldly that most of the people in Armenia are Christian only "nominally," and that the Armenian Church needs to embrace a "*new apostolate,* an evangelistic role in the life of our people."[11]

Nation, National Church, and Nationalism

Despite the discernment of churchmen such as Karekin I, however, in general a dangerous confusion and conflation of the churchly body with the ethnic community prevails in official Orthodox rhetoric and persists in the popular Orthodox mind. This matter becomes even more complicated and convoluted when ordinary people univocally identify the nation and nationhood with the nation state. Then they view the church as an organ of the nation state. Some see it as a useful functioning organ;

10. Karekin I, *Challenge to Renewal,* p. 90.
11. Karekin I, *Challenge to Renewal,* p. 87.

others, more secular sorts usually, view it as a rather useless organ, like the human appendix. In both cases, the church is diminished in stature and misunderstood in principle.

Furthermore, since at least the French Revolution, a distinction between nation and nationalism has become increasingly problematic. This is dangerous for correct thinking about the essential character of the church. Modern nations and national movements create and embrace nationalism. Nationalism becomes the "religion" of the modern nation state. And it is in some real sense obligatory, or at the very least highly convenient, for churches that have identified themselves closely with an ethnic or national group to pay obeisance to nationalism. Nationalism becomes the religion of the church as well. A golden calf is set up inside the holy sanctuary. As Schmemann says, the national idolatry subverts and threatens to replace the true worship. The very essence of the church "begins to be viewed in terms of . . . nationalism." This has marked "an alarming . . . [internal] deterioration" of Orthodoxy in the modern era.[12] It is not just that there has occurred a reduction of catholic consciousness inside of Orthodox churches. Unity also is undermined. When Orthodox churches absorb nationalism into their bloodstreams, they become supporters and even enthusiastic legitimizers of secular national movements. They contribute to the conflict between competing nationalisms.

As ecumenical actors, the Orthodox churches have infused the modern movement with a powerful ecclesiology of the essential unity of the church; but as historical actors they have been agents of church disunity. Sadly, with the fall of the Soviet Union and Communism in many of the traditional "Orthodox" lands, the old ethnocentrisms that Communist rule muted have risen up with even louder and more strident voices than before. Divisiveness and contentiousness tied to nationalism also are presently on the rise. And in almost every location, resistance has increased to letting old habits of compromise with the world die and new forms of a truly catholic and evangelical Christian life committed to unity be born.

---

12. Schmemann, *Church, World, Mission*, p. 99.

Diaspora Transmutations:
The Problems and Challenges of Denominationalism

Meanwhile, in the immediate aftermath of the Western diaspora[13] (or dispersions) of the Eastern Christian churches over the course of this past century, Orthodox life in the so-called diaspora has undergone critical transmutations, a real crisis whose effects are being felt even presently. In North America, in particular, these transmutations have struck at the very core of Orthodox belief and sense of church. Yet Orthodox have not adequately studied these changes sociologically or analyzed them theologically. The crisis has been addressed from the standpoint of canon law, however. For when the various regional and national Orthodox churches of the Old World settled and collected in North America, they quickly planted a multiplicity of overlapping jurisdictions. This created a novel situation that contradicts the rule and standard of one Orthodox bishop in each "city." Bulgarians, Serbs, Russians, Greeks, and Romanians not only brought over their own church but their own bishops, and they established new dioceses. Addressing the canonical issue was virtually unavoidable, but it is not yet resolved.

As significant and urgent as this canonical conundrum is, most who have written on the subject are in agreement that, at core, the problem is not merely juridical or jurisdictional. It constitutes, rather, a deep crisis in ecclesiology, which so long as it continues and is not effectively answered, severely weakens the Orthodox witness to unity. It is a crisis inextricably connected to religious pluralism and denominationalism.

In his classic study *The Social Sources of Denominationalism* (1929), H. Richard Niebuhr defined the nature of the denomination in terms that, despite their demurral, certainly apply to the Orthodox churches in North America. The Orthodox at New Delhi said that they would not "accept a 'parity of denomination.'" In North America, however, Orthodox *have made* this accommodation. "The cultural quality of nationalism . . . rather then its ethnic character must be considered as one of the probable sources of denominationalism," Niebuhr wrote. Denominations, like

---

13. On the meaning of diaspora and its questionable use in theological speech about the church see John Meyendorff, *Catholicity and the Church* (Crestwood, N.Y.: St. Vladimir's, 1983), ch. 6; and Vigen Guroian, *Faith, Church, Mission* (New York: Prelacy of the Armenian Church, 1995), pp. 21-31.

the national churches from which they originate, "are separated and kept distinct by differences of language and of habitual modes of thought" more than by "physical traits, and the former are only incidentally rooted in the latter."[14] In sociological terms, little distinguishes the situation of the Russian, Greek, or Armenian churches in North America from the German or Swedish Lutheran churches and the Dutch Reformed of an earlier era. Niebuhr demonstrated that the sources of American denominationalism are in the national and nationalistic character of the immigrant churches. The Orthodox national churches, like other Protestant churches that have preceded them in the American parade of churches, have carried to America within their very ecclesial bodies the basic elements out of which denominations are constituted.

The Orthodox have argued that their church is exempt from this recipe for denominationalism. They have said that the Protestant churches lacked the right ecclesiology and were bound to splinter into denominations, whereas the Orthodox ecclesiology is a prophylactic against such a thing occurring. The practical ecclesial and social realities of Orthodox existence in the Western diaspora, however, belie this claim of invulnerability to forces of division. I cannot in this short space review all the facts. The best that I can do is to identify several profound ironies in Orthodox life that are worrisome signs of a forthcoming complete accommodation to denominationalism.

First, despite their sacramentally grounded vision of the church, Orthodox in America have adopted ad hoc a distinctly American instrumentalist ecclesiology. It makes no difference whether we are speaking of Greeks, Ukrainians, Armenians, or Romanians. All use their church as a tool of ethnic self-preservation. This works for a time, but at a great cost to the integrity of the church. In the longer haul, when the ethnic identity atrophies and fades, a spiritually hollow denomination grows in the place of the former ethnic enclave. No, the hard reality is that in North America, the ethnic and national flavor of these churches is transitional. If that were understood and accepted, then the way would be cleared for a compelling vision of a united Orthodoxy in America. This would be a true unity based in the right ecclesiology and in the sacramental reality of the One Church, which even an ethnically divided Orthodoxy still honors.

14. H. Richard Niebuhr, *The Social Sources of Denominationalism* (Cleveland and New York: Meridian Books, 1957), p. 110.

Alexander Schmemann states this matter precisely: "What is required, therefore, is not only unity of cooperation *among* various national 'jurisdictions,' but a return to the real idea of unity as expressing the unity of the Church and the catholicity of her faith and tradition, not a 'united' Church, but the *Church*."[15] Then Orthodoxy genuinely would stand in its full integrity as the One Body of Christ and could convict all those who, for whatever their reasons, persist in keeping the church divided in America.

While the transplanted national church is in jeopardy of becoming a sect or denomination because it clings too strongly to its ethnic identity, I am not saying that this identity and character are valueless and that its members must simply forget it or throw it overboard and become "truly" American. Alexander Schmemann defines the Charybdis and Scylla of stubborn ethnocentrism, on the one hand, and mindless Americanization, on the other, through which Orthodoxy must find the means to steer successfully. He writes:

> For the first time in its whole history, Orthodoxy must live within a secular culture. This presents enormous spiritual problems. . . . What is important . . . is that the concept of "americanization" and "American" Orthodoxy is thus far from being a simple one. It is a great error to think that all problems are solved by the use of English in services, essential as it is. For the real problem (and we will probably only begin to realize and to face it when "everything" is translated into English) is that of culture, of a way of life. . . . Deprived of this living interrelation with culture, of this claim [in old lands] to the *whole* of life, Orthodoxy, in spite of all formal rectitude of dogma and liturgy, betrays and loses something absolutely essential [in the new American milieu]. And this explains the instinctive attachment of so many Orthodox, even American born, to the "national" forms of Orthodoxy, their resistance, however narrow-minded and "nationalistic," to a complete divorce between Orthodoxy and its various national expressions.[16]

In other words, Orthodoxy should not become simply American. In fact "there is not and there cannot be a religion *of* America in the sense in

---

15. Alexander Schmemann, "Problems of Orthodoxy in America: The Canonical Problem," *St. Vladimir's Quarterly* 8, no. 2 (1964): 79.
16. Schmemann, "Problems of Orthodoxy," p. 78.

which Orthodoxy is the religion of Greece or Russia." Likewise, Orthodoxy can never be American in the way that it has been Greek, Serbian, or
Armenian. One cannot by "a surgical operation called 'americanization'
distill a pure Orthodoxy in itself, without disconnecting it from its flesh
and blood, making it a lifeless form."[17] Yet if this "americanization" is
completely resisted, atrophy and death surely will come also. Therefore,
Orthodox Christians need to employ their theology and ecclesiology with
a new and sharpened awareness in America. They must be attentive to
this truth: that in order to prosper the church has to initiate renewal and
renovation in a timely way, but that the church also has to be careful not
to set aside its old forms too quickly, thus jeopardizing its core identity.

Recent trends of fairly large-scale conversion to Orthodoxy in
America present the opportunity for renewed mission and witness to the
unity of the church. But they also present the danger of blindly following
the path to a wholly denominational mentality. Ironically, the national
Orthodox Church's resistance to assimilation in an "alien" culture makes
it an especially attractive retreat for disaffected, disillusioned, or embit-
tered Protestants and Roman Catholics. These new converts often bring
with them virulent strains of voluntarism and a desire to transform their
newly adopted church into another sort of enclave other than the traditional ethnically defined Greek, Russian, or Syrian parish. They can dominate in the parish, push to the sidelines the old and atrophying ethnic
identities and habits, and create for themselves a safe refuge from the secular culture or a strategic citadel from which to wage the culture wars.
Perhaps, this constitutes the very worst sort of Americanization of Orthodoxy and transmutation into sect or denomination. Yet, ironically, this
possibility comes about precisely because the national church long ago
lost its sense of mission, whilst in America the ethnic parish never learned
how to catechize effectively.

Conclusion

Despite this somewhat grim analysis and prognostication, I want to insist
one last time that I embrace the Orthodox claim that the right ecclesiology can make a vital difference in the shape the church takes in the

17. Schmemann, "Problems of Orthodoxy," pp. 77, 78.

world. I believe that ideas and dogmas have consequences. What those consequences will be, however, depends upon human decisions freely reached and open to the guidance of the Holy Spirit. Orthodoxy's best gift to the modern ecumenical movement always has been itself, not a theory of the church, but the *ancient living* church that it is. There is no guarantee that Orthodoxy can resist the same schismatic and divisive forces that afflict all the rest of Christendom. To a large extent, the Orthodox churches already have compromised themselves to these forces, whether here in North America or abroad. In this respect, the admonition and call of New Delhi that "nothing less [is required] than a death and re-birth of many forms of church life as we have known them," applies just as much to the Orthodox Church as to the other churches. Orthodox must bravely follow the Pioneer of their faith on a journey from old and familiar places and ways into God's unpredictable future.

Ecumenism and the Rocky Road to Renewal

WILLIAM J. ABRAHAM

Much of contemporary Christianity has collapsed into a nebulous network of competing renewal movements. So many streams have flowed into the main river that it is now flooded and bursting its banks. At the last count I located over thirty-two renewal groups within mainline Protestantism. Thinking more nationally and globally, much of the history of the church in the twentieth century could be charted by tracking the lives of those renewal movements that have been most visible, namely, the Ecumenical movement, the Civil Rights movement, the Charismatic movement, the Feminist movement, the Church Growth movement, and the like.[1] The end result is ecclesial chaos, for different renewal movements have radically different agendas, and they often work at cross-purposes to each other. They also consume enormous amounts of energy and money.

By renewal movements I mean organized or semi-organized groups that emerge to address this or that problem in the church at large. Characteristically they work out of an assumed network of presuppositions that involve three distinct elements. They offer a description of the current scene that highlights a particular problem; they provide a diagnosis of what has gone wrong; and they develop a patchwork of insights and practices that operates as a prescription or cure. Not surprisingly, renewal movements quickly shade off into reform, revisionist, and restoration move-

---

1. For a review and analysis of competing visions of renewal see my *The Logic of Renewal* (Grand Rapids: Eerdmans, 2004).

ments, for the particular schemas of description-diagnosis-prescription spread out like weeds in novel and surprising directions.

The ecumenical movement clearly represents a paradigm case of a renewal movement in twentieth-century Christianity. Leaving aside the description of the wider background situation at the end of the nineteenth century, we can see that its great architects began by highlighting the problem of disunity within the church and then sallied forth to address this issue in a thoroughly persistent manner. Over time they invented a series of institutional mechanisms to bring about the visible unity of the church. The favored mechanisms to date have been local, national, and worldwide councils, research committees, study groups, conferences, annual prayer meetings, official reports, and bureaucratic offices. It is small wonder in these circumstances that ecumenism might not turn up on most people's list of renewal movements. The mechanisms invented have, as it were, taken on a life of their own and overshadowed the original vision; the instruments of renewal have become identified as mere instruments; the original vision of renewal is lost from view.

In the originating ecumenical vision of the twentieth century, it is very clear that ecumenism was invented not just to solve the problem of unity but also to advance the evangelistic work of the church. One major argument for unity was that unity is a significant condition of successful evangelism. Christians should be one that the world might believe.[2] For many, this was the crucial theological motivation winning them to ecumenism.

Yet the connection between ecumenism and evangelism was eroded over the generations. The story behind this development is very complicated.[3] As already noted, ecumenism became so demanding that it became an end in itself for many. There was a time, in fact, when ecumenism was the ticket to preferment and status, if not job security, within the church. Ecumenical institutionalism was a safe haven for steady minds and safe hands. Over time, many ecumenists shifted understandably to fold evangelism into the wider category of mission. In turn, other ecumenists reduced mission to ministries of peace and justice. Thus the

2. John 17:21.

3. Whatever the original motives and reasons for ecumenism, it became clear over time, if it was not clear from the beginning, that the oneness or unity of the church was axiomatic in any serious ecclesiology. Thus in what follows I may be underestimating the strictly theological and ecclesiological factors in play.

internal borders of ecumenical thought and practice twisted and turned in ways that undermined the originating intention to tie ecumenism tightly to evangelism. This left many committed to the original vision of ecumenism out in the cold. Not surprisingly, many gave up on ecumenism. Ecumenism had gone sour for them, and they could no longer invest time and energy sustaining it.

One of the most startling developments over the last thirty years has been the loss of passion about ecumenism within mainline Protestantism. It is not too brutal to say that ecumenism is now brain dead.[4] Folk still pay lip service to it, but the first love, if it ever existed, is gone. Compared to the fifties and sixties, the best and the brightest in the younger leadership of the church have abandoned the ecumenical seas and gone sailing in other waters. Currently, the reward system for top-ranking pastors operates in a world where any commitment to ecumenism is idling.

Aside from losing the allegiance of those Christians whose first commitment in mission was evangelism, at least four factors are at play here. First, massive decline in the mainline churches has led to a scramble to stem the losses that were first seriously registered in the 1980s. Human agents have limited amounts of energy; much of the energy of the current generation has been redirected to addressing the problem of decline. As a result, ecumenism was shunted off the working priority lists of action.

Second, one highly favored way to address decline was to turn to the Church Growth movement. Thus ecumenism ran quickly into conflict with another significant renewal movement of the twentieth century. The Church Growth movement impacted the fortunes of ecumenism in two ways that were profoundly subversive. Through the voluminous writings of its chief architect, Donald A. McGavran, mainline church leaders met a determined critic of the instruments of modern ecumenism. McGavran excoriated the World Council of Churches again and again for its neglect

---

4. It is a mark of the enormous strength of ecumenism in the mid-twentieth century that it survived the onslaught of its critics in North America. For a long stretch, the ecumenical movement, and more particularly, the World Council of Churches, was seen as the conduit for communism and all sorts of other nasty conspiracies that were thought to be abroad in the world. Thus opposition to ecumenism was a central feature of the Cold War in the West. Given that some evangelicals shared such worries, and given the rise of evangelicalism within the mainline tradition, it may well be the case that the echoes and traces of older voices may have been a significant factor in the decline of ecumenical enthusiasm in the 1980s and 1990s. I leave this aside in the present analysis.

of evangelism and church growth.[5] Coming from an insider, that is, a member of the more "liberal" Disciples of Christ, this criticism cut deeply into the credibility of the ecumenical movement. Furthermore, Church Growth research and strategies were constituted by a radical pragmatism and empiricism that made ecumenism purely instrumental. Thus the concern with church growth could be very easily turned against ecumenism. After all, if disunity and diversity are causally effective in growing congregations, then so be it. What matters above all else is the making of disciples. If effective strategies in this domain conflict with the ecumenical movement, then we must ditch ecumenism. The prevailing consensus among many mainline pastors is that unity, rather than fostering the growth of local congregations, hinders it. Anecdotal testimonies and the decline figures, say, for the United Church of Canada, only serve to confirm this observation.

Third, mainline churches themselves have embraced diversity with a vengeance. In part, commitment to diversity has stemmed from the impact of the Civil Rights movement, which drew attention to the moral failures of the American church overall in the area of race relations. In time, the commitment to diversity was reinforced by the Feminist movement and by other liberation movements that made the moral and theological repair of the faith a consuming priority. As a result, race, gender, and ethnic identity became so pivotal that transgression of these boundaries overrode any other commitment that got in their way. Ecumenism, as generally and indeed properly understood, that is, as the quest for visible, organic unity, became sidelined. Alternatively, the ecumenical vision was skillfully reworked and reinterpreted so that it could be a vehicle for the new theological positions that did not have an inadequate overall vision of unity.

Fourth, in and around these swirling winds lay an even deeper problem, namely, the problem of theological disagreement on how to respond to modernity. The crucial issue overall was how far to resist or to accommodate the challenges of the Enlightenment. The best way forward, so many thought, was to embrace whatever version of theological pluralism

5. McGavran graphically captured the crucial issue for many when he identified three billion who had never heard of Christ. See, for example, Donald A. McGavran, "Today's Task, Opportunity, and Imperative," in Ralph D. Winter and Steven C. Hawthorne, eds., *Perspectives on the World Christian Movement, a Reader* (Pasadena, Calif.: William Carey Library, 1981), p. 541.

would work; that is, the strategy was to save as many theological options as possible. Thus a valiant effort has been made to develop an ecclesiology of hospitality that will make room for liberals and conservatives, for radicals and orthodox, for traditionalists and revisionists, and so on. The ecclesiology on offer is in fact a mere baptizing of the status quo; it is not a genuine unity of mind, body, and soul. While this vision has rightly called attention to neglected factors in the dialectic of unity and diversity, it does not offer a fully comprehensive vision of unity as a whole.

In reality, pluralism is a stopgap arrangement that cannot survive intellectual scrutiny. To be sure, the ideology of pluralism still lives on fitfully, but pluralism is at bottom incoherent. At one and the same time its proponents develop an ecclesiology that is officially inclusive but cannot find a ready home for a critical constituency in its own ranks. Pluralists cannot find a ready place for those forms of orthodoxy that are not prepared to jettison cardinal Christian doctrines like the resurrection, the incarnation, the Trinity, and the like.[6] In principle many orthodox Christians are not satisfied to finesse the issue by opting for a hermeneutical laxity that in reality abandons the substance of Christian doctrines but keeps their verbal form now recast as metaphor, symbol, or religious myth. So pluralism offers an inclusivism that is exclusivist at its very core. While pluralism can pretend to be inclusive, under the surface it is deeply troubled by the existence of Evangelical and Orthodox groups that are committed to a more robust ecclesiology and who cannot in good conscience accept that what they see as heresy has the same status as the canonical faith of the church.

The result has been an accident waiting to happen. Sooner or later the mainline traditions have had to face the danger not just of death by decline but also of death by implosion. Some mainline Protestant denominations are seriously threatened by disunity from within. The tripwire for this crisis turned out to be sexual morality represented by passionate differences over chastity, marriage, and homosexuality, but these in most cases do not begin to capture what is at stake for mature observers. What is at stake below the surface are issues of authority, divine revelation, and ecclesiology. These matters remain utterly unresolved. Hence, contemporary mainline Protestantism is faced with an acute paradox that puts it be-

6. I am not saying that one cannot find an artificial place for these groups, but it is a fitful place marked by unease, suspicion, and not a little paranoia.

tween a rock and a hard place. It has effectively abandoned the quest for visible unity within Christianity as a whole, but it is equally driven by an intense commitment to maintain visible unity within its own ecclesial boundaries. We shall return to this issue later.

It would be fascinating to extend this analysis and explore the problems that now face Roman Catholics, non-mainline Evangelicals,[7] Pentecostals, and Eastern Orthodox in the arena of ecumenism.[8] However, to do this would be a distraction. I want to focus instead on the challenge to ecumenism arising from the emergence of confessional groups within the mainline tradition.[9] It is commonly thought that the current quest for doctrinal renewal poses a very serious, fresh threat to ecumenism. I want to challenge this thesis.

By confessional groups I mean here those groups that have the following four features. First, they are committed to revisiting the classical confessional commitments of their denominations. Thus they are not content to ignore or bypass the originating doctrinal proposals that brought them into existence. Second, they are committed to a generous orthodoxy as developed in the great creeds of the church. They are not satisfied with revisionist and radical versions of Christianity that dismiss the great doctrines of the church as morally oppressive, intellectually incredible, socially and pastorally irrelevant, and the like. Third, they are committed to staying within their current denominations. Thus they have deliberately rejected the separatist option. Fourth, they place their confessional and doctrinal commitments within a wider vision of the church and of its renewal. Thus they welcome any and every manifestation of the work of the Holy Spirit that makes the church all that she is meant to be.

We can promptly understand how this form of renewal can pose a threat to ecumenism. Given the first commitment, that is, the intention to revisit the traditional denominational doctrines, it looks as if we are

7. The current squabbles over Open Theism in the Evangelical Theological Society have barely registered as a serious ecumenical problem.

8. The unease within Eastern Orthodox ranks is especially interesting. Much of it, in my view, stems from an intense recovery of nerve within the heartlands of an Orthodoxy that is intimately committed to local nationalisms. For a wonderful review of this development see Victoria Clark, *Why Angels Fall* (New York: St. Martin's, 2000).

9. I have given a preliminary account of this development in "Confessing Christ: A Quest for Renewal in Contemporary Christianity," in *Interpretation* 51 (1997): 117-29.

back in the nasty old world of denominationalism, the world that has been the inveterate barrier to the serious practice of ecumenism. I immediately grant this perception, and I readily concede that there is a real problem here. The problem cannot be solved, moreover, by dropping this first commitment. For many doctrinal renewalists, revisiting originating doctrine is crucial to their position for at least two reasons.

First, it is precisely the traditional denominational doctrines that provide the critical lifeline to debates about the doctrinal identity of the denominations to which they are faithful. Thus, for United Methodists, for example, one crucial debate concerns precisely what, if any, constitutes the confessional content of the United Methodist Church.[10] The debate about pluralism is a debate about the canonical identity of the tradition that cannot bypass the originating doctrines of the tradition itself. Those who reject "orthodoxy" invariably eliminate or explain away this material. Hence to sidestep the relevant denominational doctrines is to handicap the debate at the outset and to hand victory on a plate to those who have reworked the identity of the denomination to suit their own agendas.

Second, it is precisely in this older material that doctrinal renewalists have a pivotal lifeline back into the classical faith of the church, a faith that they see as integral to the full healing and renewal of the denominations in which they serve their risen Lord. This material, however archaic or odd its verbal vehicle may be, can still operate as a very important means of grace today. It would be foolish in the extreme to set such material aside. Nor in fact should we do so, if we are serious about ecumenism. Ecumenism requires not the setting aside of such material in a cavalier fashion but the ultimate reconciling and even reworking of that material in any future visible church. Hence, contrary to first impressions, the revisiting of the traditional canonical doctrines of the various denominations can be of real service to ecumenism.[11]

On the one hand, revisiting the relevant canonical doctrines secures

10. Three texts deserve mention at this point: William J. Abraham, *Waking from Doctrinal Amnesia* (Nashville: Abingdon, 1995); Scott J. Jones, *United Methodist Doctrine: The Extreme Center* (Nashville: Abingdon, 2002); and Richard Heyduck, *The Recovery of Doctrine in the Contemporary Church* (Waco, Tex.: Baylor University Press, 2002).

11. One thinks immediately of the important doctrinal rapprochements between Eastern Orthodox Christians and Coptic Christians on Christology and between Lutherans and Roman Catholics on justification.

the theological integrity of ecumenism by taking doctrines seriously, by recognizing the potential limitations of current denominational positions, and by facing fully and squarely the issues to be resolved over time. On the other hand, reappropriating the canonical doctrines paves the way for the full and intentional embrace of the great faith of the church, as secured, say, in the Nicene Creed, by bringing out just how pivotal that faith has been in the history of mainline Protestantism. Such work gives the lie to the common reduction of mainline Protestantism to moralistic legalism, offbeat theology, effervescent piety, social action, bureaucratic efficiency, evangelistic strategy, liberal spirituality, happy-clappy liturgy, ministries of peace and justice, and the like.

Classical ecumenists should, therefore, rejoice that a denomination like the United Methodist Church is awakening from its doctrinal amnesia and coming to terms with its doctrinal history, its cerebral sloppiness, its intellectual laziness, and its doctrinal indifference. Other groups, like Presbyterians and Lutherans, may be sufficiently robust doctrinally to be worried about a false kind of doctrinal precisionism at this point. It would be a grave mistake to foist this worry on others who are recovering their doctrinal nerve and seeking by the most obvious means at their disposal to recover from a bad bout of doctrinal irreverence and theological carelessness.

I readily grant that there are dangers afoot here. Historically, renewal movements within the Western church have been acutely disruptive and divisive. To confine ourselves to the Anglican tradition, both Methodism and Anglo-Catholicism were a great threat to the unity of the Church of England in their day. In the former case, despite John Wesley's best intentions and efforts, renewal gave birth to a whole family of new denominations, which in turn have failed to come together despite a century of ecumenical endeavors. Anglo-Catholicism shook the Anglican tradition to its foundations, and, in the person of John Henry Newman, lost one of the greatest theologians of the nineteenth century to Rome.[12] Thus we can surely agree that doctrinal renewal today can pose a similar threat to unity. When combined with elements mightily at work in the current scene, the dangers of doctrinal revitalization to ecumenism can be

---

12. For a fascinating interpretation of Newman that highlights the divisive potential of Newman's Anglo-Catholic theological vision, see Frank M. Turner, *John Henry Newman* (New Haven: Yale University Press, 2002).

great. We can well imagine what an aggressive doctrinal vision wedded to a secularist mentality of church growth will do to ecumenical renewal. Such a shotgun wedding will abort ecumenism by making a virtue out of proclaiming a confident self-identity tailor-made to capture one corner of the religious market. However, there are no problem-free solutions to the issues addressed by any form of renewal. Mature renewalists are acutely aware of the pathology of renewal and expect trouble at every turn. They are not going to be discouraged by this kind of development. Sufficient unto the day are the troubles thereof.

Thus far I have laid out three distinct but related theses. First, renewal is a very marked feature of the contemporary situation, so much so that Christianity as a whole in the West has collapsed into a coterie of caucuses, movements, and interest groups. Although it is not often seen in this manner, the ecumenical movement is a paradigm case of a renewal in the church as a whole. Second, ecumenical renewal has run into serious difficulties over the last twenty years or so. It has run out of energy and been displaced by concerns that have surfaced in competing renewal movements, most especially in the Church Growth movement. Third, the recent emergence of confessional renewal movements within mainline Protestantism, while they may initially appear to be an additional threat to ecumenism, need not at all be so. On the contrary, confessional renewal dovetails with robust forms of ecumenical renewal and should be seen as complementary rather than competitive. More positively, confessional renewal is one crucial ingredient in ecumenism.

This last point deserves further exploration. We should note immediately that many forms of renewal naturally foster robust forms of ecumenism. The Charismatic renewal of the last half-century has, in some cases, worked wonders for the practice of ecumenism. Many Protestant charismatics were initially taken aback when they encountered Roman Catholics who were deeply committed to the renewing work of the Holy Spirit in worship, in spiritual revitalization, in recovery of the manifold gifts of the Spirit, and in the deepening of Christian affection. I witnessed this firsthand in Ireland in the 1970s. On all sides stereotypes had to be abandoned, inadequate accounts of the history of the church had to be reworked, and painfully fresh insights had to be thought through with care. A sense of living unity in worship, often a relief from the artificiality of official ecumenical services, provided an alternative vision of what might be possible up ahead for ecumenism.

Equally, it is interesting that many renewal groups have recently sought out each other for advice and counsel, culminating recently in a joint national gathering of theologians in renewal in Dallas in 2002, and a joint national conference later in the fall in Indianapolis. This represents the culmination of many years of informal conversation and networking. Some will be tempted to read these gatherings as seeking safety in numbers, whistling in the dark together, or old-fashioned politics in action. However, this is much too cynical a reading of the situation. In reality it is a sign of the drive to unity inherent in the comprehensive renewal of the church. It is much more accurate to read this development as a new expression of ecumenism, a migration of ecumenical renewal from its current (and sadly failing) embodiment to a more nourishing embodiment. We are entering a period of fresh incubation in ecumenical renewal whose outcome is not yet visible.

We can make this claim because it is vital to distinguish between ecumenical renewal and the instruments or embodiment of ecumenical renewal. The tendency to conflate these is very natural, and it is a mistake commonly made by renewal movements. In the nineteenth century, when the code name for renewal was revival, many revivalists collapsed revival into the practices of revival worked out by Charles Finney.[13] It became popular to confuse revival with the instruments of revival like altar calls, pointed preaching on the atonement, specific patterns of repentance, and certain kinds of music. Thus revival was falsely constituted by the practices and the particular theology worked out by Finney. Not surprisingly, many Christians who found Finney's practices suffocating and spiritually inadequate rejected revival when they rejected his practices. They were not able to distinguish revival from its instruments.

The same mistake has been made in ecumenism. Because astute critics have had to reject the current instruments of ecumenism, they unwisely think they are rejecting ecumenism. Folk confuse ecumenism with the practices and theology of, say, the World Council of Churches, or this or that ecumenical figure. So when they become disillusioned with, say, the current trends and practices of the World Council of Churches and its present leaders, they feel they have to abandon ecumenism. We can understand how this happens psychologically; our empathy cannot, how-

13. Charles Grandison Finney, *Lectures on Revivals of Religion* (Cambridge, Mass.: Harvard University Press, 1960).

ever, override the elementary conceptual mistake that is all too visible. The failure of the current instruments of ecumenism should drive us not to despair but to fresh repentance, deeper reflection, and more sensitive engagement. It should also lead us to explore the pathology of renewal as that relates to ecumenism.[14]

Ecumenical renewal is best understood as a quest for the unity that the Holy Spirit wills for all disciples of Jesus Christ. Ecumenism in its essence is a charismatic phenomenon or process; it is constituted by the intention to receive the gift of unity bestowed on us by the Holy Spirit. Ecumenism is driven at its deepest level by recognition that disunity is sin; it is contrary to the will of the risen Lord who has redeemed us. More positively, it is driven by a vision of God's people as one people throughout the earth, abiding in one body, sharing one faith, blessed by common sacraments, preaching one gospel, and so on. Mere human schemes, institutions, and practices can never achieve such unity; it is a precious gift of the Holy Spirit that can be resisted as well as implemented. Thus the current instruments may fall by the wayside and even become the enemy of ecumenism. Mature ecumenists will be on the lookout for such negative possibilities. They can do so while remaining persistent in their ecumenical passion and unrelenting in embracing whatever new instrumentalities the Holy Spirit may create to achieve what is imperative in renewal as a whole.

We are now in a position to return to a topic left dangling in midair earlier. We noted the striking challenge facing mainline Protestant church leaders who have given up on the quest for visible, organic unity within Christianity as a whole, but who are deeply committed to visible, organic unity within their own denominations. What is needed, surely, is that the quest for unity be tackled as a seamless whole. Rather than local problems of unity acting as an excuse for opting out of the global quest for unity, solving the local problems should proceed simultaneously with a recommitment to global ecumenism.

We need to walk carefully here and not overestimate what is at issue. There are some who trace virtually all the problems in the contemporary

14. The standard problems of renewal show up all too clearly in the history of ecumenism: judgmentalism, pride, power politics, wishful thinking, insensitive institutionalization, financial mismanagement, self-serving bureaucracy, ideological rationalization, and the like.

church to the problem of disunity. The dysfunction produced by disunity is the root cause of other problems of the church; these problems, so the argument goes, can only be addressed in, with, and through resolving the divisions of the church. Ecumenical renewal is, in the end, the only renewal game in town. This strikes me as false and misleading. Ecumenical renewal is indeed a pivotal aspect of comprehensive ecclesial renewal, but there is much more to ecclesial renewal than resolving the problem of disunity. Moreover, we can grant that local disunity is likely to be intimately linked to global disunity in the obvious sense that resolution at the global level is highly likely to be related to resolution at the local level, and vice versa. So current church leaders should seize the challenge of local disunity as a spur to recovering their nerve in ecumenism more generally. We can at least hope that work on one will have knock-on effects on the other.

Clearly the road ahead in all forms of renewal is a rocky one. We can be sure that some will be tempted to despair and that others will be distracted by new problems that few will anticipate. Only a deep acknowledgment of the depths of human sin and a resolute dependence on the matchless ingenuity and power of the Holy Spirit will carry us through. Renewal of any kind is a long-haul, intergenerational process where we live in faith, hope, and love. The journey will continue to be perilous and rocky; the destination up ahead is more than enough to make it worthwhile.

Agents of Unity: Problems and Prospects for a Broadened Ecumenical Participation

P. MARK ACHTEMEIER

The recently published *Growth in Agreement II* presents some of the fruits of a worldwide ecumenical effort that has concentrated its energies largely on upper-level conversation among official delegates of ecclesial communions and international ecumenical agencies.[1] This "top-down" model of dialogue and conversation has produced significant results: the text of *Growth in Agreement II* runs over 900 pages. But as the introduction to that book also acknowledges, these achievements have presented the churches with a growing challenge with the reception and implementation of these ecumenical accords within their grassroots life and ministries.[2]

This essay will offer reflections on the problems and propose possibilities for a different kind of ecumenical engagement, one that involves agents other than the customary cast of denominational and agency representatives. We will consider the potential, and potential difficulties, involved with trying to engage parachurch organizations, denominational renewal movements, and independent congregations as agents in ecumenical work. In an effort to keep the discussion focused, we will consider a specific example of each type of potential agent. While these re-

---

1. Jeffrey Gros, FSC, Harding Meyer, and William G. Rusch, eds., *Growth in Agreement II: Reports and Agreed Statements of Ecumenical Conversations on a World Level, 1982-1998*, WCC Faith and Order Paper No. 187 (Grand Rapids: Eerdmans, 2001).

2. Gros et al., *Growth in Agreement II*, p. xvi.

flections will of necessity be grounded in a North American context, one hopes that they will find resonance in other settings as well.

A Parachurch Initiative:
Evangelicals and Catholics Together

"Evangelicals and Catholics Together: The Christian Mission in the Third Millennium" (ECT) is a joint statement released in March of 1994 over the signatures of fifteen prominent Roman Catholic and Evangelical leaders in the United States.[3] Growing out of a series of private meetings spearheaded by Richard John Neuhaus and Charles Colson, the statement was not produced under the official auspices of any sponsoring church bodies. In its opening paragraph the document states, "This statement cannot speak officially for our communities. It does intend to speak responsibly from our communities and to our communities."

For all its modesty about its lack of official ecclesiastical status, the document does nevertheless propose areas of doctrinal agreement that both Catholics and Evangelicals can affirm: it professes a common missionary hope for the spread of the gospel throughout the world; it issues a call for ongoing theological dialogue over areas of theological disagreement; and it proposes principles to guide cooperative witness by Catholics and Evangelicals throughout the world. In addition, the lengthiest section of the statement outlines a detailed public agenda of cooperative moral and political witness in the North American context.

The release of ECT prompted widespread discussion and some exceedingly sharp criticism, especially in certain evangelical circles.[4] Indeed, two of the document's original framers subsequently withdrew their signatures in response to harsh criticism emanating from within their own Southern Baptist Convention. The document's call for ongoing theological conversation has to date born fruit in the October 1997 release of a subsequent statement, "The Gift of Salvation," that in a manner reminiscent of the Lutheran-Catholic *Joint Declaration on the Doctrine of Justifi-*

---

3. The text of ECT is reproduced in *First Things* 43 (May 1994): 15-22; also available online at http://print.firstthings.com/ftissues/ft9405/articles/mission.html.

4. For a summary of such criticism and an evangelical response, see J. I. Packer, "Crosscurrents among Evangelicals," ch. 6 in Charles Colson and Richard Neuhaus, eds., *Evangelicals and Catholics Together: Toward a Common Mission* (Dallas: Word, 1995).

cation treats matters of grace, salvation, and justification. These issues had been particularly central in Evangelical criticisms of ECT.[5]

ECT is best understood as a parachurch initiative, as neither the Center for Religion and Public Life with which Neuhaus is associated, nor Colson's Prison Fellowship Ministries, is officially associated with any particular church body.[6] That being the case, what can we learn from ECT about the potential for parachurch organizational involvement in ecumenical initiatives?

The largest obstacle standing in the way of significant parachurch ecumenical involvement is precisely the lack of official, accountable connection between these organizations and the various ecclesial communions. That means the effect of such parachurch engagement will necessarily play an indirect role in the work of reconciling particular church bodies.

But being indirect does not mean it is insubstantial. The most prominent feature of the ECT document is the proposal it makes for cooperative witness and mission work among the communities of its signatories. While such cooperative work does not in itself constitute the fullness of church unity, it is not irrelevant to it either. The 1961 New Delhi Declaration describes truly united churches as "having a corporate life reaching out in witness and service to all," and as being able to "act and speak together as occasion requires for the tasks to which God calls his people."[7] The achievement of such a common witness can surely be seen as a stage on the way to full communion.

It is not only the call to cooperative witness and service in ECT that is significant, but the *kind* of cooperative mission envisioned. In a 1995 speech, World Council of Churches General Secretary Konrad Raiser proposed a "paradigm shift" in ecumenical work at the world level, which would henceforth address as its primary concerns the "de facto apartheid

5. The text of "The Gift of Salvation" appears with an introduction by Timothy George in *Christianity Today*, December 8, 1997, pp. 34ff; reproduced online at http://www.christianitytoday.com/ct/7te/7te034.html. Also *First Things* 79 (January 1998): 20-23.

6. J. I. Packer characterizes ECT as a parachurch initiative in Colson and Neuhaus, *Evangelicals and Catholics Together*, pp. 164f.

7. Report of the Section on Unity, Third Assembly of the WCC, New Delhi, 1961; reproduced in Michael Kinnamon and Brian Cope, eds., *The Ecumenical Movement: An Anthology of Key Texts and Voices* (Grand Rapids: Eerdmans, 1997), p. 88.

between rich and poor" and the "progressive degradation of the whole ecosphere."[8] The ECT document calls in similar fashion for cooperative witness and service, but in pursuit of a significantly different (not necessarily opposed) agenda. ECT calls among other things for the churches to work to found politics, law, and culture upon a substantive understanding of moral truth, to establish religious freedom against the claims of secularism, to advance the protection in law of unborn human life, to secure substantive moral formation and parental choice in education, to promote a free society and market-based economy that carefully balances the claims of economics, politics, and culture; and to seek governmental support and strengthening of mediating structures in society such as families, churches, and voluntary associations. Whatever one thinks of its politics, ECT demonstrates how parachurch ecumenical involvement can effectively broaden the range and scope of cooperative witness and service among the churches, thereby drawing into the ecumenical sphere groups of Christians and even whole churches who might find a more restrictively focused agenda alienating. It is certainly the case in my own Presbyterian Church (USA) that support for ecumenical work among conservative and evangelical Presbyterians has been significantly undermined by the perceived identification of world ecumenism with the social agenda of Protestant liberalism. Broadening ecumenical cooperation beyond this narrowly defined agenda opens the way for the entry of denominational constituencies long alienated from the ecumenical movement.

Cooperative witness and service, of course, tend to break down without a foundation in common belief. Here, too, the ECT declaration is illuminating. The text itself makes no attempt to gloss over significant theological differences between Roman Catholics and Evangelicals. But it does lift up a common core of beliefs — at the center of which stands the Apostles' Creed — that the two groups can affirm in common.

In a commentary on the document, Charles Colson cites C. S. Lewis's invocation of "Mere Christianity" as a substantial body of common faith that orthodox Christians of all stripes have in common.[9] ECT, says Colson, "was drafted by believing Catholics and believing Protestants, people at the center of their communions, who realize that they

---

8. Lecture at Rome's Centro Pro Unione, cited in George Weigel, *Witness to Hope: The Biography of John Paul II* (New York: HarperCollins, 1999), p. 763.

9. Colson and Neuhaus, eds., *Evangelicals and Catholics Together,* pp. 34-40.

have more in common with one another than with the borderline liberals of their own traditions." He goes on to say,

> What we emphasize is that evangelicals and Catholics affirm many of the same truths. The deity of Christ, his death on the cross for our sins, his resurrection from the dead, his Second Coming, the infallibility of Scripture — these truths, affirmed in "Evangelicals and Catholics Together," provide a solid foundation for all Christians. Those who can affirm these truths have something in common of monumental significance.[10]

ECT thus suggests the substantial viability of "mere Christianity" as a doctrinal foundation for the involvement of evangelical parachurch groups in ecumenical endeavors, and as a basis upon which to build subsequent theological dialogue. It is worth noting in support of this point that the American Evangelical community itself quite comfortably spans a significant number of denominational boundaries. This is made possible by a central core of shared theological commitments that in a certain sense precede denominationally distinctive stances. It is noteworthy in this context that the Evangelicals comprising the list of original signatures and endorsements of ECT are drawn from the ranks of Southern Baptists, Anglicans, Presbyterians, Methodists, Nazarenes, Assemblies of God, etc.

A Renewal Ministry: PFR

We turn our attention now to the prospects for engaging intradenominational renewal groups in ecumenical work. Our aim is not to lift up their current ecumenical engagement, of which there is very little, but rather to identify the promise that such groups might hold for supporting and fostering efforts toward reconciliation of the churches.

Presbyterians for Renewal (PFR) describes itself as aiming to foster a Presbyterian Church (USA) that

> boldly proclaims Jesus Christ the incarnate Son of God as the only Savior and Lord of the world; confidently relies upon Scripture as the authority for our faith and life; effectively equips disciples to live abundantly in Christ; intentionally develops godly leaders for future

10. Colson and Neuhaus, eds., *Evangelicals and Catholics Together*, p. 36.

generations; consistently supports congregations as the primary agents of God's mission in the world; willingly relies upon healthy governing bodies for accountability, mutual encouragement, and shared witness; courageously embraces action for social justice and evangelism as essential dimensions of our primary task, to proclaim the Good News; faithfully lives with holy abandon in the power of the Holy Spirit, willing to risk all and serve all in order to show the love of Christ to all.[11]

In pursuit of these ends PFR pursues a number of ministries in the areas of youth work, clergy and seminarian support, education, publishing, issues advocacy, and political activism.

If one were to inquire why, at the present time, ecumenical work is wholly off the radar screen of an organization like PFR, one suspects the answer would center around two primary points. The first is a matter of the organization's nature: PFR is an intra-denominational ministry that does not, and indeed cannot, speak in representative fashion for the Presbyterian Church as a whole. The organization has no ability to play an official representative role ecumenically. The second reason for its ecumenical disengagement stems from the organization's vocation: PFR understands its mission as a ministry to one particular denomination, and consequently has no need or calling for ecumenical engagement with other Christians beyond the bounds of Presbyterianism.

Is it possible to make a counter-case for the ecumenical relevance of PFR and other intra-denominational renewal groups? Such a case might center around three points.

First, it is clearly the case that PFR has little role to play in the brand of top-down dialogue among official church delegates that has formed the solid core of the modern ecumenical movement. But as David Yeago points out, the successful forging of "official" ecumenical agreements has turned out to be only one part of the ecumenical challenge, and probably the easiest part at that.[12] The grassroots reception of ecumenical accords has emerged as a significant stumbling block to the long-term progress of the ecumenical movement.

When this "other" aspect of the ecumenical challenge is brought into the picture, the nature of an organization like PFR becomes not a hindrance but a positive asset to ecumenical engagement. Renewal minis-

11. From the PFR website, http://www.pfrenewal.org/about/mission.htm.
12. David S. Yeago, Chapter 3 above.

tries of this sort are nothing if not shapers of the grassroots culture of ecclesial communions, and as such are ideally situated to undertake the long, arduous work of changing the hearts and minds and self-understandings and prejudices that so often block the reception of ecumenical agreement. The key to this lies in making the case to such organizations that this kind of ecumenical advocacy is an indispensable component of a biblically faithful effort at church renewal.

This leads to the second point to be made in favor of PFR's ecumenical relevance, and has to do with the organization's calling. As a ministry to and for its own denomination, nowhere does it show ecumenical engagement in its list of objectives for the renewal of the Presbyterian Church. But a challenge needs to be raised whether it is possible to speak in comprehensive terms of denominational faithfulness *without* speaking about purposeful engagement toward fellowship with other believing Christians. As an organization committed to fostering a truly faithful Presbyterianism, PFR perhaps needs to be gently encouraged to ponder how such faithfulness could possibly be conceived in isolation from Jesus' heartfelt petition "that they may be one, even as we are one."

In short, the absence of any reference to ecumenical engagement in the goals of an organization like PFR suggests the possibility of a different kind of ecumenical dialogue in which PFR could be an active participant. Such a dialogue would be aimed, not at forging doctrinal agreement over contested issues that divide the churches, but at fostering a theological consensus concerning the necessity for ecumenical engagement in any adequate understanding of Christian faithfulness. Such a conversation might also pursue a deeper understanding of how PFR's own vocation within the Presbyterian Church could contribute in a practical way to a faithfulness of that kind.

Suggesting the possibility of such a dialogue raises the interesting question of who the other dialogue partners might be. There is certainly a case to be made that the denomination's own ecumenical office ought to play a major role in initiating such a conversation. But would it be in any way conceivable to imagine that this sort of initiative — intended to foster commitment to the ecumenical process across a wide variety of fronts — might comprise a part of that reconfigured Petrine ministry of worldwide Christian unity that Pope John Paul II has so remarkably invited all of us to imagine along with him in the text of his 1995 encyclical, *Ut unum sint?*

A final and somewhat obvious comment relating to PFR's potential

as an ecumenical agent also warrants mention. PFR is not the only renewal organization in the Protestant mainline. It has numerous counterparts who share very similar values and interests in a host of other communions. Like the Evangelicals who have come together across
denominational lines to participate in efforts like ECT, it would surely be
possible for PFR to form helpful partnerships with its counterparts in
other Protestant communions, and even within the Catholic Church.

An Independent Congregation:
The Father's House Vineyard Christian Fellowship

Located in Cedar Rapids, Iowa, the Father's House (FH) is a self-
governing congregation that avails itself on a voluntary basis of "oversight
and encouragement" by a Regional Coordinator of the Association of
Vineyard Churches. The latter association had its origins in the mid-
1970s in a single "Vineyard" congregation in Los Angeles. From there it
has grown to a network of over 850 Vineyard-affiliated churches worldwide.[13] The church website reveals an institution that holds to quite a
typical "evangelical" and trinitarian confessional stance, offers charismatic
worship with contemporary music, and is overwhelmingly focused on
cultivating the personal religious experience of individual believers.

On the face of it, the prospects for such an independent congregation to serve as an agent of ecumenical unity seem rather dismal. A single,
self-governing congregation seems, after all, about as far removed from
the goals of the worldwide ecumenical movement as it is possible to get.
Surprisingly, however, the congregation proclaims itself committed to
church unity:

> We value UNITY. We are convinced that all who belong to Christ are
> one in His Body, the Church. We aim to maintain unity by honoring
> all who call on Jesus and by intentionally seeking racial and denomina-
> tional reconciliation within all parts of His Church.[14]

The church website further lists "unity within the whole body of Christ, a
relationship with other local churches" as one aspect of what participants

13. http://www.crvineyard.org/HISTORY.htm
14. http://www.crvineyard.org/VALUES.htm

in a Vineyard Christian Fellowship "typically experience."[15] For the sake of the present discussion, two features of this remarkable affirmation are worth attending to carefully.

The first is the model of union that forms the theological basis of this particular ecumenical self-understanding. It is what Avery Dulles has characterized as "spiritual ecumenism,"[16] based on the conviction that truly faithful believers are united with Christ and with one another in an invisible, spiritual fellowship — regardless of the status of their current institutional affiliations. Such an invisible fellowship has tangible effects on church life, as evidenced by FH's determination to honor "all who call on Jesus" and to seek "racial and denominational reconciliation." It thus becomes clear that this "independent" congregation is not so much ecumenically isolated as it is proceeding according to an understanding of ecumenical engagement that is radically different from what has informed the world ecumenical movement. Churches that hold to a "spiritual" understanding of Christian unity are numerous, and their existence suggests the possibility of a committed theological conversation between these churches and others who understand the ecumenical imperative quite differently.

The second notable feature of the FH's commitment to unity is that it is resolutely and exclusively *local*. Careful examination of the website reveals that the "denominational reconciliation" to which the FH community commits itself is not fullness of fellowship at the level of hierarchies and institutions, but cordial, cooperative relationships with neighboring congregations. Now, on the one hand, such a construal of church reconciliation seems disastrously one-sided, reducing the whole panoply of ecumenical challenges to a matter of middle-class niceness at the local level. But, on the other hand, the very one-sidedness of this construal serves to accentuate the overemphasis on the opposite side of the spectrum that has characterized the world ecumenical movement, and which now results in tremendous difficulties with the process of reception of official ecumenical agreements. Is it not the case that successful ecumenical advance will require coordinated and intensive efforts on both ends of the spectrum, and for that reason there may be a great deal to learn and profit from the involvement of churches like FH which specialize, as it were, in the local dimensions of the problem?

15. http://www.crvineyard.org/HISTORY.htm
16. Colson and Neuhaus, eds., *Evangelicals and Catholics Together,* pp. 120f.

Let me conclude this discussion of the local dimensions of ecumenism with a story. A friend of mine, a Presbyterian pastor in Miller, South Dakota, received a call this past spring from the local Catholic parish. The Catholics were planning a prayer service for the Presbyterian church and its ministry, and wanted to find out what might be a good date for their Presbyterian neighbors to join them for this special occasion. Later that spring this same Roman Catholic church also held a large bake sale to help raise money for a local Baptist congregation that was building a new sanctuary. I would submit that efforts such as these require our attention no less than the production of top-level concordats of theological agreement. One can only hope and pray that such creative movements of the Holy Spirit may grow and flourish, until Christ's prayer comes to fruition "that they may all be one."

Speaking for the Spirit
in the Time of Division

TELFORD WORK

The NRSV renders Acts 15:28, "For it seemed good to the Holy Spirit and to us to lay upon you no greater burden than these necessary things." Our traditions have appropriated this text in ways that suggest a more colorful range of paraphrases:

> "The Holy Spirit has authorized us to lay these necessary things upon you."

> "We have authorized the Holy Spirit to lay these necessary things upon you."

> "We have authorized the Holy Spirit to lay these necessary things upon everyone."

> "The Holy Spirit and we hereby micromanage you and anathematize them."

> "We, the Patriarchate of Jerusalem, hereby declare Antioch our turf. (They'll return the favor later.) With this canon, we authorize and anticipate seven future ecumenical councils."

Many thanks to Jonathan Wilson and Bruce Fisk of Westmont College for their patient reading and perceptive criticisms on an earlier draft of this essay, and to the ecclesiology study group of the Center for Catholic and Evangelical Theology, for whom this paper is prepared, for their critical suggestions and corrections.

"We, the Magisterium, hereby faithfully develop the unchanging deposit of the apostolic faith along an infallible, irreformable trajectory that leads from Jerusalem to Rome."

"We who sit on James's throne hereby obscure the gospel of justification by faith alone with the following early Catholic dogma."

"The Jerusalem Presbytery issues the following committee resolution on behalf of the session of the Reformed Church in Palestine. It would keep from offending your brethren if, until they are more firmly established, you would exercise your freedom in the following way."

"The Holy Spirit and we refute all past, present, and future local claims to autonomy by laying these burdens upon you."

"We usurp your congregations' right to autonomy by imposing these unnecessary burdens."

"I, Luke the evangelist, hereby paper over the crisis between Jewish and Gentile Christianity to make the church more appealing to Rome."

"Having been baptized, filled, and slain by the Holy Spirit, we offer this word of knowledge to our sister churches. (Paul has a word too, but he wants to send it himself.)"

"It seemed good to the Holy Spirit and to us to lay upon [women leaders, divorced pastors, homosexual believers] no greater burden."

This little text is a battleground, ammunition, and prize in countless ecclesiological wars. To cite it is to claim divine authority for one's words. Many have presumed to do so.

What are the conditions, if there are any, under which a group of Christians can *speak* to the church on behalf of the Holy Spirit who dwells within it? And what are the conditions for communities to *receive* those findings in that same Spirit?

Most answers are given in terms of political structure: One must speak as a council of apostolic successors, or as the successor of Peter himself, or as a local congregational assembly, or as some other formally authorized and politically delineated Magisterium. Or in terms of doctrine: One must speak in the apostolic tradition as witnessed in Scripture and organized in the normed norms of biblical creeds. Or in terms of charisma: One must be speaking from the anointing of the Holy Spirit. Each has its merits. Yet, what if all these proposals have missed something so basic that without it they are doomed to failure, and so elusive that its absence has characterized many of the church's teachings, despite their triumphs?

This essay explores the ecclesial and theological conditions for speaking and hearing in the Spirit by examining the Council (or Conference)[1] of Jerusalem, to which all Christian traditions have appealed as having paradigmatic authority for ecumenical discernment and problem-solving.[2] *The theme of the passage — God's sudden inclusion of the Gentiles apart from observance of Torah — ties the character and salvation-history of God into every aspect of the Jerusalem meeting and its letter: its setting, communities, articulation, tradition, and reception.* My interpretation argues for an approach to ecumenism that respects the central concerns of the "Pentecostal" (Lesslie Newbigin) or "Baptist" (James McClendon) tradition — that is, the free-church tradition — without absolutely privileging them. Furthermore, it confirms Robert Jenson's proposal that the basic flaw in ecumenical (i.e., Catholic and Protestant) theology is an inadequately Christianized doctrine of God.[3]

---

1. Raymond E. Brown warns of confusing the "meeting" of Acts 15 with the ecumenical councils of the later church. In later Catholic usage, one might call this a *primatial* council. See Raymond E. Brown, *An Introduction to the New Testament* (New York: Doubleday, 1997), p. 306.

2. In recent thought, see John Howard Yoder, "The Hermeneutics of Peoplehood: A Protestant Perspective," in *The Priestly Kingdom: Social Ethics as Gospel* (Notre Dame: University of Notre Dame Press, 1984); Dalton Reimer, "Phases in Problem Solving: A Biblical Model for the Christian Community," *Direction* 19, no. 2 (Fall 1990): 3-17; Luke Timothy Johnson, *Scripture and Discernment: Decision Making in the Church* (Nashville: Abingdon, 1996); Stephen E. Fowl, *Engaging Scripture: A Model for Theological Interpretation* (Malden, Mass.: Blackwell, 1998).

3. Robert W. Jenson, *Unbaptized God: The Basic Flaw in Ecumenical Theology* (Philadelphia: Fortress, 1992). Jenson earlier alluded to this claim in a response to an earlier paper of mine, "Gusty Winds or a Jet Stream? Charismatics and Orthodox on the Spirit of Tradition," delivered in 1999 for the American Academy of Religion Evangelical Theology and Orthodox Theology groups.

Setting

A Failure and Triumph of Vision

The controversy is fundamentally eschatological, in at least two respects. The first respect concerns the issue around which the debate revolves: Does salvation require circumcision? How should Christian practice of the Law reflect the new creation's inauguration? The second respect concerns the role of prior authorities: What authority do these believers have to teach the Law? How do the old structures of authority function in restored, apostolic Israel? Despite their outward differences, these two questions are deeply related, even two respects of one common question.

The Pharisee believers' answer to both is "business as usual." The Torah retains its prior authority in the life of Jesus' people, and its teachers retain their authority to interpret it. The Gentile influx is a new blessing, but it runs along the old lines. Luke is not subtle in implying that the Pharisees' reading of both Law and eschaton fails the fruits-test (15:2). This is true both doctrinally and politically. The cause of the crisis and its threat of schism is the Pharisee believers' failure to discern their new location in the new creation.

So the church gathers and answers in a more eschatologically discerning way. Its leaders come to see the recent events as a Rubicon already crossed. That insight is already familiar to the reader of Acts: "*This is that* spoken of by the prophet Joel." "I do a deed *in your days,* a deed you will never believe." "All the prophets who have spoken, from Samuel and those who came afterwards, also proclaimed *these days.*" "*After this* I will return, . . . says the Lord, who has made these things known *from of old.*" With every event the momentum shifts palpably from old to new as the God of the excluded unveils his cosmic act of inclusion. Eschatological vision brings clarity to the otherwise perplexing issue of Gentile observance of Torah in Christ.

Moreover, eschatological vision construes the Kingdom's authorities in a particular way that looks unlike the Catholic, Protestant, and Orthodox visions that command the lion's share of later theological and ecumenical attention. This is so because the Spirit's unfolding revolution constantly stretches, undermines, and renews old structures of authority. The changing shape of Israel transforms not only Israel's pre-Christian authority structures (e.g., the Christian priests and Pharisees of Acts), but even the apostolic structures already in place at Pentecost.[4] By the middle of Acts, Peter and the Twelve are the "old guard," still ruling over the restored Israel. The newcomers, Barnabas, Paul, and James, have joined the movement since (and on account of) the resurrection. As Acts moves on, Peter decreases, James presides, and Paul increases.

Not Developmentalism, Primitivism, or Radicalism

There is no guarantee that yesterday's authorities will be playing the same roles tomorrow. Doing the job of the first-century church demands a continuing openness to the unpredictable consistency of the Holy Spirit's ever-new work. Thus the very consistency of the task of discernment keeps us from simply grounding a normative method of discernment on original authority structures. Both the primitivism of Baptist and Reformed polity and the developmentalism of Catholic and Orthodox polity dogmatically reject just such prerogatives of the new creation's Creator.[5] They must statutorily reject any pneumatic innovations that might jeopardize the structures on which their theological and denominational distinctives rest. Yet Luke's narrative repeatedly recounts just such innovations.

Yet unpredictable consistency is not unqualified radicalism either. The new creation is renewal, not rejection, of older creation (which is not simply "old creation"). God has chosen both the old guard and the new to be part of the next stage. Furthermore, the two look out for each other: the old guard speaks on behalf of the new (15:7-11), and the new speaks on behalf of the old (15:13-21).

---

4. Consider the roles of three newcomers to church leadership: Barnabas, Paul, and James. Or the Antiochene church's very existence, predicated on nameless refugees from Judea who preached the gospel to Greeks even before Peter's vision. Or the founding of the "diaconate" (Acts 6:1-7). Or the overall shape of the church in Acts 28 compared to its shape in Acts 1.

5. Orthodox developmentalism resembles primitivism in some respects and Catholic developmentalism in others, and Orthodox Christians would be unhappy with the term. Nevertheless, the Orthodox vision does not share the political open-endedness of this vision.

God of the First and Last

To appreciate and honor God's unpredictable consistency in the economy is to appreciate and honor God's unpredictably consistent character. Here I will appeal to two ecumenical authorities: Lesslie Newbigin's *Household of God*[6] and Robert Jenson's *Unbaptized God*. For both, the root cause of the ecumenical impasse and its ultimate solution are eschatological, pneumatological, theological.

Newbigin maintains that the elusive key to the Protestant-Catholic impasse may be the radical "Pentecostal" strand of ecclesiology that eschewed ecumenism in his day. In its appreciation both of God's spontaneity and of the church's eschatological nature, it alone respects the "dangerously revolutionary implications" of the Spirit's work.[7]

Jenson roots the Protestant-Catholic impasse not on the surface issues over which the two sides usually disagree, but in an incompletely Christianized Hellenistic theology still exerting influence throughout the Orthodox, Catholic, and Protestant traditions.[8] By stopping short of its missionary calling to criticize old gods, the Gentile Christian movement failed to overthrow the god of the philosophers in its own thinking. God was still conceived as immune from time, rather than originating it, directing it, and participating in it.[9]

The Catholic tradition (and in a different way, the Orthodox) historicizes the eschaton in order to defend its magisterial authority to write and interpret Scripture. The Protestant tradition dehistoricizes it in order to relativize any temporal authority, even (at the extreme) Scripture itself, so that divine presence is always a discontinuous event. The "Pentecostal" strand, which James McClendon (a Baptist) identifies with what

6. Lesslie Newbigin, *The Household of God* (New York: Friendship, 1954). See in particular the chapters "The Community of the Holy Spirit" and "Christ in You, the Hope of Glory."

7. Newbigin, *The Household of God*, p. 106.

8. For Newbigin, the foe is division; for Jenson, Hellenism; for McClendon, Constantinianism. These different agendas drive somewhat different categories. Eastern Orthodoxy remains out of sight for Newbigin, but in his analysis it is most at home in the Catholic type. Jenson includes Eastern Orthodoxy in his project, sensing both promise and failure there, and locates Baptist ecclesiology under the Protestant umbrella. Again, McClendon endorses the Pentecostal type over the Protestant.

9. Jenson, *Unbaptized God*, pp. 137ff.

he calls "the baptist vision,"[10] inverts the normativity of worldly time over eschaton that drives both of these approaches. Because time's Creator is its eschatological Indweller and Goal, history is a theologically and teleologically determined category.

McClendon characterizes the baptist vision in terms of parallel eschatological claims. First, "this is that" (cf. Acts 2:16 on Joel 2:28-32). The church of the apostles *is* Israel, and *is* the church today. This is not because it lies along the trajectory of institutional apostolic succession. Nor is it because the Word breaks into human history only in discrete events of revelation, which leave the world's linear chronology otherwise intact. It is because "then is now." "The church now *is* the primitive church; *we* are Jesus' followers; the commands are addressed directly to *us*," says McClendon. "And no rejoinder about the date of Jesus' earthly ministry versus today's date can refute that claim" (1986, p. 33).[11] To conflate McClendon and Jenson, we are the world's time, its metanarrative, the people in whom God's story becomes the human story. Jerusalem's apostles and elders are among the ancient people of God whom the blood of Christ and the wind of the Spirit have been regathering from the ends of the earth. And *today*, when *we* assemble and proclaim the will of the Holy Spirit, we do so as the primitive and final church, sharing the common task of discerning the times and telling the gospel as we travel along its divine, human narrative.

Primitivism would seem the inevitable implication of this eschatology. For example, as the necessary condition for speaking for the Spirit, John Howard Yoder proposes a formal *process* patterned closely on the New Testament church rather than either a hierarchically mediated formal apostolic structure or a biblically mediated event of divine inbreaking. That process takes the form of conversation, in a context of forgiveness, through listening to several witnesses (cf. Matt. 18:15, 18), according

10. While the baptist vision is manifested most often in the traditions of the Radical Reformation, McClendon's featured baptist visionaries are Jonathan Edwards, Dietrich Bonhoeffer, and Dorothy Day, as well as the communities of the Pentecostal movement. See James Wm. McClendon Jr., *Ethics* (Nashville: Abingdon, 1986) and *Doctrine* (Nashville: Abingdon, 1994), p. 343. Furthermore, many Baptists do *not* share the vision, especially those formed theologically by classical Protestantism.

11. I have developed McClendon's claims according to eschatological categories in *Living and Active: Scripture in the Economy of Salvation* (Grand Rapids: Eerdmans, 2001), ch. 3 ("The End of Scripture"), and will not repeat them here.

to functions discharged by various organs within the community.[12] Such a conversation will necessarily include agents of prophetic direction (1 Cor. 14:3, 29), agents of scriptural memory (Matt. 13:52), agents of linguistic self-consciousness (teachers, James 3:18), and agents of order and due process (Acts 15:13, 28). "The attestation, 'It has been decided by the Holy Spirit and by us' . . . was a testimony grounded in the formal validity of the conversational process, not in the status of James' throne."[13] Our community is the community of James's original conversation. *This is that.*

Yet even if the free-church vision is right, it demands that we say more. Do not Israel's synagogues, and both Roman and Protestant Magisteria, have all these agents? Then how could *their* ecclesial claims be less authentic?

It is here that Newbigin's "Pentecostal" label is more apt than McClendon's "baptist" label.[14] By appealing to inadequate doctrines of God as the ultimate causes of Christian division, Newbigin and Jenson lead us away from the temptation of supplying conditions for pneumatic speaking that are merely hierarchically, or conversationally, or congregationally political, and from the opposite temptation of denying conditions outright. The Triune God's actions drive us to claim with and for Jerusalem's apostles and elders that *communities and individuals speak for the Holy Spirit insofar as they correctly discern God's character and purposes.* Insofar as the Spirit's spokespeople are appreciating the revealed mystery of the immanent, economic Trinity, their words have divine as well as human authority. "The one whom God has sent utters the words of God, for it is not by measure that he gives the Spirit" (John 3:34). While this verse literally applies only to the Son, in whom apostolicity centers (John 3:35), God has now breathed the Spirit upon Jesus' disciples, individually (John 19:30)[15] and collectively (John 20:22). The divinity of prophetic and apostolic speech is a gift of the Holy Spirit.

Insofar as the Spirit's spokespeople *fail* to honor that mystery, how-

---

12. Yoder, "The Hermeneutics of Peoplehood," pp. 26-28.

13. Yoder, "The Hermeneutics of Peoplehood," pp. 29-34.

14. I develop this distinction in "Reordering Salvation: Church as the Proper Context for an Evangelical *Ordo Salutis*, in *Ecumenical Theology in Worship, Doctrine, and Life: Essays Presented to Geoffrey Wainwright on his Sixtieth Birthday* (New York: Oxford University Press, 1999), pp. 182-95.

15. Thank you, David Yeago, for this insight.

ever, their words and actions, however formally authoritative, are not binding. No polity, process, or proof text can make them so. Rather, these agents are merely "apostles from human authorities" (Gal. 1:1 NRSV) and "*reputed* pillars" (Gal. 2:9) who open themselves to rebuke by the Lord's greater authority.

Such rebukes may not look like hierarchical magisterial hermeneutics. They may not look like free-church conversational hermeneutics. Yet they *are* binding: "We must obey God rather than human beings" (Acts 5:29). Paul, the untimely apostle, is right to condemn even Peter at Antioch (Gal. 2:11) and to judge while absent (1 Cor. 5:3-4). John the prophet is told to judge entire communities in Jesus' name and from a distance (Rev. 1–3).[16]

The structural variety of pneumatic speech does not mean that church structures are unimportant! Jesus' ministry, the entire New Testament, and the church's history all prove otherwise. What it means is that church structures are important in surprising ways. The Spirit's work takes unpredictably consistent turns that can be reliably discerned but never ensured, manipulated, or foreseen. God writes precisely the story Aristotle describes: "One in which each new event is genuinely unpredictable beforehand, but afterward recognized as what had to happen."[17]

If McClendon's baptist vision were merely a reiteration of the futurist (or is it realized?) eschatology of free-church primitivism, it would betray both God's unpredictable consistency and Newbigin's vision of three inadequate types that must defend their existence by appealing to ultimately inadequate criteria for ecclesiological security. Yet McClendon's baptist vision is wider and more Pentecostal than his terminology at first implies. In the final theological exercise of his career, McClendon rejects the normativity of congregational autonomy. He calls catholicity (in W. B. Gallie's phrase) an "essentially contested concept." No party of Christians fully appreciates its meaning, not even his own. Nor does he believe the problem can be solved by adding up the various insights or splitting the differences, if that were even possible. To learn the depth of the church's catholicity demands a shared struggle among all who now

16. Yet, contrary to some Protestant usage, the condemned spokespeople do not forfeit their standing as *apostles* and *churches* (Rev. 3:1). They are invited to have their official authority restored in the new and always renewing order of the church of Jesus Christ.

17. Jenson, *Unbaptized God,* p. 131, quoting *Peri Poietikes* 1452a, 3.

see only in part what we will someday fully understand.[18] The wholeness of "all in each place" demands tolerance, conversation, openness to the future, humility before God — and ultimately ecclesial death and resurrection.

This leads to the next aspect of the Jerusalem meeting: the politics of its communities.

Communities

Are the Antioch and Jerusalem Communities Divided?

One community, the Judean church, has disturbed another by criticizing its constitutive practices. The affected community invites the instigator to help resolve its problem (15:2). Mutually acknowledged authorities from both communities deliberate and come to consensus. How could this story of partisans acting within a fellowship guide the practices of opponents in divided churches who seek unity according to different and incompatible visions?

The differences between then and now are not so vast as they might seem, for until the meeting's conclusion, the communities do not know they are united. In fact, they are *divided* — engaged in deep soteriological dissension (15:2a, 7a) that goes to the heart of the gospel, and political dissension that goes to the nature of Christian authority. Some in Jerusalem undoubtedly see the meeting as a test of Antioch's orthodoxy, not unlike its testing of Samaritan Christianity in Acts 8. On the other hand, Peter and Paul see it as a test of *Jerusalem's* orthodoxy. Peter, who knows from experience, accuses the assembly of "trying God," ominously echoing Luke 4:12. Luke is tactfully silent about Paul's conduct at the meeting (and if Galatians is an indicator of that conduct, wisely so), but Paul may be even more suspicious of James than James of Paul.

Our situation is actually quite similar. Idealized readings of Acts 15, whether Orthodox, Protestant, or Catholic, clothe prior expectations of swift ecumenical success and prior commitments to clear ecumenical failure in auras of orthodoxy. But these fail to discern the times then and so

18. McClendon, *Witness: Systematic Theology,* vol. 3 (Nashville: Abingdon, 2001), pp. 338-39.

misinterpret the times now. Our divided communities cannot help but acknowledge a share of ecclesial standing in each other. Yet by no means are we assured of each other's fundamental health. We have had no small dissension and debate (15:2). The first century's crisis of authority is our own.

If so, then we face a possibility that has been rarely exploited. What if we truly envisioned each other as the partisans of Acts 10–15, rather than the apostates of 1 John 2 or the factions of 1 Corinthians 1? On the grounds of Luke-Acts, is it legitimate for us to acknowledge, even provisionally, each other's authenticity and authority?

Are the Communities Equals?

It is commonly assumed that Antioch and other new communities orbit the Judean center like little planets around a star. Yet Acts 15 portrays a startling degree of *symmetry* between the two communities, a symmetry that reflects the political consequences of the Spirit's unfolding revolution. A Judean inquiry into Antiochene practices prompts what is possibly an Antiochene inquiry into Jerusalem's own. There is dissension and debate at Antioch, and much debate in Jerusalem. A question from Antioch to Jerusalem prompts a response from Jerusalem back to Antioch. Two apostles go up to Jerusalem; two teachers go down to Antioch. Barnabas and Paul, outsiders from Cyprus and Tarsus, testify sandwiched between Peter and James, the ultimate Galilean insiders. Jerusalem affirms the apostolic teaching in Antioch (cf. 13:39-41); Antioch affirms the apostolic teaching in Jerusalem (15:31); both reject the "Judaizing" teaching of unauthorized teachers. Timothy, the story's half-Jewish poster child, personifies the new harmony and interdependence between Jew and Gentile (16:1-5).

To be sure, this symmetry is lopsided. *Jerusalem's* teachers presume to go to Antioch; Antioch sends its apostles to *Jerusalem; Jerusalem* sends a letter advising its neighbors. Of all the world's cities, it alone is indispensable to Jesus' plan (Acts 1:8). Yet even here, Luke is intent on subverting the kind of magisterial triumphalism that later takes hold among some of the apostles' and elders' successors. The center of the church is, ironically, the center of churchly opposition to God's will. If Antioch consults Jerusalem because its people have longer histories with Jesus, they do so in vain, for the assembly can cite no dominical teaching to solve the problem. Luke shows Paul and company going through Samaria and Judea, triangulating against the circumcision party and winning the battle for public opinion (15:3). Jerusalem has the last word on the matter in part because Jerusalem is the last church to *get it* — the last truly to perceive and proclaim the new vision of the Holy Spirit that its sister communities already share.

How seriously have magisterial churches taken this fact?

However, for all the irony, Jerusalem's word remains respected, and its faculty of discernment is ultimately vindicated. If the communities are equals, Jerusalem is the first among them.

How seriously have free churches taken *this* fact?

Jerusalem's eschatological primacy is critical. Constantinianism massively centralized authority along Roman lines; anti-Constantinianism massively decentralized it along European and then American lines. Both visions come from a church that had long neglected Israel as the ethnic and geographical origin, center, *and* goal of the world's salvation, and had learned to envision themselves in terms of the world's kingdoms. Luke's end-times are different from either the Constantinian or anti-Constantinian endgames. Here Jerusalem is neither the seat of the Magisterium, nor one more local church in exile, but the center of a fellowship, itself magisterial, that is reaching out to the ends of the earth (Acts 1:8). It is not *transferring* to the ends of the earth — either to St. Peter's Basilica or to my local sanctuary — but resides in "the dwelling of David" (Amos 9:11 LXX in Acts 15:16).

Therefore the council respects the Spirit's present and future initiative by acknowledging the Law's new role, *and* respects the Spirit's past initiative by acknowledging the synagogues in which Moses is preached (15:21). Subsequent ecumenical decrees have not always been so sensitive to the theological, ethical peculiarities of Israel's people, and so they have exacerbated the most basic Christian division of all. Our Greek, Latin, European, American accents have often garbled the words of Jesus the Nazarene, and sometimes we have substituted the words of our unbaptized gods.

Articulation

What Action Do the Authorities Actually Take?

The council's decree, if it should even be called that,[19] arguably does not impose a rule beyond the prior practices of Christian God-fearers at Antioch.[20] It seems to be an acquittal, so to speak, of Antioch's practices in light of Scripture. The Holy Spirit's decision has already been delivered, in Antioch and Caesarea. The initiative belongs to God, the response to the Antiochian and Judean churches. The apostles and prophets are no more authorized to create new commandments than to relax old ones. That prerogative belongs only to God. So "the Holy Spirit and we have decided" names two chronological moments, not one. The council is interpreting, not legislating. Here we find a surprising resemblance to Paul's own teaching on circumcision, which does not in the end forbid the practice (Gal. 6:15). He too is interpreting rather than legislating.[21]

Such reserve is short-lived. The Spirit's agency eventually comes to be identified with the Magisterium's, and the church begins to invoke the spirit of Acts 15:28 for a far wider variety of canonical discourse. Many supposedly necessary things have come along since the Jerusalem Council. The habit of imposing further uniformity of faith and practice across the Catholic Church comes early, e.g., settling paschal dating controversies through threats of excommunication in the second century, and actual excommunication at Nicea. Moreover, following Montanist excesses, enthusiasm for the Spirit's consistency soon quenches enthusiasm for his unpredictability. Holy Tradition assumes an irreversibility that would have made the Judean teachers blush. The baptist/Pentecostal vision

19. See Peder Borgen, "Catalogues of Vices, the Apostolic Decree, and the Jerusalem Meeting," in Jacob Neusner et al., eds., *The Social World of Formative Christianity and Judaism* (Philadelphia: Fortress, 1988), pp. 126-41, for a rejection of the idea that the letter from Jerusalem is a "decree." Borgen considers the letter's "necessary things" to be an affirmation of prior Jewish and catholic Christian proselyte tradition, which condemns pagan vices, rather than a new apostolic decree (p. 133).

20. Whether these are "ethical" or "ritual," if these distinctions are even helpful, is immaterial to this point.

21. The parallels may be more than formal. Paul's Galatian teaching on pagan vices (5:19-23) echoes the letter's "ethical" necessities (Acts 15:29). If the letter from Jerusalem lies behind the letter to the Galatians, then Paul remains compliant with James's will. But Paul spins boldly, to be sure!

fades, and the stage is set for the Orthodox-Protestant-Catholic show-down.

We need not deny the profound insight and blessing of many of these later actions to ask how often the later church has really been doing what the apostolic church does in Jerusalem. After all, presuming to speak for God magisterially, imposing uniformity of practice, and citing precedent too confidently are the very acts that create the crisis in Antioch. In seeking to imitate the apostles and elders, we have too often resembled the unauthorized Judean teachers.

Tradition

Are Texts Enough?

Two moments of discerning the Spirit, articulation and reception, meet in a third: the process of promulgation or tradition. Here too we find an important quality of Jerusalem's practice. The council's response does not offer the Antiochians any reasons for its conclusions.[22] The reader of Acts may know something of the mind of James,[23] but readers of the Jerusalem letter do not. Instead, Jerusalem sends *teachers* to Antioch. This holds at least twofold significance for ecumenism.

First, Antioch is free to use its own theological reasoning to support its sister church's practical and theological claims. It is advised to appreciate God's character and purpose as Jerusalem does, but it may do so from a different perspective. Likewise, the greatest triumphs of ecumenical discourse, the Nicene-Constantinopolitan Creed and the Chalcedonian Formula, famously omit the reasons for their assertions. Their economy has given them enormous versatility and persuasive power across cultures, eras, and theological traditions. When the church has canonized its theo-

---

22. This surprising omission may be additional evidence that the necessities of the letter are prior practices in Antioch, which would not need explaining.

23. But not much: Are these Torah regulations for "aliens in the land"? or rabbinic traditions about what was forbidden to all Noah's children? Or pragmatic considerations designed to ease friction with Jewish believers and unbelievers? What is clearer from the text than from most of the commentaries is that the regulations recognize the Gentiles' new incorporation as the turning point in the eschatological fulfillment of God's promises to Israel.

logical reasoning along with its theological conclusions, the results have been less successful.

Second, lasting unity comes not merely by joint assent to dogmatic texts, but by *mutual personal presence* in tradition and reception. The right to eat at each other's table means little if no one bothers to exercise it. It is not enough that Paul and Barnabas return with the right hand of fellowship, for the dynamics that aggravated the first crisis would still be ready to stir the next one. So Paul and Barnabas return with Judas and Silas, who strengthen the tenuous bond between the sister churches with their teaching and prophecy. They learn as they teach — and help the still wary communities keep an eye on each other. (As they say in arms control, "Trust, but verify.")

Nothing breaks down barriers like truly shared lives. Here we sense what Yoder was claiming, though it is better expressed in pneumatological terms:[24] *Those indwelt by the Spirit can best discern when they live out the fellowship of the Spirit.* The *practice* of community is essential to spiritual articulation, tradition, and reception, especially across the boundaries that divide. Ecumenism has been stronger on the first two than the third (for instance, in the reception of *Baptism, Eucharist and Ministry (BEM)*, which was largely intra-denominational).[25]

Despite its reputation for sectarian divisiveness, the free-church tradition has wisdom to contribute on this topic. McClendon describes three meanings of catholicity that emerged in the early church. The first, catholicity-as-authenticity, describes the wholeness of any community that embodies a wholly Christian way of life. The second, catholicity-as-universality, describes the full extension of Christian existence over space and time, "the entire authentic new people of God" of which local congregations could be a part. The third, catholicity-as-party, describes the concrete tradition that uses catholicity as a proper noun, a label that distinguishes the true church from other, defective varieties of Christianity.

24. Yoder appeals to these too, but delineates them formally along primitivist lines ("The Hermeneutics of Peoplehood," p. 29).

25. I am willing to be corrected on this point. But the initial recommendations of the *BEM* document were that the representatives of the separated communities were to take the findings back to their own communities, not to each other's. Of course, the Jerusalem meeting did not provoke a schism, at least not at the time, so the communities shared common personal authorities. The common authorities of divided Christian communities may be merely textual.

Each represents not just a vision of catholicity, but a *strategy* for achieving unity. In the third, those lacking full catholicity are exhorted to leave behind their lack and rejoin the true fellowship. The second finds ground for proclaiming "mystic sweet communion," but no concrete instructions for realizing it. The first pursues "the character that is complete or authentic or prototypically Christian," which cannot but bring together the communities that practice it, especially when they practice it together. To John Henry Newman's (and many others') strategy of universality through partisan solidarity, McClendon and Yoder prefer the "baptist path" of universality through authenticity. It is, they say, one pursued in apostolic times and among monastics, Czech Brethren, Anabaptists, General Baptists, Campbellites, and all communities that struggle for "unity first of all with one another" (though less among today's Baptists than their spiritual ancestors).[26] McClendon admits that unity through authenticity may not be the whole prescription, but he rightly senses it is an essential and oft-neglected one.

Reception

What Are the Conditions for Reception?

Reception of the Jerusalem letter has a structural, indeed liturgical, component: "Having gathered the congregation together, they delivered the letter" (Acts 15:30). This structure goes beyond the written text's performance to include the community's reception of Judas and Silas and their exhortations (15:31-32). Yet here too, polity is no guarantee, even when liturgically focused. It has taken anonymous refugees in Antioch and dreams from heaven to bludgeon the church's chief authorities into perceiving an event that had been announced in the scriptures for centuries and already accepted even in Samaria and Syria.

If a certain political structure is neither a necessary condition nor a necessary consequence of pneumatic speaking, then how can authentic speech be known for what it is? Only in the same Spirit in which it was

---

26. McClendon, *Witness*, pp. 335-37, drawing on McClendon and Yoder, "Christian Identity in Ecumenical Perspective," *Journal of Ecumenical Studies* 27, no. 3 (Summer 1990): 561-80.

given.[27] The conditions for reception of God's speech are as theological as those for its articulation and tradition. *It is critical to the authority of the Spirit's spokespeople that their words are authenticated by those who know God's protological character and eschatological end.*

In Acts 15, such authentication is neither particularly rare nor particularly common. On the one hand, it has been going on for some time: In Antioch before Peter's vision; at Cornelius's house; throughout Phoenicia and Samaria. On the other hand, the battle is hard-won. And here too Luke overturns our expectations: Jerusalem is the *last,* not the first, to receive authentication, because Jerusalem is the last community to appreciate this aspect of God's history.

What Counts as Success?

The Jerusalem council has rightly been viewed as a triumph of fellowship over division. But just how complete a triumph is it? Certainly circumcision is soon ruled out as a means of Christian salvation. Yet the euphoria of Acts 15:31-33 is fleeting. Reception of the exhortation is far from uniform. It is authoritative and popular in Jerusalem, at least through Acts 21. It is binding in Antioch and as far west as Lystra. It may even be echoed in *Didache* 6.[28] Yet in Corinth (cf. Acts 19:10), the dietary rules are different. Paul may simply have left Jerusalem's sphere of influence to concentrate on nations farther west.[29] Furthermore, the Jerusalem church is unable or unwilling to defend Paul's reputation as Acts progresses, and James confronts him with the letter in 21:20-25 as if he has not even seen it. The lingering distrust costs Paul dearly on his return to Jerusalem. Relations between Christians and Jews only deteriorate from there, and Paul eventually shakes the dust of the synagogue off his feet (28:25-28).

The later textual tradition of Acts 15 reflects an even wider variety in reception, with serious ecumenical consequences. The famous incompatibilities between the Alexandrian and Western manuscript traditions of the apostolic decree are more than a headache for biblical critics. They reflect

---

27. Newbigin, *The Household of God,* p. 107.

28. "As regards diet, keep the rules so far as you are able; only be careful to refuse anything that has been offered to an idol, for that is the worship of dead gods."

29. Brown, *An Introduction to the New Testament,* p. 309.

an apostolic and patristic church willing to interpret the Jerusalem Council so freely as to change the language, add or drop individual items so as to turn a focus on "ritual" into a focus on "ethics" (or vice versa),[30] and ignore inconvenient prohibitions. Whatever the reason for the divergences (scribes "interpreting" the apostolic words, or Luke revising his own manuscript, or any of the other competing theories[31]), the fact remains that traditions of textual mutation survive in the canon itself. The *Filioque* (which, after all, may fundamentally be a translational issue) pales by comparison.

The exhortation's uneven reception helps us set realistic expectations for ecumenical discourse. Apparently we may interpret ecumenical speech to the point of limiting its synchronic and diachronic scope, and even to the point of changing its very language, without inevitably violating authority or breaking fellowship. Juxtaposing Acts 15 and Galatians 1–2 suggests how much canonical latitude we have. By contrast, actual insubordination to proper authority or break in fellowship constitutes an outright failure to discern somewhere in the process. God's people have then failed either to speak for the Spirit, or to hear in the Spirit.

Even the greatest successes of Constantinian Christianity must on these grounds be judged *relative* failures. This is true even of its crown jewels, the creeds and canons of Nicea 325 and Constantinople 381, on account of the *Filioque* (not because of the textual change itself, but because of the way it has been received so far).[32] Here — *even* here — the theological conditions for discerning have not been fully met. God has not been perfectly understood.[33] The consequences have been incompletely edifying — which is to say that they have been disastrous.

Jenson concludes his project with the dream of a church that looks forward to God as clearly as it looks back to him, and "thus experiences the temporal unity of its own communal self as the personal unity of the risen

---

30. The two terms overlap more than is often appreciated in the critical literature. If the *Didache* is a witness to the apostolic letter (see ch. 6), it already interprets it in an "ethical" direction.

31. Bruce Metzger, in *A Textual Commentary on the Greek New Testament,* 2nd edition (Stuttgart: German Bible Society, 1994), pp. 222-36, lists a dizzying array of proposals.

32. On the other hand, the "Clarification on the Filioque" from the Secretariat of Christian Unity in Rome represents a more positive stream in the *Filioque*'s history of interpretation.

33. Perhaps, as Jenson claims, because the God of the East and West has remained incompletely Christian.

Son."[34] While we do look forward and back in that way, we do it *imperfectly*, and so we are imperfectly one (cf. John 17:23). Like people who ruin the stories they tell, churches have repeatedly proven inadequate to the narrative treasure entrusted to them. Perfect timing is not a quality of the apostolic community that was lost; it was a quality the apostles and prophets never had in the first place. We, like they, lose our place, step on our lines, and argue over the details. Newbigin is right that the more apostolic the church has been, the more it has found its division intolerable.[35]

Yet the categories of *relative* success and failure are an unlikely source of hope. Our long track record of both has somehow sustained us. Our divided communities *have* common authorities. We *do* submit to the authorities of other communities insofar as we hear our Lord's voice in theirs. With God's help, we still manage to stammer out the divine wisdom of our apostolic and prophetic ancestors. For all our disagreement, we finally tell *one* story, about a Jesus whom we recognize in each other's tellings, and so our stories are finally one in his. The strong family resemblances among Christian canonical practices — Bible, sacraments, and so on — indicate that (contrary to Bruce D. Marshall's fear in *First Things*)[36] God has *not* abandoned the divided churches of Jesus Christ. Our common narrative practices do sometimes, incompletely, meet the conditions for articulation, tradition, and reception in the Holy Spirit.

The persistent authority of the church's Scriptures, its rules of faith (embodied in the Apostles' and Nicene Creeds, only the latter of which is inextricably tied to conciliar Constantinianism), its sense of the faithful, its special and general spiritual gifts, its fruit of the Spirit — all of these indicate a living faculty for discernment. Furthermore, our use of these common resources as guides to the whole Christian life shows a common grasp of the connection between the *faith* of the church — that is, its appreciation of the character and purpose of the triune God of Israel — and the *authority* of the church.

This suggests a range of relative authority for the claims that pass

34. Jenson, *Unbaptized God,* p. 147.

35. Newbigin, *The Household of God,* p. 173.

36. Bruce D. Marshall, "Who Really Cares about Christian Unity?" *First Things* (January 2001): 29-34, here 29. This is not to deny Marshall's contention that today's divided church suffers from being under God's judgment. Today's Corinthians are indeed falling ill and dying. Yet they are still "the church that is at Corinth . . . sanctified in Christ Jesus, called to be saints," and hopefully blessed with grace and peace (1 Cor. 1:2-3).

the tests of discernment, and even for those that fail them and divide us. It also suggests that the greatest chance of ecumenical success may come from an approach to fellowship that respects the limits and peculiarities of our speaking. Ecclesial discourse, both ecumenical and local, has often pursued and claimed maximal authority. Consequently it has often overstepped its bounds, presumed its authority, enjoined inappropriate uniformity, created crises, and divided believers. This tendency to overstep is nothing new: "Unless you are circumcised according to the custom of Moses, you cannot be saved."

Conclusion

It is time to add my paraphrase to the list that introduced this exercise:

> "Greetings from the Jewish brothers and sisters in leadership, to the Antiochian and Syrian and Cilician Gentile brothers and sisters. We hear that some from among us trouble and unsettle you with their words. We did not ask them to do this. So we have agreed to send teachers of our choosing back with Barnabas and Paul, whom we love just as you do. Judas and Silas have put themselves on the line for the name of the Lord Jesus Christ. They will affirm the same things in person. The Holy Spirit fell upon you, burdening you with nothing more besides these necessary things: avoiding idolatry, and blood, and what is strangled, and immorality. We agree with God's decision. Staying away from these things, you will get along fine."

Deciding more would have misread the Spirit, and might have cost Jerusalem its fellowship with Antioch, let alone with the Pauline communities. Deciding less would have left the crisis to heal itself, which of course it would not have done, and might still have cost the communities their unity. The Mother Church managed to steer clear of either course, for it both saw clearly and trusted others to see clearly what it could not see for them. The results were uneven, but successful. The new teaching strengthened rather than alienated Jerusalem and its sister churches.

Then is now. We are those churches. We bear no greater burden besides these necessary things: to see God and the world through the eyes of Jesus, to discern the unpredictable consistency of the Spirit, to write what we see, and to know when to stop.

"It Has Seemed Good to the Holy Spirit and to Us": Mission and Ecumenism in the Power of the Holy Spirit

LOIS MALCOLM

Then he said to them, "These are my words that I spoke to you while I was still with you — that everything written about me in the Law of Moses, the prophets, and the psalms must be fulfilled." Then he opened their minds to understand the scriptures, and he said to them, "Thus it is written, the Messiah is to suffer and to rise from the dead on the third day, and that repentance and forgiveness of sins is to be proclaimed in his name to all nations, beginning from Jerusalem. You are witnesses of these things. And see, I am sending upon you what my Father promised; so stay here in the city until you have been clothed with power from on high."

Luke 24:44-49

But you will receive power when the Holy Spirit has come upon you; and you will be my witnesses in Jerusalem, in all Judea and Samaria, and to the ends of the earth.

Acts 1:8

For it has seemed good to the Holy Spirit and to us to impose on you no further burden than these essentials. . . .

Acts 15:28

The Edinburgh Conference of 1910, which is seen by many as a precursor to the World Council of Churches and the contemporary ecumenical movement, was essentially a missionary conference. Ecumenism and missionary activity were intrinsically linked at that event.[1] This stands in sharp contrast to much of the situation in the world today. Those churches that place a strong emphasis on evangelism often tend not to be very enthusiastic about ecumenical activity. Indeed, much of the growth in conversions to Christianity throughout the world occurs in churches that are independent of official denominational affiliation or have only loose affiliations with a denomination, but have much evidence of spiritual activity — healings, speaking in tongues, radical conversions of life, and so on.[2] Moreover, many have noted that missionary activity and church growth tend to be aligned with the kind of explicitly delineated belief often seen to be incompatible with the sort of consensus required in ecumenical agreements.[3] Evangelical Protestant churches, which traditionally placed a strong emphasis on holding particular beliefs and living a certain lifestyle, have eschewed ecumenism but have been noted for their focus on evangelism. Indeed, some very interesting ecumenical discussions and agreements have emerged between evangelicals and Roman Catholics, focusing specifically on questions related to the meaning of evangelism and salvation — questions that take very seriously the differences between them.[4] In turn,

1. See W. H. T. Gairdner, *Echoes from Edinburgh, 1910: An Account and Interpretation of the World Missions Conference* (New York: Fleming H. Revell, 1910) and Hugh Martin, *Edinburgh, 1837: The Story of the Second World Conference on Faith and Order* (London: SCM, 1937).

2. See, e.g., Philip Jenkins, *The New Christendom: The Coming of Global Christianity* (Oxford: Oxford University Press, 2002); see also Samuel P. Huntington, *Clash of Civilizations and the Remaking of World Order* (New York: Touchstone, 1997) and Peter L. Berger and Samuel P. Huntington, eds., *Many Globalizations: Cultural Diversity in the Contemporary World* (Oxford: Oxford University Press, 2002). See also David Martin, "The Evangelical Protestant Upsurge and Its Political Implications," in *The Desecularization of the World: Resurgent Religion and World Politics,* ed. Peter L. Berger (Washington, D.C.: Ethics and Public Policy Center and Grand Rapids: Eerdmans, 1999).

3. See the early argument made by Dean M. Kelley, *Why Conservative Churches Are Growing: A Study in Sociology of Religion* (New York: Harper & Row, 1973).

4. See, e.g., "The Gift of Salvation" (a document signed by 19 "evangelicals" and 15 Catholics), *First Things* 79 (January 1998): 20-23. See also *The Nature and the Mission of the Church: Conversations between the World Evangelical Fellowship and the Roman Catholic Church,* ed. George Vandervelde, *Evangelical Review of Theology* 23, no. 1 (January 1999): 6-91.

the Roman Catholic Church has recently placed a great emphasis on "evangelization" and *catechesis* (that is, basic instruction in the Christian faith).[5] At the same time, however, it has increasingly called attention to her differences with her "separated" brothers and sisters.[6] Furthermore, those within the mainline church who call for a renewal of interest in missionary activity often call for ecumenical activity that is more focused on strategic tasks and goals[7] rather than, say, a sacramental understanding of the church's unity.[8] By contrast, those who tend to affirm ecumenism often tend to eschew aggressive evangelistic efforts. Indeed, churches affiliated with the World Council tend to emphasize either social justice concerns or ecumenical agreements over doctrinal matters — but not explicit missionary activity. In many cases, there are good reasons for this, given inappropriate forms of evangelistic activity especially in contexts where there already is an established church.[9]

These observations raise a number of pertinent questions for mainline churches and those interested in ecumenism: What value do they place on missionary activity? And given the diverse ways "mission" can be defined, how should "mission" be defined in the first place? And, how is such activity to be related to ecumenical endeavor?[10] What is the ratio-

---

5. See, e.g., Avery Dulles, "John Paul II and the New Evangelization," *Studia Missionalia* 48 (1999): 165-80. See also Thomas Stransky, "The Mission of the Church: Post–Vatican II Developments in 'Official' Roman Catholic Theology," *Evangelical Review of Theology* 23 (January 1999): 52-69.

6. See, e.g., the Papal encyclical *Ut Unum Sint*. See also the response from Paul Meyendorff and William Rusch, "Response of the Faith and Order Commission of the National Council of Churches of Christ in the USA to the Papal Encyclical *Ut Unum Sint:* On Commitment to Ecumenism," *Mid-Stream* 38, nos. 1-2 (January-April 1999): 170-73.

7. See, e.g., Craig Van Gelder, ed., *Confident Witness — Changing World: Rediscovering the Gospel in North America* (Grand Rapids: Eerdmans, 1999); George Hunsberger, *Bearing the Witness of the Spirit: Lesslie Newbigin's Theology of Cultural Plurality* (Grand Rapids: Eerdmans, 1998); Darrell Guder, *Missional Church: A Vision for the Sending of the Church in North America* (Grand Rapids: Eerdmans, 1998). See also Charles Arand, "Grass Roots Ecumenism," *Concordia Journal* 25 (July 1999): 232-43.

8. See, e.g., the understanding of the church depicted in Ephraim Radner, *The End of the Church: A Pneumatology of Christian Division in the West* (Grand Rapids: Eerdmans, 1998).

9. See, e.g., the essays in *Pluralism, Proselytism, and Nationalism in Eastern Europe,* ed. John Witte and Paul Mojzes, *Journal of Ecumenical Studies* 36 (Winter-Spring, 1999): 1-286.

10. For treatments of this question, see, e.g., *Ecumenism and Mission: SEDOS*

nale for either missionary or ecumenical work? Are the two even related in any organic sense? Finally, since "reception" and "authority" have been such central themes in the discussion of the appropriation of ecumenical documents, is there any link between these themes and the missionary and catechetical tasks of the church? The pertinence of these questions in the United States is intensified by the numerical decline of mainline denominations and the observation that many have made that we are now in a "post-Constantinian" world in which a Protestant establishment no longer exists in the United States.[11]

An Interpretation of Acts 15

It is in relation to this context that we examine what Acts 15:28 might have to say to us today.[12] This verse is part of a letter sent by the Jerusalem church to the church in Antioch to address the specific question of whether new Gentile converts needed to be circumcised and follow Mosaic Law. The issue had been of "no small discussion and debate" in the Antioch church (v. 2; cf. 12:18-19). The missionaries who had started the church, Paul and Barnabas, were therefore sent, along with other congregational leaders, to Jerusalem for some guidance on the matter. After much deliberation, the Jerusalem church sends back a group — including Paul, Barnabas, and leaders from Jerusalem — with the decision found in v. 28 that the Gentile converts are to have no further burden imposed upon them "than these essentials." What is most interesting for our pur-

---

Ariccia Seminar, May 1999 in *SEDOS Bulletin* 31 (June-July 1999): 163-207. Note also the essays on *Mission Seen through Harare,* ed. Jorge Luiz F. Domingues, in *International Review of Mission* 49 (Spring-Summer 1999): 5-134.

11. The most influential text on this is Loren B. Mead, *The Once and Future Church: Reinventing the Congregation for a New Mission Frontier* (Washington, D.C.: The Alban Institute, 1991). For theological comment, see Stanley Hauerwas, *Resident Aliens: Life in the Christian Colony: A Provocative Christian Assessment of Culture and Ministry for Those Who Know That Something Is Wrong* (Nashville: Abingdon, 1989) and Douglas John Hall, *The End of Christendom and the Future of Christianity* (Valley Forge, Pa.: Trinity Press International, 1997). For a sociological perspective, see Dean Hoge, Benton Johnson, and Donald Luidens, *Vanishing Boundaries: The Religion of Mainline Protestant Baby Boomers* (Louisville: Westminster/John Knox, 1994).

12. I offer a similar reading of Acts 15 in "Conversion, Conversation, and Acts 15," *Word and World* 22, no. 3 (Summer 2002): 246-54.

poses is that this verse is found right at the heart of Acts, in the middle of the book itself. It signifies the shift that the church takes from being centered in Jerusalem to being flung across "the ends of the earth" (1:8).[13] After this, Paul is the central hero of Acts, with his missionary activity at the heart of its narrative. The Jerusalem apostles are last mentioned in 16:4; after this, they disappear from Luke's story in Acts.

This verse, on the one hand, is part of a missionary story. But it also depicts a decision made by a church council, which many identify as the first "Apostolic" council that would be a precedent for later ecumenical councils. We have an incident that is both missionary and ecumenical. How does Luke depict both types of activity? What is their purpose? And how are they related to each other? What is most intriguing is that the focal point of the story is centered elsewhere — in the activity of the Spirit. And while mission and ecumenism are central parts of this story — and they indeed are intrinsically related — they are, in Acts, simply a part of a much larger, and we could add grander, vision of the "promise of the Father" that Jesus speaks of at the end of Luke: that the disciples would receive the "Holy Spirit with power" and that this Spirit would enable them to be his witnesses "in Jerusalem, in all Judea and Samaria, and to the ends of the earth." (Acts 1:8).

As Beverly Gaventa has pointed out, the chief character — the chief agent — in the book of Acts is God.[14] And the God Luke presents is not some abstract numinous power only indirectly perceived. The drama of Acts revolves precisely around what happens when people — as communities and individuals — receive and experience this "Holy Spirit with power" and what happens when they try to manipulate or resist it. Indeed, the first thing Paul, Barnabas, and the others do when they arrive in

---

13. Joseph Fitzmeyer observes: "The issue that the incident in the Antiochene church raises sparks what is for Luke a very important development in his story of the early church. It falls designedly in the center of Acts. In my translation, chaps. 1-14 have 12,385 words; chaps. 15-28, 12,502 words. So what is now recounted is the turning point of Luke's story, when the apostolic and presbyterial college of Jerusalem officially recognizes the evangelization of Gentiles, which has been initiated by Peter and carried out on a wide scale by Barnabas and Paul. It leads to the definitive break of the Christian church from its Jewish matrix." *The Acts of the Apostles: A New Translation with Introduction and Commentary* (Doubleday: The Anchor Bible, 1998), pp. 538-39.

14. See Beverly Gaventa, *The Acts of the Apostles: A Commentary* (Nashville: Abingdon, forthcoming), and Joseph Fitzmeyer, *The Acts of the Apostles* (New York: Doubleday, 1998).

Jerusalem is to report "all that God had done with them" (15:4). But they receive in Jerusalem a very different reception from the one they received in Phoenicia and Samaria: there the believers responded to their report about the "conversion of the Gentiles" with "great joy" (v. 3). By contrast, in Jerusalem they are greeted with a challenge from believers "who belonged to the sect of the Pharisees." The challenge is this: that the new Gentile converts in Antioch must be "circumcised and ordered to keep the Law of Moses" (v. 5). This challenge creates a stir, and the apostles and elders of the church meet together to consider the matter (v. 6).

After some debate, Peter stands and gives a speech in defense of the new converts. He begins by appealing to the fact that God had chosen him to be the one to bring good news to the Gentiles. Whether or not this is historically accurate, the point in Luke's account is to connect Peter's speech in this incident to his early speeches in Cornelius's household and later to the Jerusalem church justifying his eating with Gentile converts in that household.

Recall that Acts 10 depicts how Cornelius receives a vision to invite Peter to his household and Peter receives a vision in which he is told to eat what is ritually unclean for him to eat as a Jew. What ensues is the conversion of Cornelius's household after a speech by Peter in which he tells them about Jesus of Nazareth and the message that "everyone who believes in him receives forgiveness of sins through his name" (10:43). After the speech, the members of Cornelius's household receive the gift of the Holy Spirit even before they are baptized. Peter later has to justify to the Jerusalem church why he stayed and ate with the members of that household, even though they were uncircumcised (11:1-18). His key warrants justifying his behavior are the vision itself in which he is told three times to eat what is unclean (11:5-10) and then told by the Spirit not to "make a distinction between them and us" (11:12), and the fact that God gave the members of Cornelius's household the same gift of the Holy Spirit given to the Jewish Christians on the day of Pentecost (11:15-17).

Peter's speech with regard to the church in Antioch draws on warrants similar to those he used to defend his actions in the Cornelius event. As with his defense of his actions in the Cornelius household, he focuses on what God has done. Echoing his argument, he observes that God "[gave] them the Holy Spirit, just as he did to us" (15:8). This God "made no distinction between them and us" (v. 9) — a warrant that is key not only to defending actions with Cornelius in Jerusalem but in the very speech he gave in Cornelius's household in which he claimed that "God shows no partiality, but in every nation any who fears him and does what is right is acceptable to him" (10:34, 35).[15] Indeed, he asks his hearers — in a fashion very similar to his query in 11:17 ("who was I that I could hinder God?") — why are you putting God "to the test by placing on the neck of the disciples a yoke that neither our ancestors nor we have been able to bear?" (v. 10). Note that to put God to the "test" means to mistrust God.[16] Peter then concludes with a final warrant: the appeal that "we will be saved through the grace of the Lord Jesus, just as they will" (v. 11).[17] Although this is not quite Paul's distinction between faith and works, it is an assertion that salvation for humanity resides solely in the "grace of the Lord Jesus" (*dia tes charitos tou Kyriou Iesou*) and not in any works of the law.

When Peter finishes speaking, the assembly grows silent. Then Barnabas and Paul stand up to report "the signs and wonders that God had done through them among the Gentiles" (v. 12). This appeal to "signs and wonders" is especially significant in Luke and Acts where divine sanction comes primarily from the miracles that either Jesus or — after his ascension — the new believers enacted.[18]

When they finish, James stands up to give a speech. If Peter was an important authority for the early Jewish Christians to have speak on behalf of the new Gentile converts, then James is probably an even more im-

15. Cf. Romans 2:10-11 where "partiality" is used as an abstract noun (*prosopolempsia*). The LXX phrase *prosopon lambanein* translates the Hebrew panîm nasa', "lift up, raise the face (of someone). Cf. Leviticus 19:15: "you shall not lift up the face of (the) poor," i.e., you shall not show partiality to the poor. See also Deuteronomy 10:17; 2 Chronicles 19:7; Sirach 35:12-13. "According to ancient Near Eastern customs the greeting to a superior would include the bowing of the head, if not full prostration; and lifting up the face would mean full acceptance of such obeisance. As used by Peter, it means that God does not favor only Jews, but also respects Gentiles who call upon him." Joseph Fitzmeyer, *Acts of the Apostles*, pp. 462-63.

16. On "testing" God, see Exodus 15:22-27; 17:2, 7; Numbers 14:22; Isaiah 7:12; Psalm 77; Wisdom 1:2.

17. Cf. Romans 3:24; 4:16; 5:21. Note that the timeless aorist infinitive is used (*sothenai*) to express "salvation" in an eschatological sense.

18. Note the importance of "signs and wonders" in Acts. See also 2:22: "with mighty deeds, wonders, and signs, which God wrought through him in your midst" and 19:11 where reference is made to "portents and signs." See also 2:43; 4:30; 5:12; 6:8; 7:36; 14:3; 15:12. The phrase is used to describe Jesus' miracles (e.g., in Luke 10:13; 19:37). In the LXX, it often describes God's mighty acts on behalf of Israel (e.g., Exod. 7:3; Deut. 4:34; 28:46; 43:11; Ps. 135:9; Isa. 8:18).

portant authority — identified even by Paul as "the brother of the Lord" (Gal. 1:19; 2:9, 12). He begins by referring to how Peter (called Simon here) has related how "God first looked favorably on the Gentiles, to take from among them a people for his name" (v. 14).[19] James uses the phrase "a people for his name," a term reserved for Israel (cf. 3:11), to include the Gentiles. He then quotes Amos 9:11-12 to demonstrate that God's plan has always included the Gentiles. God, he contends, will rebuild the fallen "dwelling of David" so that "all other peoples may seek the Lord — even all the Gentiles" (vv. 16, 17). To reinforce the point he adds that the Lord "has been making these things known from long ago" (vv. 17b, 18). A comparison of James's appropriation of Amos with either the Septuagint or the original Hebrew suggests that he has revised both originals — the latter even more than the former — but his intent in doing so is clear: to demonstrate that Amos had already foreshadowed how God would incorporate the Gentiles into Israel.[20] Having given this defense, he concludes by stating that he has decided that "we should not trouble those Gentiles who are turning to God" (v. 19); "turning" here refers to their conversion. He then introduces the four things the new converts are to abstain from: idols, fornication, whatever has been strangled, and blood. These are what according to Jewish law all people should abstain from, and not only the Jews (vv. 20-21).[21]

When he finishes his speech there is more deliberation. Then the leaders of the Jerusalem church choose two representatives to go with Paul and Barnabas to the church in Antioch (Judas called Barsabbas and Silas) with a letter that gives the same decision James arrived at in his speech: that the new converts are to have "no further burden than these essentials," that is, the four restrictions listed in James's speech. The letter states that the representatives were "unanimously" chosen (v. 25), and it

---

19. James's words allude to the OT; see Deuteronomy 14:2 (LXX): "the Lord your God has chosen you to be a people set apart from all nations" *(laon periousion apo panton ton ethnon)*; 7:6; 26:18-19; Exodus 19:5; 23:22. Luke is applying a term used for Israel only to include the Gentiles.

20. Note that James transposes the Amos 9:11-12 of the LXX for his purposes and that the sense of the original Hebrew has a completely different meaning.

21. See also 15:29; 21:25. In Leviticus 17:8–18:30 these regulations are for Israel and foreigners. James retains a law for Gentile Christians in line with Mosaic law but that does not impose circumcision (cf. Philo *Migration of Abraham* 89-94; Josephus *Antiquities* 20:38-48).

introduces the final decision with the phrase "it has seemed good to the Holy Spirit and to us" (v. 28).

This latter phrase is very important for our understanding of the Holy Spirit's role in this event. Luke does not want to present this simply as a political decision or consensus reached by the Jerusalem leaders but rather as something that, in Luke Timothy Johnson's words, interweaves "elements of divine intervention and human discernment so that the decision of the church appears finally neither as an abject submission to the divine impetus by politically motivated leaders, but as a *dialectical synergism of God's intrusions and human faith.*" The phrase "it has seemed good to the Holy Spirit and to us" suggests this synergism: not that the Holy Spirit and the church leaders are equal partners. Rather, "the church's decision is one that has finally *caught up with and therefore confirmed a decision made already by God.*"[22]

This chapter may be combining two original events in the Jerusalem church, one having to do with the question of whether Gentile converts needed to be circumcised and keep Mosaic law (cf. the issue reported by Paul in Gal. 2:1-10) and the other having to do with a decision regarding diet and marital unions for local churches in Antioch, Syria, and Cilicia.[23] But that must not detract from seeing the role this event plays in the book of Acts. As we have noted, this incident occurs at the center of Acts. It is found after the accounts of the movement of Philip into Judea and Samaria (8:5-40), Saul's conversion (9:1-31), Peter's encounter with Cornelius (10:1–11:18), and Paul's first missionary journey in Asia Minor (13:1–14:28), and before the rest of Paul's missionary journeys culminating with his arrest and trial in Jerusalem. What this decision makes official is the fulfillment of the Holy Spirit's promise that the believers would be

---

22. Luke Timothy Johnson, *The Acts of the Apostles,* Sacra Pagina Series (Collegeville, Minn.: Liturgical Press, 1992), p. 279, emphasis mine. See also C. K. Barrett: "This must be regarded as the outstanding example of Luke's insistence that all developments in the church's life were directed by the Spirit. . . . the [very] unanimity of the church bore witness to a decision already reached by the Holy Spirit." *Acts: The International Critical Commentary* (Edinburgh: T. & T. Clark, 1998), p. 744. Note also F. F. Bruce's comment: "This assigning to the Holy Spirit of prior authority in the issuing of the decree is eloquent of the practical awareness of his presence in the primitive church (cf. 5:3; 9; 13:2; 16:6f.)." *The Acts of the Apostles* (Grand Rapids: Eerdmans, 1990). I am grateful to Beverly Gaventa for these references.

23. Fitzmeyer, *The Acts of the Apostles,* p. 553.

witnesses not only in Jerusalem and in all Judea and Samaria but to "the ends of the earth" (1:8).

But this movement from Jerusalem to Judea and Samaria to the ends of the earth is not merely a human event. The promise is precisely the promise that the new believers would receive "power" when the Holy Spirit came upon them (1:8). And that power is defined in very specific ways. When the Holy Spirit first descends upon the believers in Jerusalem on the day of Pentecost it comes with a "sound like the rush of a violent wind" and tongues of fire descend upon them. Filled with the Holy Spirit, they speak in many languages; Jews from other nations hear them speaking in their own languages. According to Peter, this fulfills Joel's prophecy that God's Spirit would be poured out on "all flesh" — sons and daughters, young and old, and even slaves, male and female (Joel 2:28-32). After the Pentecost event Peter gives a speech that tells the story of Jesus of Nazareth and urges his hearers "to repent and be baptized . . . in the name of Jesus Christ so that your sins may be forgiven" (2:38). Luke informs us that three thousand persons are added to the group of new believers. This new community shares "all things in common" (2:44), selling their possessions and distributing to all as they have need (2:45; 4:32-35). Miracles also happen in this new community — a man who was lame from birth is healed (3:2-10) along with many other healings and exorcisms (5:16).

At the heart of all this activity is the Holy Spirit. Though not always followed in the same sequence, the pattern for becoming Christian entails repenting, being forgiven, being baptized, and receiving the gift of the Holy Spirit (2:38; cf. 8:5). And the Spirit received actually encourages the new communities and individuals within them to move in the directions outlined in 1:8: from Jerusalem to Judea and Samaria to the ends of the earth. Note that the rest of Acts follows the pattern outlined in 1:8: from the community's experience of the Holy Spirit at Pentecost (2:1-13) to the preaching and ministry of Peter and others among the emerging community of believers in Jerusalem (2:14–8:3) to the movement of missionaries into Judea and then Samaria (8:4-25), and finally the move out into the "ends of the earth" starting with the Ethiopian eunuch (8:26-40) and the conversion of Cornelius and his household (10:1–11:18) and ending with Paul's arrival in Rome after many missionary adventures (28:14). At each point, it is the Spirit who propels the churches' expansion — and not only in a general way, but with concrete, specific directives. The Spirit tells Philip to go to the Ethiopian eunuch's chariot (8:29) and respond to his questions. The Spirit tells the church to set Paul and Barnabas apart as missionaries (13:2). And the Spirit even forbids Paul to go in certain directions (16:6, 7; 21:4). Finally, in Acts 15, Peter appeals to his experience of seeing Gentile converts receive the Holy Spirit just as Jewish Christians had. In turn, the apostles and elders of the Jerusalem church, with the consent of the whole church, appeal to the Holy Spirit's participation in their deliberation.

This drama of the Spirit's activity in Acts is heightened by various attempts to manipulate or resist it.[24] All attempts to manipulate the Spirit's power for personal gain are eschewed. In fact, Ananias and Sapphira both die because they keep back part of the proceeds of property they have sold for the community (5:1-11). Simon the sorcerer is rebuked for wanting to manipulate the power given by the Holy Spirit in the laying on of hands (8:20-23). But perhaps the greater blasphemy is that of resisting or opposing the movement of the Holy Spirit — of being "uncircumcised in heart and ears" (7:51), having hearts that are dull, ears that are hard of hearing, and eyes that are shut, as Paul quotes Isaiah (Isa. 6:9-10 in Acts 28:26-27). Indeed, Acts is full of stories of arrest, persecution, and imprisonment because of resistance to Jesus' name (e.g., Acts 4:1-22; 5:17-41; 22–26; cf. Luke 6:22).

The phrase "it has seemed good to the Holy Spirit and to us" is found at the heart of the Spirit's movement in Acts. The Spirit of Jesus that fell upon the first Jewish-Christian community is the same Spirit that is now moving among Gentiles, causing them to become believers. This fulfills the Father's promise that the Spirit would come upon the disciples giving them power to "proclaim" to the "ends of the earth" that "repentance and forgiveness of sins" is given in the name of Jesus.[25] At issue is

---

24. Note the warning in Luke that "whoever blasphemes against the Holy Spirit will not be forgiven" (Luke 12:10). See also Acts 5:1-11; 7:51; and 8:14-24. Note that the denial of Jesus was forgiven (Luke 22:54-62; 23:32).

25. Note these themes in Luke: (1) Jesus' life, death, and resurrection fulfill "the law of Moses, the prophets, and the psalms" (Luke 24:44). (2) "Repentance and forgiveness of sins is to be proclaimed in his name to all nations, beginning in Jerusalem" (v. 47). (3) Jesus appears to the disciples for forty days "speaking about the kingdom of God" (Acts 1:3). (4) Before he is "lifted up" and "a cloud" takes him out of the disciples' sight he promises them that (5) they will "receive power when the Holy Spirit" comes upon them as the Father promised (Luke 24:49; Acts 1:7) so that (6) they could be his "witnesses" in Jerusalem, in Judea and Samaria, to the ends of the earth (Acts 1:8).

simply the question of whether Christian believers will "test" God and hinder this movement, or whether they will participate in the Spirit's power.[26]

What Does Acts 15:28 Have to Say to Us?

In the middle of the century, Rudolf Bultmann made much of the chasm between the worldview of the biblical texts and that of the contemporary world.[27] Indeed, much has been written about how we might bridge that chasm with hermeneutic insights and strategies.[28] The question of how to appropriate biblical texts — and their depiction of God's presence and activity — is not insignificant especially if one wants to understand what the Bible has to say about how God is present and active in the world today, a world greatly informed, for example, by a scientific worldview.[29]

But when one observes the actual experiences of God most Christians have in the world today — and not only Christians but adherents of other forms of religious or spiritual practice — one discovers that we may, in fact, have more in common with the world depicted in the biblical texts than initially meets the eye. Harvey Cox, who wrote *The Secular City* in the 1960s, has recently written a book on Pentecostalism in which he writes:

> Even before I started my journey through the world of Pentecostalism it had become obvious that instead of the "death of God" some theologians pronounced not many years ago, or the waning of religion that sociologists had extrapolated, something quite different has taken

26. See Galatians 2:1-10 for Paul's version of this story. Although there are evident differences in the detail of the accounts they essentially arrive at a similar conclusion. Nonetheless, much more could be developed about the similarities and differences in the theology that informs these two accounts. For a discussion of Paul's position on this, see J. Louis Martyn, *Galatians: A New Translation with Introduction and Commentary* (New York: Doubleday, 1997).

27. See among others Rudolf Bultmann, *Jesus and Mythology* (New York: Scribner, 1958).

28. See, e.g., Paul Ricoeur, *Figuring the Sacred: Religion, Narrative, and Image* (Minneapolis: Fortress, 1995).

29. See, e.g., John Polkinghorne, *Belief in God in an Age of Science* (New Haven: Yale University Press, 1998).

place. . . . Instead before the academic forecasters could even begin to draw their pensions, a religious renaissance of sorts is under way all over the globe. Religions that some theologians thought had been stunted by western materialism or suffocated by totalitarian repression have regained a whole new vigor. Buddhism and Hinduism, Christianity and Judaism, Islam and Shinto, and many smaller sects are once again alive and well. . . . We may or may not be entering a new "age of the Spirit" as some more sanguine observers hope. But we are definitely in a period of renewed religious vitality, another "great awakening" if you will but on a grander scale.[30]

The very theological and sociological prognosticators who predicted that ours would be a highly secularized world at the turn of this century are now observing something very different. It is true that secularizing forces remain very powerful indeed. The mobility entailed by a global market economy and the ways cultures are influenced by an international mass media often lead to the decline of traditional beliefs and practices. Nonetheless, these very forces are often also correlated not only with the rise of various forms of spiritual practice — often highly individualistic in their orientation — but with the rise of highly conservative forms of religious community as well.[31]

Perhaps we have more in common with the early believers in Acts than initially might meet the eye. Like Paul at the Areopagus in Athens, we too are surrounded by the "extremely religious" (17:22), who are interested in spending their time "in nothing but telling or hearing something new" (17:21). Like Peter in the household of Cornelius or before the Jewish community, we too have to grapple with both our own and our communities' understandings of what is right belief and practice as we encounter the way the Spirit works in the lives of people from around the world who are very different from us. We have not escaped the problems of idolatry and blasphemy. Recall that Paul's distress over the idolatry in

---

30. Harvey Cox, *Fire from Heaven: The Rise of Pentecostal Spirituality and the Reshaping of Religion in the Twenty-First Century* (Reading, Mass.: Addison-Wesley, 1995).

31. Note that sociologists are rethinking the "secularization" hypothesis. See Peter Berger, ed., *The Desecularization of the World: Resurgent Religion and World Politics* (Grand Rapids: Eerdmans, 1999). Contrast this with his earlier work: *The Noise of Solemn Assemblies: Christian Commitment and the Religious Establishment* (Garden City, N.Y.: Doubleday, 1961) and *The Sacred Canopy* (New York: Doubleday, 1969).

Athens compelled him to give his speech at the Areopagus. But if pagan idolaters are rejected for wanting to manipulate divine power for their own personal interest, then so are the Sadducees and Pharisees — and even the early Jewish Christians — who "test" God by opposing the new things the Holy Spirit is doing among them. Whether or not they believe in the resurrection, angels, or the Spirit (see, e.g., Acts 23:8) the issue remains the same. As Karl Barth noted, contrary to Bultmann: the distance separating us from hearing what the biblical texts have to say is neither temporal nor spatial but our own inability to accept God's judgment and mercy, or in Luke's terms the call for repentance and forgiveness that comes with the story of Jesus of Nazareth.[32]

So we return to the questions we raised at the beginning of the paper. Acts 15:28 pertains to both missionary and ecumenical matters. It is a *missionary* decision having to do with whether new converts should keep Mosaic Law or not, along with other rules about diet and sexual conduct. It is also an *ecumenical* decision reached unanimously, which has — at least informally — been seen as a precursor to later councils. But this verse is missionary and ecumenical in an even deeper way. It pertains to the way the Holy Spirit propels the movement of the church in Acts outward — from Jerusalem to the ends of the earth. The character and goal *(telos)* of this movement are ecumenical, pertaining to the whole *oikoumene*, the inhabited region of the world. But if the Spirit propels the missionary nature of this movement, then the Spirit also warrants its ecumenical character and goal. The Spirit is present not only in the languages of those present at Pentecost but in the households and congregations where new Gentile converts receive the Holy Spirit just as the early Jewish Christians did. Further, this presence of the Spirit among both Jews and Gentiles — and young and old, men and women, slaves and free persons — merely fulfills the prophetic promises in the Old Testament that God would "pour out my Spirit on all flesh," that God makes "no distinction" and shows "no partiality." Finally, perhaps the most central warrant is that only Jesus' name brings salvation — we are saved only by the "grace of the Lord Jesus" as Peter stated in his speech — and that no other criteria will suffice.[33]

32. See Karl Barth, *Church Dogmatics*, vols. 1-4 (Edinburgh: T. & T. Clark, 1936-1962).

33. Note that these three warrants are deeply Lukan: (1) the presence of the Spirit in the church; (2) the fulfillment of OT promises; and (3) the centrality of the message of repentance and forgiveness in Jesus' name.

In other words, the focus of all missionary and ecumenical activity in Acts is not the actions of key individuals or even communities in deliberation, but the activity of the Spirit promised after Jesus' ascension.[34] It is this Spirit of Jesus who unifies, and the unity the Spirit brings is neither a rigid conformity nor a bland homogenization.[35] When the Spirit descends at Pentecost, everyone speaks in a different language, and although hearers perceive the same "tongues of fire," what they hear is their own language. Linguistic and cultural differences occur at the heart of the Pentecost experience. And throughout Acts, there clearly is a place for deliberation and resolve and colorful personalities. Peter reflects upon and justifies his responses to the Spirit's activity among Gentile converts, offering arguments based on OT tradition, his experiences with these new converts, and his developing understanding of what Jesus' message of repentance and forgiveness entails. James also thinks through arguments for how to deal with new Gentile converts drawing on the OT tradition and coming to his own resolve on the matter. The congregation in Jerusalem clearly undergoes an explicit process of deliberation, and Paul and Barnabas clearly have strong missionary personalities that can, indeed, conflict. But throughout all of this drama, it is God and the Spirit who nudge and guide this reflection and activity, and whatever "unanimity" is reached in community decision-making. This Spirit does not efface individual or communal deliberation but enables it to do what it could not do without its power.

This Spirit is obviously linked with "signs and wonders" — gushes of wind, tongues of fire, miraculous healing and exorcisms. We have already noted that the Spirit urges people to do things — to go places and meet people. The power the Spirit enacts is not ethereal or ephemeral but concrete, specific, and definite.[36] It is the same kind of power that was clearly evident in Jesus' ministry. Recall that Peter describes in his speech before Cornelius' household that Jesus of Nazareth was anointed by God "with the Holy Spirit and with power" to go about "doing good and healing all who were oppressed by the devil" (Acts 10:38). The disciples are promised this same power, and throughout Acts there is clear evidence

34. For a recent argument on the importance of the ascended Spirit of Jesus for the church, see Douglas Farrow, *Ascension and Ecclesia: On the Significance of the Doctrine of the Ascension for Ecclesiology and Christian Cosmology* (Grand Rapids: Eerdmans, 1999).

35. For a theological account of the presence of the Spirit, see Michael Welker, *God the Spirit*, trans. John Hoffmeyer (Minneapolis: Fortress, 1994).

36. Welker makes this point throughout *God the Spirit*.

that they are able to heal and exorcise demons in the same way Jesus did in his ministry. In fact, even magicians and sorcerers want to get a hold of this power. But in the same way that Jesus' power was always linked with his teaching about the reign of God — a reign that brought good news to the poor, release to the captives, sight to the blind, and freedom for the oppressed (Luke 4:18, 19; cf. Isa. 61:1-2; 58:6) — so the presence of the Holy Spirit's power in the new communities of Christian believers is linked with sharing all in common and caring for the needy, as well as healing people and releasing their demons (Acts 2:42-47; 4:32-35; 5:12-16). If the mighty acts of God in the OT were linked with God's justice and merciful reign over all people, then the Spirit's "signs and wonders" are also linked with the common good and not personal interest or gain. Indeed, Paul himself eventually dies the death of a martyr, despite the obvious presence of the Spirit's power throughout his missionary work.

And yet this power truly does lead missionaries like Paul and Silas to "[turn] the world upside down" (17:6). The Holy Spirit's life and energy truly enable individuals and communities to do what they could not on their own. Thinking patterns, ways of being and acting, are radically transformed and reshaped. Peter is told to eat what he had previously thought was unclean; deep, deep patterns — even attitudes and feelings of revulsion toward certain kinds of food — are redefined. Jewish-Christian believers see before their eyes the Spirit fall upon uncircumcised Gentile converts the same way he had among them; people who were previously thought to be profoundly unholy are now temples of the Holy Spirit. And even James, a venerable leader of the Jerusalem church, and the congregation in Jerusalem itself, reach after much deliberation a new understanding of how Gentile converts are to be initiated into the faith. As new converts are added to the Christian community, believers have to think again, and think hard, about what is essential and non-essential in Christian belief and practice. And yet this transforming power is not merely a vague or nebulous "openness" to what is new. It is not merely a formal pattern for change and transformation that in itself has no core or substance. The very capacity for transformative thinking and living that the Spirit empowers is rooted in a very concrete story and message: the story of Jesus' life, death, and resurrection, and the message of repentance and forgiveness that is available for all people "in Jesus' name."[37] Although Luke does not elabo-

---

37. For a Jewish perspective, note Jon Levenson's very intriguing statement at the

rate as Paul does on how Christians are baptized into Christ's death and resurrection (Rom. 6), he does, throughout Acts, make clear that the story of Jesus' life, death, and being raised from the dead is explicitly linked with a message about repentance and forgiveness — both of which entail radical transformation at the deepest level.

We arrive now at the basis for all authority for missionary and ecumenical activity, and the possibility for its reception. Authority resides precisely in the Spirit's power and its witness to Jesus, the one who was crucified and raised from the dead. The issue of reception revolves around whether or not believers and new or potential converts will resist or oppose — or seek to manipulate — this power, or whether they will respond with repentance. In other words, the only mode of reception is repentance *(metanoia),* and that is only made possible by the forgiveness of sins.[38]

As for the early Jewish Christians,[39] the challenge for mainline churches is precisely to discern when and how the Spirit may be saying "repent and eat" so that we may perceive where the same Holy Spirit we have received is acting elsewhere in the world. And like the early Jewish Christians, we too have correctives to offer. Marcionite and Gnostic conceptions of spirituality in the early church were resisted by Christians steeped in the Hebrew scriptures. The palpable experiences new Gentile converts had of the Spirit were interpreted against the backdrop of early

end of *The Death and Resurrection of the Beloved Son* (New Haven: Yale University Press, 1993): "In light of the *universalistic* dimension of that legacy (e.g., Gen. 9:1-17) [that is, the legacy Jews and Christians share with the Hebrew Bible], it is not surprising that both Judaism and Christianity have proven able to affirm the spiritual dignity of those who stand outside their own communities. But the two traditions lose definition and fade when that *universalistic* affirmation overwhelms that *ancient, protean, and strangely resilient story* of the death and resurrection of the beloved son" (p. 232, emphasis mine).

38. See David Tiede's address on the Lutheran and Episcopal Agreement *(Called to Common Mission)* entitled "Paths as Yet Untrodden," given in St. Louis, Missouri, November 3, 2000, in which he situates that ecumenical agreement within the context of a joint missionary challenge. Note the importance of *metanoia* to his argument.

39. Unfortunately, Christians have often interpreted the conflict within the early church over whether Gentile converts needed to follow Mosaic Law in highly anti-Semitic ways; the same can be said of interpretations of Jesus' conflicts with authorities in the Gospels. A more fruitful line of interpretation would be to see what these may have to say about analogous difficulties within the Christian church. A recent attempt to rethink this legacy historically is Paula Fredriksen, *Jesus of Nazareth, King of the Jews: A Jewish Life and the Beginning of Christianity* (New York: Knopf, 1999).

Christian teaching about Jesus of Nazareth's life, death, and resurrection and his preaching about the reign of God — both of which, in turn, were interpreted against the backdrop of OT law, prophets, and psalms. But to offer these correctives in a fashion that is truly fruitful, mainline churches must heed the call to repentance that comes with the forgiveness of sins so that they do not "test" God by resisting the Holy Spirit's movement "to the ends of the earth."[40]

Ours is an age of concrete expressions of spiritual power. Perhaps a market economy, which relies on belief and wagers, lends itself to the intensification and proliferation of forms of activity that could be called "spiritual." The challenge we face may be very similar to the one the early church faced in Acts. Luke gives us clear guidelines for discerning when and how the Spirit's power is present, guidelines that impel us to move beyond our preconceived categories and limits precisely because they are rooted in the "proclaiming of the kingdom of God and teaching about the Lord Jesus Christ" (Acts 28:31). May we, like Paul, not hinder this power but immerse ourselves boldly in its healing joy.

40. For a helpful discussion, see Vigen Guroian, "Evangelism and Mission in the Orthodox Tradition," in *Sharing the Book: Religious Perspectives on the Rights and Wrongs of Proselytism,* ed. J. Witte Jr. and others (Maryknoll, N.Y.: Orbis, 1999), pp. 231-44, 398-400.

Contributors

William J. Abraham, Perkins School of Theology, Southern Methodist University, Dallas, Texas

P. Mark Achtemeier, The University of Dubuque Theological Seminary, Dubuque, Iowa

Carl E. Braaten, Center for Catholic and Evangelical Theology, Sun City West, Arizona

Brian E. Daley, S.J., University of Notre Dame, Notre Dame, Indiana

John H. Erickson, St. Vladimir's Orthodox Theological Seminary, Crestwood, New York

Vigen Guroian, Loyola College, Baltimore, Maryland

Robert W. Jenson, Center for Catholic and Evangelical Theology, Princeton, New Jersey

Lois Malcolm, Luther Seminary, St. Paul, Minnesota

R. R. Reno, Department of Theology, Creighton University, Omaha, Nebraska

Michael Root, Lutheran Theological Southern Seminary, Columbia, South Carolina

William G. Rusch, Faith and Order Foundation, New York, New York

Geoffrey Wainwright, Duke Divinity School, Duke University, Durham, North Carolina

Susan K. Wood, School of Theology, St. John's University, Collegeville, Minnesota

Telford Work, Westmont College, Santa Barbara, California

J. Robert Wright, General Theological Seminary, New York, New York

David S. Yeago, Lutheran Theological Southern Seminary, Columbia, South Carolina